STRANGE COMFORT

STRANGE COMFORT

Essays on the Work of Malcolm Lowry

SHERRILL GRACE

For Charlotte —
who is embarking on
her own long voyage !
Best wishes +
good luck —
Sherrill
2009

Talonbooks

Talonbooks

P.O. Box 2076, Vancouver, British Columbia, Canada V6B 3S3

www.talonbooks.com

Typeset in Garamond and printed and bound in Canada.
Printed on 100% post-consumer recycled paper.

First Printing: 2009

The publisher gratefully acknowledges the financial support of the Canada Council for the Arts;
the Government of Canada through the Book Publishing Industry Development Program; and the
Province of British Columbia through the British Columbia Arts Council and the Book Publishing
Tax Credit for our publishing activities.

LIBRARY AND ARCHIVES CANADA CATALOGUING IN PUBLICATION

Grace, Sherrill E., 1944–
Strange comfort : essays on on the work of Malcolm
Lowry / Sherrill Grace ; preface by Richard Lane.

Includes bibliographical references and index.
ISBN 978-0-88922-618-0

1. Lowry, Malcolm, 1909–1957—Criticism and
interpretation. I. Title.

PS8523.O96Z67 2009   C813'.52   C2009-902838-7

In Memory of Anne Yandle
(1930–2006)

Contents

List of Illustrations

Acknowledgements

For permission to quote from Lowry's works in previously published essays and in new ones, it is a pleasure to thank Peter Matson of Sterling Lord Literistic. Essays one and three first appeared as chapters in my book *The Voyage That Never Ends* published by UBC Press in 1982. Essays two and seven were published in *Canadian Literature* 71 (1976) and 142/43 (1994) respectively and are reprinted with permission. Essay four first appeared in *Challenges, Projects, Texts: Canadian Editing*, edited by John Lennox and Janet Paterson, AMS Press, 1993. Essay six was first published in *English Studies in Canada* XVIII, 4 (1992) and it won the Lorne Pierce Prize for best essay that year. Both are reprinted here with permission. Essay eight, first published in *Joyce/Lowry: Critical Perspectives*, edited by Patrick McCarthy and Paul Tiessen (University Press of Kentucky, 1997), and essay nine from the French journal *L'Epoque Conradienne* 26 (2000) edited by Claude Maisonnat are both reprinted with permission. Essay ten was published in *A Darkness That Murmured: Essays on Malcolm Lowry and the Twentieth Century*, edited by Frederick Asals and Paul Tiessen (University of Toronto Press, 2000) and it is reprinted with permission.

I am especially grateful to the late Alberto Gironella for his permission to reproduce works from his exhibition catalogue *El Via Crucis del Cónsul* with the original publication of "Ut Pictura Poesis," and I have reproduced two of those illustrations in this volume. For the photograph of the Nordahl Grieg Monument, it is a pleasure to thank the Norwegian Embassy in Berlin, and for the photograph of the CPR War Memorial in downtown Vancouver my thanks go to John Grace.

Once again, it is a pleasure to thank Christy Siegler and Talonbooks for helping me bring this volume to fruition, and I also wish to thank Mark Diotte, Tiffany Johnstone, and Monika Cwiartka for their assistance in preparing the final manuscript. Richard Lane deserves special thanks for his contributions to the study of Lowry and for taking time from a busy schedule to review my offerings here and put them in perspective in the Preface to this book. To my colleagues in Belgium, Canada, England, France, Italy, Mexico, New Zealand, Spain, and the United States I owe a special debt of thanks for the conferences, the conversations, and the wealth of insight they have shared so generously over the years. My thanks also go to the students in my 2008–09 Lowry seminars for their curiosity, enthusiasm, and lively debates about Lowry's work; these are the Lowry scholars who showed me how to read his work with today's eyes.

A Preface to Sherrill Grace

Richard J. Lane

Sherrill Grace has helped us see Malcolm Lowry in ways that would otherwise have potentially remained outside of our restricted vision: from her deciphering of Lowry's notoriously difficult handwriting and associated tracking down of inter-texts and allusions in that vast labyrinth known as his correspondence, to her extensive critical and biographical insights into Lowry's published and unpublished works. Lowry, Grace reminds us, "was one of the great interpreters of the modern world" (1992, 3), and in relation to this greatness, an interpreter and guide needs to always move on, searching for the different perspective, the unnoticed clue, the fragment that inevitably brings about a realignment of disciplinary approaches or structures whereupon we arrive at insight. Writing in another context altogether, Grace comments on the fluidity and dynamism of her critical methodology, as she examines "origins and beginnings ... shaping and exclusions and inclusions, of power balances and imbalances, of historical or literary events, as nodes, if you like, or points of intersection ... you open up these 'nodes' for investigation, rather than simply proceeding as if they didn't exist. So the methodology [...] of your own research becomes different" (1998, 8). Quoting this comment from an interview out of context opens it up for investigation; the phrase "So the methodology [...] of your own research becomes different" appears innocuous, or, a logical conclusion to the preceding sentences. Examined more closely, it is one of the most difficult things for the critic to achieve: an authentic shift in point-of-view, a genuine re-examination of blind-spots, or the aporias that stand at the heart of our method-ological certainties. What might have seemed innocuous is now uncanny, because it means that to understand Lowry, we need to constantly re-invent ourselves.

In many respects Grace has shown us Lowry anew by seeing him through the eyes of those people initially left out of the grand narrative(s) of his life, those ignored or marginalized people who crossed paths with Lowry, loved or were shocked by his intensity, his mobile, multiple personality, yet were always aware of the plasticity of his life as it became (or simply just *was*) the stuff of literary creation. The author Carol Phillips narrates just such an occasion, with the lonely Lowry finding solace in addressing an Acacia tree (which he re-named "the asperin tree"); as Grace notes, "This tree became something of a symbolic presence for Lowry, who identified it with his personal loneliness and with Christ's suffering. In a poem-letter written to her [Carol Phillips] that spring, he begins by saying that 'the asperin tree outside told me to say/her leaves were trembling for your good beauty/[...] as they have trembled since it wore the cross.' On the one hand beautiful, on the other a reminder (if not the source) of acute pain, the 'asperin tree' is a characteristically ambivalent Lowry image for the fragility of life and for a deep sense of loss, but as he develops the image it strikes an increasingly discordant note for a love letter-poem" (1991, 512). We see Lowry as Phillips saw him for that one intense moment, as the ambivalence and the discordance of his literary binding of loneliness, love, and loss registers over and over again. But we also see a scene—in a hotel room, with a lonely Lowry, a tree, and a future lover—as one that is thoroughly *textual*, moreover a textuality that has dramatic (here, surely, a Beckett play) and musical/operatic potential. The critical eye has helped us see, but the image—and its interpretation—remain complex and synaesthetic.

In seeing Lowry, Grace shows that we have to move with him: not just traversing his texts, but becoming aware of and moving with or alongside the "movement images" (of perception, action, and affection to use Deleuze's terms) that constitute cinematic reality and therefore his writing; as Grace says in the first essay, Lowry had an "affinity with a world view based upon perpetual movement," and furthermore, the architectonic structures of his writing were subject to perpetual re-building. Reading Lowry is to join him on multiple, never-ending journeys. Recursive writing uncannily evokes the image of the eye: a globe that sees the entire world on voyages of Nietzschean intensity—following also Nietzsche's concept of the eternal return. The circularity of *Ultramarine* is a clear example of the circular construction and symbolism of Lowry's texts, with its vision of "movement and the breaking of enclosing circles" where as Grace continues in essay two "lamps explode, their 'globes' flying into the sky, eyes waver, and 'diminishing' are 'catapulted east and west.'" To perceive is to see, but also to grasp; in *October Ferry to Gabriola* Grace suggests that the protagonist's perception of reality becomes distorted and the British Columbian landscape "bristles with symbols" as "signs threaten, snatches of overheard conversation are strange messages for him and films appear to mirror and comment upon his life" (essay three). Circularity is apparent here in perichoresis—rotation and the unity of the trinity—Ethan's profane illumination thereby deriving from the interpenetration of the sacred and the profane. The time-image is as important as the movement-image in *October Ferry to Gabriola*, including psychoanalytical time, and that strange temporality/memory triggered by the parallels between Ethan's past and that of Thurston's protagonist in his film *The Wandering*

Jew. Circularity, however, does not exclude history or subjective progression/regression. In comparing Lowry and Joyce in essay eight, Grace argues that "Lowry's modernism is deeply infused with romanticism" and that unlike Joyce's ahistorical synchronic vision, "Lowry's is deeply historical, diachronic, his stance prophetic and pathopoetic."

Examining Lowry involves exploring the materiality of his texts—the graphical surfaces of densely layered manuscripts and letters, of archival objects such as postcards and his personally annotated copy of *Ultramarine*—as well as his use of modernist and proto/postmodernist experimental form with its complex intertextual and conceptual interpenetrations and interconnections. In *Sursum Corda! The Collected Letters of Malcolm Lowry* (2 vols., 1995), an astounding number of letters were tracked down by Grace and added to the collection at UBC, the "editing" involved in preparing these volumes being a euphemism for detective work, transcription, translation, critical exploration, and detailed annotation among many other tasks. In essay four, Grace ponders the need for a graphological study of Lowry's writing as well as "a semiotics of the page"; "what *is* a Lowry letter?" Grace asks. The question unfolds as a meditation upon the relationship between the real and the fictional in Lowry's writing life: "Evidence suggests that Lowry not only drafted *fictive* letters (to real or fictional people) for use in his art ... but that he used *real* letters—his own and others'—in his fiction" (essay four). Grace offers multiple theories in answer to her question, her "typology of the Lowry letters as texts" containing a Borgesian set of categories that allows us to see our way through the epistolary labyrinth: real letters; undecidable letters; fictive letters; unsent letters; poem letters. Grace calls the unsent letters "the most intriguing" and also ponders the possibility that fictive/unsent letters are the categories that contain all of the others. However, Grace reminds us that "letters are more than written texts" and that Bakhtin's theory of speech genres facilitates understanding of the chiasmus between real/fiction in Lowry's epistolary universe. Of course Grace is already exploring the polyphony of Lowry's narratives, discussed fully in essay five on *Hear us O Lord from heaven Thy dwelling place.* The many surfaces of Lowry's texts give way here to the multiple voices of Lowry's musical writing, which leads Grace to questions of signification and the response, or not, of the "superaddressee."

It should come as no surprise, then, that in the baroque world of Lowry's texts a visual and aural aesthetic is at work, one in which Baudelaire's allegorical method is as useful as any contemporary theory for an extended interpretation. The "contemporary Mexican artist Alberto Gironella" (essay seven) is the first of many guides, which include in other essays included here: Joyce and expressionism (essay eight), Freud, Cocteau and Barthes (essay ten), and Debussy (essay eleven). Aural means to hear, a modernist breeze blowing through the oeuvre, but also it relates to the aura, that which Benjamin declares has given way in the age of technological reproducibility. Aura becomes distant and we can no longer experience it as mass reproduction technologies (film, photography, jazz, etc.) bring the aesthetic object closer to us. Lowry remains a romantic artist, utilizing popular mass cultural forms, yet through their literary sublation, he achieves the cultural heights of tragedy and allegory (essay seven). Grace investigates the Derridean question of framing when it comes to a postmodernist response to Lowry's sublation of modernism (Gironella's art), and the fact that *Under the Volcano* already contains both positions in a vertiginous discourse that still reaches for, or "points beyond," profane illumination. Lowry's modernism has subsumed Joyce's myth and Baudelaire's allegory: "In *Under the Volcano*, Lowry reaches back into the expressionist roots of early modernism to explore the causes of alienation, solipsism, and anguish in his hero, and *perhaps* to exorcise them in himself" (essay eight). The figure of the chiasmus—the crossing back and forth between modernism and proto/postmodernism; loss of aura and the auratic; myth and allegory; early and late/high modernism; and so on—paradoxically creates the textual author, while that most useful of critics of textuality (Roland Barthes) theorizes that it is here that the author disappears. Initially resisting Barthes's call for the return of the "documentary figure of the author," Grace journeys through Cocteau's "parody of Sophocles and ... radical rereading of Freud" in *La Machine infernale* (essay ten) to bring back the mother and the maid—as well as Lowry's self-plagiarism—into Lowry's bio/graphy. The aural can be a self-echo, an internal memory or repetition compulsion, that which is constantly re-expressed, or it is an inner voice that is always already dialogue, a deliberate choreography of the self. Debussy, who once defined a choreographer as "a man who is very strong on arithmetic" (Orledge, np) had already demonstrated in *Pelléas et Mélisande* "a special interrelationship of orchestration with dialogue/voice that is analogous with Lowry's narrative form in all his fiction" (essay eleven). Symbolist opera is a fitting medium for hearing *Under the Volcano*.

We inevitably see double when we see Lowry: we look for his hand, and we see the hand of another; we attempt to pin down the plagiarism, Lowry's original sin that can be traced right back to his juvenilia (essay nine), and we find instead a theory and complex aesthetic practice of plagiarism *and* "the need for a *Doppelgänger* figure" (essay six). Where Lowry should be, there is another, yet that other "is" somehow still Lowry. Is this a doubled or a divided subject? Is the figure of the double a *pharmakon*—a poison and a medicine (or cure)? Should the double be celebrated and welcomed, or like Oedipus, cast out, banished into exile? Oedipus appears to have become the poison, the unclean thing, by ignoring his memories, by forgetting past violent encounters, especially the battle at the place where three roads meet. One of the ways in which such forgetting is potentially avoided is by constructing memory devices, be they houses through which we conceptually pass, memories being attached to imaginary rooms, or actual physically constructed memorials, such as that installed outside of the Leys Chapel in 1922, at the school Lowry attended (essay twelve). Memorials can function more widely in the service of the state—or the colonial powers that built them throughout their Empires—or memorials can remind us, as Benjamin writes, "that the 'state of emergency' in which we live is not the exception but the rule" (392). Grace sees in *Under the Volcano* the same ethical imperative expressed here by Benjamin; she argues that *Under the Volcano* "mobilizes memory ethically in an effort to overcome willed forgetting [...] that Lowry *wants* us to remember the past, the world around us, and our responsibilities to that world, to our common humanity, our future, and future generations" (essay twelve). What is this state of emergency in Lowry's view? It is war. And it is the state of exception that can produce what Agamben calls "bare life": "When Geoffrey Firmin is shot by the military police and thrown into the barranca with other garbage (like the dead dog), he becomes a *homo sacer*. No one will be prosecuted or held accountable for his murder because he has first been reduced to 'bare life'—an espider, a Jew, a creature without identity or a real name, a thing of no value who may even be a spy and, thus, a danger to the powers that be" (essay twelve). If the coming community is going to be one which is *not* oppressive, that does *not* condemn anyone to bare life, then the "memory-text" that Grace theorizes, through her profound insight gained traversing Lowry's textual aesthetic, becomes essential reading.

RICHARD J. LANE
Vancouver Island University, Canada

Works Cited

Agamben, Giorgio. *The Coming Community*. Trans. Michael Hardt. Minneapolis & London: University of Minnesota Press, 1993.

———. *Homo Sacer: Sovereign Power and Bare Life*. Trans. Daniel Heller-Roazen. Stanford: Stanford University Press, 1998.

Benjamin, Walter. "On the Concept of History." In *Selected Writings*, Volume 4: 1938–1940, trans. Edmund Jephcott et al, 389–400. Cambridge, MA & London: The Belknap Press of Harvard University Press, 2003.

Deleuze, Gilles. *Cinema 1: The Movement-Image*. Trans. Hugh Tomlinson and Barbara Habberjam, London: Athlone, 1992.

Grace, Sherrill. "The 'Asperin' Tree and the Volcano: Carol Phillips and Malcolm Lowry." *Journal of Modern Literature* XVII.4 (1991): 501–20.

———. "Putting Lowry in Perspective: An Introduction." In *Swinging the Maelstrom: New Perspectives on Malcolm Lowry*, ed. Sherrill Grace, 3–18. Montreal & Kingston: McGill-Queen's University Press, 1992.

Orledge, Robert. "Timeless Musical Magic." In *The Royal Ballet, Covent Garden: Les Biches, L'Après-midi d'un faune, Jeux, The Firebird*, n.p. London: Royal Opera House, 2000.

Tucker, Bruce. "Oral History: An Interview with Sherrill Grace." *Canadian Review of American Studies* 28.3 (1998): 1–13.

The "Strange Comfort" of Remembering and Re-reading Malcolm Lowry:

An Introduction

Remember me. (Perhaps because I have difficulty remembering myself.)

When Malcolm Lowry wrote these words to the Norwegian writer Nordahl Grieg from Los Angeles in the spring of 1939, he was in a very bad state. His first wife had left him and, after some desperate, drunken months alone in Mexico, he had been expelled and made it as far north as Los Angeles, where he would pass through another difficult period in his life. Nordahl Grieg was one of Lowry's kindred spirits, a hero in Lowry's life, and a profound influence on and inspiration for his work. He is the real man behind the fictional hero of Lowry's "In Ballast to the White Sea"; his novel *The Ship Sails On* and Lowry's identification with its central character exerted such a strong influence on *Ultramarine* that Lowry felt his novel was little more than "paraphrase, plagiarism, or pastiche" of Grieg's novel. I cannot confirm that Lowry ever mailed this letter (*SC* I, no. 85) to Grieg and there is no reply to it with Lowry's papers, but it is a deeply moving testimony, not only to Lowry's troubled state, but also to his lasting admiration for Grieg and to the "strange comfort" he always found in writing and in other writers.

It seems fitting, therefore, to remember this letter with its anguished plea for remembrance on the occasion of Lowry's centenary because Lowry never forgot Grieg. He followed Grieg's publications and activities from afar, approved and agreed with Grieg's politics, and was shocked and saddened by Grieg's death during World War Two. Somehow he became aware of Grieg's articles on Carl von Ossietsky, and as he tells Grieg in this letter, he is delighted by Grieg's commentary on Ossietsky and "disgusted" (as was Grieg) with the famous Norwegian writer Knut Hamsun's National Socialist sympathies. But the chief burden of this letter to Grieg is Lowry's acute despair and his extreme need for the "strange comfort" he found with the writing "profession" (see his story called "Strange Comfort Afforded by the Profession"). This letter is a *cri de coeur* addressed to one of the few positive forces in his life at that time. As he tells Grieg, he feels "deeply lost," "alone & pretty ill," about "to die of grief," and "without a country" (*SC* I, 192), and Grieg represents a beacon of hope and a possible source of recognition of self:

> I have always looked on you as the greatest of living poets. Tell me where you are, where you will be. Remember me. (Perhaps because I have difficulty remembering myself.) (*SC* I, 192)

Things would soon improve for Lowry, of course. He would remarry, move to Vancouver, Canada, and write his masterpiece *Under the Volcano*, but he would always keep Nordahl Grieg's example in mind and cherish Grieg's memory so that references to Grieg surface, like a *leitmotif* in his fiction, poetry, and letters. There are several other motifs, or capillary links, that recur in his writing: some are references to actual people like Grieg, others are quotations from favourite, influential texts and films, and still others are the themes or issues to which Lowry constantly returned. Among the most important and pervasive of Lowry's themes are remembrance, war, voyages (always continuing ones), the beauty of the natural world, and mankind's careless destruction of that world. Lowry was a profoundly autobiographical and subjective writer during the late modernist period when such writing was frowned upon. However, with the passage of time and with increased critical appreciation for the *art* of autobiography and the complexity of autobiographical narratives, Lowry's themes and his way of developing them through the fulcrum of his own life have become easier to understand.

In gathering together the twelve essays chosen for this Lowry centenary volume, I have been reminded of biography and autobiography (Lowry's and my own) at many points. To go back to an early essay like "Outward Bound" and then come forward across my years of work on Lowry to "A Sound of Singing," "The Play's the Thing," and finally to "Remembering Tomorrow," is to re-view the literary critical theories and methods of the past thirty years. It is also to realize, rather dramatically, just how relevant Lowry's vision is and how enduring and responsive to multiple readings his work—especially *Volcano*—continues to be. The word universal has long been out of fashion, but it is a word that springs to my mind when I reflect on Lowry's longevity and importance as a writer. Consequently, in making my selection of essays, I wanted to capture something of the range of readings and approaches to Lowry's work that represent not only my own responses but, hopefully, those adopted by other Lowry readers over the years. I also wanted to address the question of Lowry's legacy for the twenty-first century, and this I have tried to do in the new essay "Remembering Tomorrow: Lowry, War, and *Under the Volcano*." This essay and the one on Debussy and *Under the Volcano* are published here for the first time. They could scarcely be more different from each other, but that difference simply foregrounds the scope and capaciousness of Lowry's great novel. It is impossible to exhaust *Under the Volcano* (or other superb works like *Hear us O Lord*). Each reading produces new questions and reveals fresh delights for readers, like myself, who think they *know* the *Volcano*, and today a new generation of Lowry readers is discovering Lowry for themselves and finding new ways of approaching his barrancas, volcanoes, visions of paradise and hell, and mysterious paths.

Bringing my twelve essays together in one volume has forced me to make several editorial decisions. While I have tried to retain the contemporaneity of each essay and have not made any substantive changes, I have reduced the number of illustrations that appeared with first publication and I have changed all the references to Lowry's letters to my two-volume edition *Sursum Corda! The Collected Letters of Malcolm Lowry*. The earlier *Selected Letters* contains many errors and silent deletions which skew the evidence of individual letters, so for these reasons, as also for the sake of consistency, I only cite *Sursum Corda!* References to *Under the Volcano* presented a different problem. The novel has gone through many editions over the years and different readers will own different editions of the text. The first edition of 1947 is now a rare book owned by very few and subsequent paperback editions have gone out of print; therefore, there seemed no satisfactory way of standardizing references and I have left them as they appeared in the original publication of an essay. All editions I have used are listed in Works Cited, and in each essay I have added a note to identify the edition from which I quote. I have also introduced a standard, consistent set of abbreviations and references to Lowry's works and to the Lowry Collection in Special Collections at the University of British Columbia as follows:

> Lowry Fonds—cited by box, folder, and page (where available)
> *The Collected Poetry of Malcolm Lowry*: *CP*
> *Dark as the Grave Wherein My Friend Is Laid*: *DAG*
> *Hear us O Lord from heaven Thy dwelling place*: *HUOL*
> *Lunar Caustic*: *LC*
> *October Ferry to Gabriola*: *OF*
> *Psalms and Songs*: *P&S*
> *Sursum Corda! The Collected Letters of Malcolm Lowry*, 2 volumes: *SC* I
>   and II
> The 1940 *Under the Volcano—1940 UV*
> *Ultramarine—U*
> *Under the Volcano—UV*
> "Work in Progress"—"WP"

It only remains for me to extend my thanks to the friends, scholars, and students who have shared their enthusiasm for Lowry with me and to acknowledge the funding support that I have enjoyed during many years of research. Lowry *aficionados* know who they are and they come from around the world, but my special thanks go to Miguel Mota and Richard Lane for organizing the July 2009 Centenary Conference at UBC that brought so many of us together once more (another form of "strange comfort" indeed) and prompted me to write "Remembering Tomorrow." The Social Sciences and Humanities Research Council of Canada has provided me with invaluable financial support, without which I would not have contemplated editing Lowry's letters, and the librarians in Special Collections at UBC have long welcomed me into their sanctum and generously assisted me on numerous occasions. This volume is dedicated to the memory of Anne Yandle who, as Head of Special Collections, developed the Lowry Archive, welcomed generations of Lowry scholars, and so often—literally—looked after us. Her memory is precious to so many, and she is sorely missed. Unlike Lowry, Anne would never have used Dido's words from her famous "Lament"—"Remember me!"—but remember her we do.

S.G.
Vancouver, 2009

1

The Voyage That Never Ends

Malcolm Lowry was many things—a poet, an incorrigible drunk, a weaver of impossible "biographical" legends, a syphilophobe, one of the great novelists of this century, a charming, sly, humorous man, and an interesting thinker. Because he was first and foremost an artist, he was not concerned with rigorous treatment of abstract theories, logic, or intellectual systems, and it is useless to search for a tightly argued philosophical position in his works. Nevertheless, Lowry was very much a product of the modern age—the age of Heisenberg, Gombrich and Wittgenstein—and he wrestled constantly with epistemological questions about the nature of perception and consciousness. These questions, in turn, led him to probe his understanding of temporal and spatial reality, as well as the ability of language and narrative structure to express that reality. In a 1953 letter to his editor, Albert Erskine, he wrote that he was looking for "a new form, a new approach to reality itself" (*SC* II, 537); that "new form" was to be created in "The Voyage That Never Ends."

Lowry's philosophical reflections appear in both his manuscripts and published work. For example, in a fascinating story, "Ghostkeeper," Lowry writes that "it is a pity I have no philosophical training for I unquestionably have some of the major equipment of a philosopher of sorts."[1] This late story, a species of biographical metafiction about a writer, Tom Goodheart, who is trying to write a story, is in many ways an excellent place to begin an investigation of Lowry's theories. Interspersed with parts of the "Ghostkeeper" story proper are some of Lowry's personal observations on what he described to Albert Erskine as "reality itself":

> Life is indeed a sort of delirium perhaps that should be contemplated however by a sober "healthy" mind. By sober and healthy I mean of necessity limited. The mind is not equipped to look at the truth. Perhaps people get inklings of that truth on the lowest plane when they drink too much or go crazy and become delirious but it can't be stomached, certainly not from that sort of upside-down

and reversed position. Not that the truth is "bad" or "good"; it simply *is*, is incomprehensible, and though one is part of it, there is too much of it to grasp at once, or it is ungraspable, being perpetually Protean. (*P&S*, 224)

The single most important aspect of this "reality" is its dynamism. For Lowry, the universe was in a constant process of change akin to the Nietzschean state of becoming that underlies romanticism and expressionism. His affinity with a world view based upon perpetual movement and possibility led him to philosophers like Bergson and Ortega y Gasset, to a mystic like Charles Stansfeld-Jones (the Cabbalist, Frater Achad, whom Lowry met in Dollarton in 1942), and to quasi-philosophers like J.W. Dunne, Annie Besant, P.D. Ouspensky and Hermann Keyserling.[2] For example, in his notes for the unpublished "La Mordida," Lowry supports his belief in process with quotes from Keyserling's *Recovery of Truth*:

Those who regard the harmony of the celestial spheres as an ideal state and hold it up to the living, therefore acknowledge death to be their life-ideal .... We came to the conclusion that only states of perfection of a kind that are fruit-ful, that continue motion, that offer the promise of higher development, are compatible with the meaning of life. (12:27, 1)

Viewed in these terms, the cycles and recurrences which play such important symbolic and structural roles in Lowry's fiction can be seen to represent subsidiary aspects of reality, the wheels within wheels of an eternal flux.

Another outstanding feature of Lowry's world is its signification. Once again, in "Ghostkeeper," Lowry comments upon the complexity of life and art:

In fact, no sooner did poor Goodheart come to some sort of decision as to what line his story should take than it was as if a voice said to him: "But you see, you can't do it like that, that's not the meaning at all, or rather it's only one meaning—if you're going to get anywhere near the truth you'll have twenty different plots and a story no one will take." And as a matter of fact this was sadly true. For how could you write a story in which its main symbol was not even reasonably consistent, did not even have consistent ambiguity? Certainly the watch did not seem to mean the same thing consistently. It had started by being a symbol of one thing, and ended up—or rather had not yet ended up— by being a symbol of something else. (*P&S*, 219)

To Lowry it seemed as if nothing could be explained away as mere accident. Everything connects or corresponds to form a highly significant whole; everything has meaning. Lowry gives creative form to his sense of interconnection and significance by using journeys, metaphors of paths, ladders, wheels, and fresh and intriguing symbols like that of the Panama Canal. Even in the strange books of Charles Fort, whose data on fires Lowry used in *October Ferry*, he found a fascinating collection of "facts" which he could draw upon to suggest that the visible world contains signs and connected events which logic cannot explain.

By 1928, when he first read Conrad Aiken's "House of Dust" and *Blue Voyage*, Lowry was already interested in questions about individual consciousness and perception. Like the symbolists, he was unwilling to allow mechanistic limitations to the human psyche, and his obsession with the creative and intuitional power of the mind is symptomatic of early twentieth-century neo-romanticism. Moreover, Lowry came to believe that the development of consciousness is never complete; therefore, his "Voyage That Never Ends" is, on one level, the never-ending effort of the individual to develop consciousness and thereby achieve understanding of a dynamic universe.

The fusion of opposites was another of Lowry's central ideas through which he related his concept of active, evolving consciousness to his picture of a many-levelled, intricately connected world. Influenced by his reading of P.D. Ouspensky (*Tertium Organum* and *A New Model of the Universe*, originally published in 1920 and 1931 respectively), Jones, and Coleridge (in particular *Aids to Reflection*), Lowry viewed life in terms of polarities that must be balanced. He felt that the activity of unifying or balancing opposites reflects the vitality of the universe and illustrates the creativity of the mind. Because Lowry believed man could penetrate deeper and deeper into the mystery of reality by means of an ever-expanding consciousness, he was convinced that to misuse this power would quickly render a potentially paradisal existence infernal.

Briefly, then, Lowry's philosophy, although eclectic, achieves a degree of unity through the considerable synthesizing powers of his imagination. Most importantly, he believed that reality must be understood as being in constant motion, "perpetually Protean," and that man's moral duty is to live in harmony with this universal motion through constant psychic growth. The past, while it threatens to enclose and paralyse the movement of the mind, he viewed as synonymous with the self created thus far in time; therefore, by understanding the past, a man understands the self he has created and becomes free to continue his growth. From this Lowry concluded that the writer's task is to strive constantly to capture in art the protean nature of reality. In practical terms, of course, he set himself an impossible task because the artist must select, begin, and end, but the effort to achieve this goal explains much about Lowry's narrative strategies, style, and what he called the rhythm of "withdrawal and return" that characterizes his work. Even his creative method, his way of writing, is congruent with these beliefs and artistic goals.

Lowry's manuscripts and notes offer valuable insight into the way he wrote. Very rarely did he cut material from his manuscripts without incorporating it, in another form, elsewhere in the text so that his work continued to expand. The extant notes for each of his novels indicate that he began with a central episode for the book, as well as each chapter, and then built upon this foundation by adding blocks of descriptive and narrative material at either end. Frequently, he would shift the position of whole passages. In *Under the Volcano*, for example, paragraphs which he had first placed in one chapter were later moved to another. He never seemed satisfied with the symbolic resonance or, to keep the architectural analogy, with what he called the "churrigueresque," or overloaded, façade of his work.[3] His imagination continually discovered new connections and unexplored resemblances among words, images, and events. Symbols, allusions, motifs, were constantly inserted—almost like mortar—at strategic points in the manuscripts. Even individual sentences illustrate the way he added phrase after phrase, adjective after adjective, to his initial idea as if to probe, develop, and expand every nuance of meaning.[4] Nevertheless, the writing was never careless or hurried: he rewrote sentences and paragraphs many times, and marginal notes indicate that he had complicated reasons for every punctuation mark.

Two features of Lowry's creative method stand out as especially significant. Firstly, he put a book together passage by passage almost as if it were a house or a pier; secondly, his work never seemed, to his eyes, complete. Even *Under the Volcano* was unfinished, because, for Lowry, a work of art was like a building that was constantly being built. Despite the hopelessness of the attempt, the fact that the work could never be finished or made permanent was its greatest source of value. In *Dark as the Grave*, Sigbjørn Wilderness emphasizes that the artist must constantly rebuild his ever-changing work of art, and he goes on to explain that:

> Part of the artist's despair ... in the face of his material is perhaps occasioned by the patent fact that the universe itself—as the Rosicrucians also held—is in the process of creation. An organic work of art, having been conceived, must grow in the creator's mind, or proceed to perish. (*DAG*, 154)[5]

The key to Lowry's art, then, the unifying idea of his metaphysics and aesthetics and the insight upon which he based his vision of life and his masterwork "The Voyage That Never Ends," is that "an organic work of art ... must grow in the creator's mind, or proceed to perish." Because symbols, images, and words are constantly expanding, Lowry's attempt to capture this activity in art becomes absurd. Commenting upon this absurdity in "Ghostkeeper," he writes:

> The minute an artist begins to try and shape his material—the more expecially if that material is his own life—some sort of magic lever is thrown into gear, setting some celestial machinery in motion producing events or coincidences that show him that this shaping of his is absurd, that nothing is static or can be pinned down, that everything is evolving or developing into other meanings, or cancellations of meanings quite beyond his comprehension .... In any case the average short story is probably a very bad image of life, and an absurdity, for the reason that no matter how much action there is in it, it is static, a piece of death, fixed, a sort of butterfly on a pin .... But the attempt should be—or should be here—at least to give the illusion of things—appearances, possibilities, ideas, even resolutions—in a state of perpetual metamorphosis. (*P&S*, 223–24)

The attempt must be made because, in Lowry's terms, the most realistic work of art is the one that imitates the flux of noumenal and phenomenal reality.

Lowry founded his aesthetic upon a belief in the infinite variation and movement of life. Just as his universe is an intricately connected, supremely meaningful structure, so his fiction is a multi-levelled world in which time and space are unlimited. By penetrating the future or reliving the past, by interpreting coincidences and events as signs and portents, by travelling mentally and physically, the Lowry protagonist inhabits and *becomes* a dynamic, mysterious universe. Finding watches, crossing borders under the scrutiny of customs officials, riding in buses, ferries, boats and planes, looping-the-loop, visiting the ruins of Pompeii, even contemplating the stacks of polished glasses in a bar, becomes, within Lowry's artistic system, a metaphor for a mystical journey, a metonymy for a larger reality.

Lowry clearly stands apart from the main body of Western philosophic and aesthetic thought. So convinced was he of the goal-less motion of life that he could not envision a final static eternal heaven any more than he could imagine "a perpetual spiritual orgasm."[6] Time could not be spatialized in Platonic terms, and art, mirroring reality, must not hypostatize life. He also stands somewhat outside Leavis's "great tradition," although the experimental quality of certain of his texts does not make him either an anti-realist or a thoroughgoing modernist. As Malcolm Bradbury makes clear, Lowry shares much with the Romantics,[7] and yet his increasing interest in metafictional forms points to his affinities with some postmodernist writers. I return to this question of fictional mode in other essays because it is important to place Lowry in this wider context, but for the moment, it is enough to point out that Lowry was moving away from traditional realist concepts of plot, character, and language. In *October Ferry*, for example, Ethan reflects on the "reality" of films or novels and decides:

> A novelist presents less of life the more closely he approaches what he thinks of
> as his realism. Not that there were no plots in life, nor that he could not see a
> pattern, but that man was constantly in flux, and constantly changing. (*OF*, 61)[8]

The only artistic form which Lowry felt could possibly embody his vision and offer "a new approach to reality itself" was the cyclical voyage ever-renewed. Lowry's need for constant creative activity is manifest in the "never-ending" aspect of the voyage, for the protagonist's quest, like that of the artist or any individual, lacks a final goal—unless it be the knowledge that the voyaging must continue. His "realism" lies in the artist's endeavour to recreate in the very form of his art the "perpetually Protean" nature of life. In the effort, according to Lowry, the artist would destroy himself. Without doubt Lowry's vision of reality, his desire to pack everything in and to keep everything moving, helped to destroy him.

"The Voyage That Never Ends" developed slowly in Lowry's mind, and his plans for the work were never finalized. To trace the evolution of the "Voyage," it is necessary to go back to 1940 when Lowry conceived of a Dantean trilogy to follow on from *Under the Volcano*.[9] Later, in 1946, he described his plan to the publisher Jonathan Cape:

> [I] conceived the idea of a trilogy entitled *The Voyage That Never Ends* for your firm (nothing less than a trilogy would do) with the *Volcano* as the first infernal part, a much amplified *Lunar Caustic* as the second, purgatorial part, and an enormous novel I was also working on called *In Ballast to the White Sea* ... as the paradisal third part, the whole to concern the battering the human spirit takes ... in its ascent towards its true purpose. (*SC* II, 503–4)

Certainly, *Lunar Caustic*, in its present form, is at least as infernal as it is purgatorial, and it is difficult to imagine how Lowry would have altered its ambiguous, if not downright dark, vision simply by amplifying. As he later came to see, the novella belonged to a later stage in the "Voyage." In fact, the early Dantean conception of the sequence has a finality and a naiveté about it which could not possibly have suited Lowry's complex evolving system, and this is nowhere more clear than in the story of the "paradisal third part." His one-thousand-page manuscript of "In Ballast to the White Sea" was destroyed (except for a few charred fragments) when the Lowry cabin burned in 1944.[10] According to Lowry, it was to have told the story of a young man's salvation from inertia through a coincidental meeting with an older writer for whom he has a mysterious affinity (see *SC* II, no. 467). That older writer was modelled on the Norwegian Nordahl Grieg.

Some time before his arrival at Cambridge in 1929, Lowry had discovered Grieg's novel *Skibet Gaar Videre*, translated in 1927 as *The Ship Sails On*. The nineteen-year-old Lowry, who had been to the Far East in 1927 on the *Pyrrhus* and was writing a novel (to be called *Ultramarine*) about his experiences, was shaken by Grieg's portrayal of young Benjamin Hall's first voyage and by Grieg's grimly moralistic picture of a sailor's life. Despairing of news from his girl at home and disillusioned by the brutality and boredom of the ship, Hall has his first sexual experience with a prostitute, contracts syphilis, and nearly commits suicide. Grieg's book, written in a straightforward realistic mode, reveals a profound philosophical pessimism in scattered remarks such as—"Life had played one of its scenes over again, a new spiral had wound its way upward, and now he found himself looking down into it"—and in the underlying suggestion that time repeats inexorably and that life is a maelstrom of meaningless change—that life, like the ship, moves on oblivious of private pain.

The influence of *The Ship Sails On* is most obvious in the subject of *Ultramarine*.[11] Lowry's fascination, however, was not simply with the congruity of Grieg's book with his own experience. It is a minor step from the idea of "the ship sails on" to "the voyage that never ends." In the summer of 1930, Lowry had signed aboard a tramp steamer bound for Norway in order to meet Grieg, and it was from this voyage, and the eerie significance of discovering *The Ship Sails On* while he was working on *Ultramarine*, that he conceived "In Ballast to the White Sea." Nordahl Grieg had provided Lowry with the first evidence for his Pirandellian belief that he was, in a sense, a character in someone else's novel. This idea became both an obsession and a basic premise in "The Voyage That Never Ends."

Despite the loss of "In Ballast to the White Sea," plans for a major opus grew. Although the Dantean parallel became too restrictive, Lowry continued to talk about his work in terms of hell, purgatory, and paradise. It was characteristic of his creative method and aesthetic beliefs that his evolving plan should attempt to include every new idea. In the autumn of 1951, he wrote to his agent, Harold Matson, that his reconstituted literary continuum would include

> Five, perhaps six interrelated novels, of which the *Volcano* would be one, though not the best one by any means, the novel you suggested I should write some years back, a sort of Under *Under the Volcano*, should be ten times more terrible (tentatively it's called *Dark as the Grave Wherein My Friend Is Laid*) and the last one *La Mordida* that throws the whole thing into reverse and issues in triumph. (The Consul is brought to life again, that is the real Consul; *Under the Volcano* itself functions as a sort of battery in the middle but only as a work of the imagination by the protagonist.) Better still: some years back I was not equipped to tackle a task of this nature: now, it seems to me, I've gone through the necessary spiritual ordeals that have permitted me to see the truth of what I'm getting at and to see the whole business clearly. (*SC* II, 436)

On 22 November 1951 he sent Matson the detailed description of his ambitious plan. "Work in Progress" contains a thirty-four-page discussion of "The Voyage That Never Ends" and twenty-nine pages devoted to *Hear us O Lord* and "Forest Path." Although Giroux was deeply impressed, Harcourt Brace was unable to support Lowry. Happily, Random House offered Lowry a contract enabling him to work with his former editor and friend, Albert Erskine. The 1951 outline in "Work in Progress" (hereafter "WP") is as follows:

THE VOYAGE THAT NEVER ENDS
THE ORDEAL OF SIGBJØRN WILDERNESS   1
UNTITLED SEA NOVEL

LUNAR CAUSTIC
UNDER THE VOLCANO   The Centre

DARK AS THE GRAVE WHEREIN MY FRIEND IS LAID
ERIDANUS   } Trilogy
LA MORDIDA

THE ORDEAL OF SIGBJØRN WILDERNESS   2[12]

The untitled sea novel is, of course, *Ultramarine*, which Lowry felt needed considerable rewriting. *Lunar Caustic*, instead of functioning as a purgatorio in a trilogy, now precedes *Under the Volcano*, which assumes a focal position midway in the "Voyage." By this time Lowry thought of *Dark as the Grave*, "Eridanus," and "La Mordida" as a "trilogy" within the "Voyage" and worked on them concurrently.

This ordering, however, was far from final. During the 1950s—in fact, until his death—Lowry struggled with *October Ferry*, which gradually consumed the material for "Eridanus," thereby causing another major shift in the "Voyage." According to Margerie Lowry, he later altered the position of "La Mordida," putting it before "Eridanus" (now called *October Ferry to Gabriola*). The "Voyage" would therefore proceed thus:

"Ordeal 1"

Ultramarine
Lunar Caustic

Under the Volcano

Dark as the Grave
"La Mordida"
October Ferry to Gabriola

"Ordeal 2"

This order seems logical because "La Mordida" is a continuation, in time and place, of *Dark as the Grave* whereas *October Ferry* leads on into the future. There are other indications in the manuscripts, discussed below, which further corroborate these late changes, but Lowry would no doubt have revised his plan still further had he lived.

Lowry held high hopes for his ambitious masterwork. The "Voyage" was to be an image of life, viewed as "primarily (among other more pleasant factors) ordeal, a going through the hoop an initiation, finally perhaps a doing of God's will" ("WP," 3), and a genuine portrayal of life in all its monotony and simple joy. It was to be many other things as well: a great love story, a quest for faith, and certainly Lowry's own testament to the wonder of man and universe. Towards the end of "Work in Progress" he declared: "He who, even in extreme youth, turns to page 870 passim of the Voyage That Never Ends, such is my ambition, will not go unrewarded, or uncomforted, or empty away" ("WP," 30). Incredible as it sounds, given the fact that *Under the Volcano* took ten years to write, he actually estimated that the entire "Voyage" might require five years to complete!

Without doubt, "The Ordeal of Sigbjørn Wilderness" is the most fascinating of the "Voyage" fragments. In July 1949 Lowry injured his back in a fall from his Dollarton pier, and during a brief stay in hospital, he experienced hallucinations and visions and heard voices.[13] Lowry was deeply moved by this experience not least because it related to work he was doing at the time (*SC* II, 183). Art had seemed to influence life. Lowry in turn used the hospital experience to provide a setting for both parts of the "Ordeal" and, thereby, a framing device for the entire "Voyage."

"The Ordeal of Sigbjørn Wilderness" consists of a very raw draft—notes, Lowry's discussions with himself, and quotations from Arthur Lovejoy and Annie Besant (13:7, 151 pages). The intention was for the protagonist, like Lowry, to injure himself in a fall and to hear voices from his past while he was confined to hospital. Among the voices is that of a college friend, James Travers, who had committed suicide. The typescript contains frequent references to Lowry's other novels, and the Travers scenes foreshadow *October Ferry to Gabriola.* As Muriel Bradbrook points out, the suicide of his Cambridge friend, Paul Launcelot Charles Fitte, haunted Lowry all his life, causing him recurrent feelings of guilt and responsibility.[14] Consequently, he wove the event into the "Voyage." As far as the "Voyage" is concerned, however, Fitte (as Travers or Cordwainer, as he would be called in *October Ferry*) was not to be dead in any final sense, but passed on to another plane from which he could commune with the living. Sigbjørn Wilderness himself was to cross the border from life into death after the accident because "the Ordeal of Sigbjørn Wilderness is the ordeal of death itself ... albeit in fact ... the protagonist, who has suffered a near fatal accident, does not actually die" ("WP," 1). During this death-in-life crisis Sigbjørn reviews his entire existence, not haphazardly, but with events carefully selected and edited. This "transcript," giving form and meaning to his life, comprises the novels of "The Voyage That Never Ends"; "the action properly speaking begins with the second novel, the untitled sea novel, i.e., with an actual voyage" ("WP," 1).

The "Ordeal" involves one of the most unusual and challenging concepts in modern fiction. Part one was to take Wilderness from the accident to the threshold of death and the beginning of the novel sequence. Part two, emerging from the last novel, was to bring the protagonist back to life, back to his wife, back to his home, back to a balanced existence. Lowry's summary of the "Ordeal" in "Work in Progress" places the entire project in context:

> Should the plan as I now conceive it be carried out the end of La Mordida would merge into Sigbjørn Wilderness's recovery in hospital after his near fatal accident, though this, far from banal as it sounds, is actually one of the most original scenes in the Voyage. Wilderness has been placed (the accident is in Eridanus from his own self-built pier, and the opening passage of the whole work describes the flux and flow of the inlet as portrayed in the Forest Path to the Spring) shortly after the book opens in a Catholic hospital. After he has been there some days and seems to be recovering there is evidence of the most extraordinary psychic phenomena in his cell as a consequence of which—though he has injured his spine—he is considered possessed by the devil, people are removed from the adjacent wards, and he is transferred to the Protestant City Hospital. It is during this period, already beyond life, and as if he is trying to present to God some meaning in his ways on earth, that the other books, starting with the sea voyage which merges into the other hospital experience of

Lunar Caustic, the Volcano, etc., and ending with La Mordida are as it were dreamed, or lived through, merging in turn again into the psychic experiences. As he wakes, certain in his own mind that he has had among other things direct evidence of life beyond the grave and the survival of the soul ... he slowly realises that no one will believe him should he try to convince anyone of the supernatural side of his experience, not even his wife .... On the other hand he has been given his life and his health back as by a miracle, and he determines to spend the rest of it more wisely and unselfishly and usefully and the book closes once more, as it began (and as it is portrayed in the Forest Path to the Spring) on a note of happiness, with Wilderness watching the tide bearing the ships out upon its currents that become remote, and which, like the Tao, becoming remote, return.[15] ("WP," 31–32)

This passage clearly demonstrates Lowry's desire to contain the delirium of life within a literary form capable of dramatizing the necessary process of spiritual growth. On its simplest level, that form represents the patterned narrative of Wilderness's mind as he withdraws from the hospital situation into the wider reality of his imagination, finally to return to life "as by a miracle." Control or balance is all. Even at the moment of death, man must shape "his-story" because, according to Lowry, it is this shaping of life-into-art-into-life that gives meaning to existence: "Not only the editor, but man himself is a cutter and a shaper; indeed as Ortega observes, a sort of novelist" ("WP," 2). Sigbjørn Wilderness is both the author reliving his life in *Under the Volcano, Dark as the Grave,* and the other novels, and the protagonist in the "Ordeal," where his life is being written; therefore, he is contained not only within his own books but also within the imagination of the writer of the "Voyage." This concept of fabulation as a metaphor, not only for the activity of the human mind, but also for life is the cornerstone of Lowry's "Voyage."

Describing the "real protagonist of the *Voyage*" in his letters as "not so much a man or a writer as the unconscious," Lowry goes on to say that

Wilderness is not, in the ordinary sense in which one encounters novelists or the author in novels, a novelist. He simply doesn't know what he is. He is a sort of underground man. Also he is Ortega's fellow, making up his life as he goes along, and trying to find his vocation .... According to Ortega, the best image for man himself *is* a novelist, and it is in this way that I'd prefer you to look at him .... Moreover he is disinterested in literature, uncultured, incredibly unobservant, in many respects ignorant, without faith in himself, and lacking nearly all the qualities you normally associate with a novelist or a writer .... His very methods of writing are absurd and he sees practically nothing at all, save through his wife's eyes, though he gradually comes to see. I believe I can make him a very original character, both human and pathetically inhuman at once. I much approve of him as a doppelgänger. (*SC* II, 538)

Lowry approves of Sigbjørn as a *Doppelgänger* because this character is more than a conventional persona; he is a double, Lowry's other self. But his inspiration for this concept of man as novelist comes from José Ortega y Gasset's *Toward a Philosophy of History*, which he discovered in 1950 (*SC* II, 253–55). According to Ortega, "body and soul are things: but I am a drama, if anything an unending struggle to be what I have to be."[16] Wilderness, then, is a dramatization of the unconscious of the master-creator of the "Voyage," and as such he represents humanity in the process of creating history. If Lowry had lived to complete more of the "Voyage," the position and importance of the Wilderness protagonist would have imparted, as Barry Wood suggests, a strong metafictional quality to the entire "Voyage,"[17] and for this aspect of the fiction the protagonist's (or Lowry's) autobiography is immediately relevant, not because it is of personal significance but because it is the type of the general human story. Through Wilderness and the "Ordeal," Lowry was deliberately moving the "Voyage" novels further and further away from conventional realist narratives of three-dimensional, consistent characters (an aspect of fiction which he claims—in his famous letter to Cape about *Volcano*—never greatly interested him) and ever closer to the depersonalized centres of consciousness found in *Tristram Shandy*, *Finnegans Wake*, and *Gravity's Rainbow*, as well as some recent metafiction.

Lowry's description of the "Voyage" proper begins with a discussion of *Lunar Caustic*. The relationship between the sea novel and *Lunar Caustic* was to be like that between *Volcano* and *Dark as the Grave*—the protagonist in *Lunar Caustic* was to be the author of the sea novel. Lowry foresaw the finished *Lunar Caustic* as "a novel of almost total blackness" ("WP," 4). At the same time, it was to be purgatorial, hell being set aside for subsequent novels: "in one way—though originally designed to succeed it—will be seen to lead up inevitably to *Under the Volcano*" ("WP," 5). There is little further description of the book in "Work in Progress," but Lowry expatiated upon his *grand guignol* plans in complementary notes (36:5).

Apparently Lowry wished to incorporate as much material from the lost "In Ballast to the White Sea" into *Lunar Caustic* as possible. The hero, now named Thurstaston (another Wilderness projection), dreams of his university days and his youthful fixation on an older writer.[18] All this was to occur in a flashback while Thurstaston lies in hospital suffering from *delirium tremens*. Furthermore, he fears he has been contaminated by a homosexual, that his only son is dead, and that his wife has been unfaithful! The projected *Lunar Caustic* was to contain many parallels with Lowry's other novels, among them the hospital setting, which links it with the "Ordeal," and with the fact that the insane asylum, though like a "marathon of the dead," has windows that connect it with more propitious locales:

> But what is below is like what is above. The window that gives on the East River is the counterpart of the window that gives on Eridanus inlet when we have at long last, as it were, emerged into Paradise! (36:5, 8)

At this point he planned that the ending of *Lunar Caustic* should be set in a Catholic church (not the bar where Plantagenet withdraws in the published novella), "thus paralleling the end of *Dark as the Grave*" (36:5, 17).

Lunar Caustic, as published, suffers from the lack of convincing explanation for the hero's suffering, but *Lunar Caustic* rewritten along the horrifying lines sketched in the notes would have run the risk of becoming grotesquely melodramatic. Perhaps sensing these problems, Lowry devised an etiology for his protagonist: Thurstaston was to be a murderer (which is hardly surprising when one remembers the guilt of Ethan Llewelyn and Geoffrey Firmin, and the fantasies of Dana and Sigbjørn):

> I had better explain this so-called murder (which will involve another flashback) because it is a key to the whole Voyage, and it is also the key to the Consul's character and his guilt. It must be remembered that Thurstaston will turn out to be, like the Consul, Wilderness' "creation" .... But we shall learn in *Dark as the Grave* that it is Wilderness that has really committed the murder. (36:5, 10)

This "murder" is the suicide of a young Cambridge student for which Thurstaston feels responsible. Subsequently, Thurstaston/Sigbjørn's life has been one long atonement. In this way *Lunar Caustic* would double back on the "Ordeal" and dovetail into *Volcano* and *October Ferry*:

> In the Ordeal of Sigbjørn Wilderness, the first part, the man he thinks he has murdered actually speaks to him ... and forgives him, telling him that his, Wilderness', atonement has long been made but that his continuing remorse is forcing him, the dead man, to follow him everywhere.[19] (36:5, 12)

Lowry quickly dismisses *Under the Volcano* in "Work in Progress" and moves on to his plan for *Dark as the Grave Wherein My Friend Is Laid*. For the most part, the plot is identical with the published version, but there is one interesting exception. Lowry wanted to incorporate a new major character, M. L'Hirondelle, who was to be a film-maker and owner of the tower in Quauhnahuac where the Wildernesses stay. L'Hirondelle spots Sigbjørn in the airport on the way to Mexico and retrieves the manuscript, which Sigbjørn left in the bar, of the *Valley of the Shadow of Death* (the title for *Under the Volcano* in *Dark as the Grave*). L'Hirondelle, who knew Sigbjørn as a young man, turns out to be the prototype of Jacques Laruelle. Once all the characters have arrived in Quauhnahuac, "M. Laruelle and the Consul meet ... in the person of M. L'Hirondelle and Sigbjørn Wilderness, quite near the ravine of the Consul's demise" ("WP," 14). Sigbjørn was definitely to live within his own book. Despite eight pages of analysis and description, "Work in Progress" does not substantially clarify the many problems surrounding *Dark as the Grave*. Lowry reiterates what is obvious from the published text—that the novel is "a quest for faith"—but it is impossible to see how his plans, as set forth in "Work in Progress," would have significantly improved it. As far as I am aware, the proposed sections involving L'Hirondelle were never written.

Lowry devotes only one page of "Work in Progress" to an outline of "Eridanus," which was to be the next novel in the sequence. Briefly, the Wildernesses, still in their tower in Quauhnahuac, have invited L'Hirondelle to dinner, and the evening is spent "invoking" their happy life in Eridanus. Although the framing device of the dinner party seems never to have been started, the descriptive passages in "Eridanus" grew into *October Ferry*. Lowry's intention in 1951 was to use the idyllic "Eridanus" material as an "intermezzo" between the hells of *Dark as the Grave* and "La Mordida." The trilogy would thus have had a brief breathing space in the middle as well as an emphatic reminder of what the characters stood to lose. The three books, *Dark as the Grave*, "Eridanus," and "La Mordida," were to span seven months (seven being an important Lowry number) from November 1945 to May 1946.

"'La Mordida' is a continuation in time of *Dark as the Grave* and a resumption of that story" ("WP," 23). The work, a sprawling 422-page typed draft (12:9–26), exists as a collection of notes, quotations, and prose passages scarcely approximating a novel. Recorded is a thinly fictionalized account of the Lowrys' misadventures in Mexico in 1946 and their ultimate deportation. Sigbjørn and Primrose leave Quauhnahuac for a holiday in Acapulco where they are placed under hotel-arrest for a breach of visa regulations and for an unpaid fine. The remainder of their stay is spent in futile visits to the authorities while Sigbjørn withdraws to the bottle. His drinking signals yet another stage in the ordeal of life, another withdrawal before the next successful return to equilibrium. The withdrawal, however, was intended to be still more hellish than either *Volcano* or *Dark as the Grave*. Once again, the "mordida" in question is Sigbjørn's personal remorse and guilt.

The book was not to be the unrelieved nightmare that this synopsis suggests. The drama of the story—and Lowry believed it would be "an extremely exciting story, more so than *Under the Volcano*" ("WP," 29)—was to arise first from a sense of ironic contrast and, second, from a quality of "self-cancelling melodrama" ("WP," 29). Constant contrasts, amounting to counterpoint, would be created by the repetition of scenes from the other novels within the distorted, all-threatening context of "La Mordida"—scenes in prison, in a church, by the sea, in a bottle, and on the inevitable buses. The "La Mordida" bus rides were to outdo anything previously portrayed, as Lowry suggests in this description of the sense of melodrama he was seeking:

> the suspense, which seems to build up and up and up during the time of their ordeal, reading through my notes for this part, seems to me to hint of something new, or something old, that has not been thought worth developing in literature—I believe, from something I read recently, that Howells would have given me full marks—which is the drama of actual life, of stagnation, hopelessness, of monotony, the awful suspicion added to day after day, that they are never going to get their passports back at all, the self-cancelling melodrama of

D.W. Griffith-like last-moment arrivals at the Consul's office—having almost every day either by bus or car climbed the 10,000 feet up to the Tres Marias, and descended the 4,000 from Quauhnahuac to Mexico City—only to find that the Consul [not Geoffrey but the American Consul helping them] has let them down again, that no one is there: and yet they are under arrest, and are deprived of all freedom, the withdrawals and returns repeating themselves endlessly, more and more wearily, without apparent meaning. ("WP," 29)

Despite these elaborate plans and high hopes, "La Mordida" remains a tedious venture. However, Lowry's notes for the novel refer to two dream chapters that were to operate as escapes from the reality of his characters' incarceration (36:7, 1). One was to be "Through the Panama," the other was to be a story with a Haitian setting called "Battement de Tambours," which Lowry never began, and these chapters might have alleviated the monotony of the plot. The ending, in which the protagonists escape across the American border, fuses the story with the "Voyage." Beneath a brilliant night sky, Sigbjørn, with his wife in his arms, realizes that his soul has been reborn from all "these weavings to and fro, these treacheries, these projections of the past upon the future, of the imagination upon reality …. These dislocations of time" (12:26, 345). He has a "vision of absolute joy" and knows he will now return to rebuild his Canadian paradise.

October Ferry to Gabriola does not appear as a part of the "Voyage" in the 1951 "Work in Progress," but because of later developments and its eventual importance within the continuum, a few points should be made here.[20] The published text elaborates Lowry's concept of withdrawal and return first by examining Ethan Llewelyn's paralysing obsession with guilt, remorse, and disaster, and then by portraying Llewelyn's desperate struggle toward faith, psychological and emotional equilibrium, and the promise of joy. Although the story repeats this fundamental "Voyage" theme, it offers, with the exception of "Forest Path to the Spring," Lowry's most convincing portrayal of harmony. Links with the "Voyage" are obvious and numerous, from the ubiquitous "Frère Jacques" melody to the haunting presence of Peter Cordwainer.

The Cordwainer material is the most important link with the "Voyage" for it includes the identical psychic situation that Sigbjørn experiences in the "Ordeal" and, as previously noted, Lowry was determined to introduce the suicide-guilt configuration from the "Ordeal" into *Lunar Caustic*. The Cordwainer theme, although clearly stated in the published *October Ferry*, lacks nuance and significance, but in a letter to Erskine (*SC* II, 698–99), Lowry mentions that he planned to have Cordwainer appear to Ethan in a dream. When completed, this scene of communion with the dead would echo that in the "Ordeal" and further unify the "Voyage."

More interesting still is the draft of a dream chapter in which Ethan experiences his own death. The chapter, entitled "The Perilous Chapel," exists in a rough pencil draft which was apparently never typed. This heavily annotated manuscript (20:15) of twenty-six pages, most surmounted by a plea to St. Jude for help, was in no condition to be included in the published text. Nevertheless, in addition to illuminating an underdeveloped aspect of *October Ferry*, it reveals Lowry grappling with the terrors of recalcitrant prose and attempting to orchestrate his multifarious themes, motifs, and images.

"The Perilous Chapel" holograph bears scant resemblance to chapter thirty-five in the published *October Ferry*, which has the same title. The manuscript presents Ethan's dream of climbing the cliff to a mysterious chapel at its summit. A dog accompanies him on his "monumental ascent" as he battles with "death itself"— both the dog and the ascent recalling mythic and religious references in the *Volcano* while the entire scene parallels and reverses the scene of Geoffrey's death. Ethan reaches the chapel and prostrates himself before the altar upon which a single candle is burning, and here the dream acquires a nightmare quality as he experiences his dark night of the soul. Finally, the nightmare abates, and he begins his descent with the realization that reprieve from evil and death requires change: "The change had to be made now, to be made in Gabriola, or they would lose their future, as well as any but the most disastrous meaning in their past" (21:15, Q). He reaches the beach at the foot of the cliff amidst visions of angels drawn from Swedenborg and, having awakened from his ordeal, he is ready—like the Ancient Mariner—to bless and to love. Not only has Lowry conceived of a striking parallel to Geoffrey's final vision, but also the chapel with its single candle recalls the planned propitious close of *Dark as the Grave*, and the overall sense of withdrawal and return intensifies and recapitulates the central dilemma of the "Voyage." Here, the protagonist has died in order to be reborn, and he is reborn into the knowledge that the voyage never ends. With this movement of the protagonist from dream to waking, from death to rebirth, Lowry would have merged the end of *October Ferry* with part two of "The Ordeal of Sigbjørn Wilderness," from where the voyaging would have continued, ever renewed, always outward bound.

As Robert Giroux predicted in his 11 December 1951 letter to Harold Matson, "The Voyage That Never Ends" did promise to be an outstanding literary project, not only for the fifties, but also for the century (see *Selected Letters*, 445). The fragmentary remains of Lowry's masterwork provide a clear sense of the scope and unity of Lowry's system through configurations of symbols, recurring allusions and motifs, repetition of events (such as visits to bars and churches, bus rides, lighting candles, dreams, ascending mountains, and so on), and the inescapable presence throughout of an encyclopaedic perceiving consciousness. Lowry's unifying principle of repetition is nowhere more obvious, however, than in the repeated narrative pattern of withdrawal and return, and whether the movement of withdrawal from reality occurs on a epistemological or a psychological level, or more simply on the level of ordinary personal relationships, it is always a negative state characterization by narrative and stylistic stasis and by a character's emotional, spiritual, or physical death. Return from this state, like the flow of the tides, brings movement, clarity, balance, and joy—"as by a miracle."

Each of the "Voyage" novels creates a stage in Sigbjørn Wilderness's journey through life—the initiation, repeated ordeals with failure and retreat, followed by success and development, that in turn give way to fresh defeat. At each stage the same lessons recur: man must learn to change and evolve by courageously accepting his past and joyously creating his future. With *Ultramarine* the voyage begins. In *Lunar Caustic* the hero descends into a hell of self that climaxes in the apocalyptic vision of *Volcano*. In *Dark as the Grave*, a new effort begins that, with constant setbacks, will be renewed in *October Ferry to Gabriola*. Together Lowry's novels express his myth which is the story of life repeated over and over again in "The Voyage That Never Ends."[21]

(1982)

NOTES

[1] "Ghostkeeper" was first published in *American Review* 17 (Spring, 1973): 1–34, and reprinted in *Psalms and Songs*, ed. Margerie Lowry (New York: Meridian, 1975), 202–27. All references are to *Psalms and Songs*. The story is an intriguing example of Lowry's type of metafiction. It moves from polished prose passages, to notes, to trial dialogue, as the protagonist, Bill Goodheart, writes his story within the story in which he is being written. "Ghostkeeper" recalls "Through the Panama" in style, but it is more interesting for Lowry's comments on life and art. For further discussion of the story see Barry Wood's, "Malcolm Lowry's Metafiction: The Biography of a Genre."

[2] Dunne's book on serialism, *An Experiment with Time*, first published in 1927, enjoyed great popularity during the thirties, and Jones became a close friend who gave Lowry access to his library of mystic lore. The influence of Dunne and Jones is discussed in chapters three and five. The influence of Ouspensky is diffuse and harder to assess, but see *A New Model of the Universe* (New York: Vintage Books, 1971), chapter ten, where he discusses the relationship of time, space, and consciousness within his holistic vision of an "eternally changing universe."

[3] Lowry uses the term "churrigueresque" to describe *Under the Volcano* in his famous letter to Jonathan Cape; see *Sursum Corda!* I, 521. It is an architectural term describing the Spanish baroque style which reached its height in Mexico in the late seventeenth and early eighteenth centuries.

[4] Brian O'Kill claims that Lowry typically avoids "the closed unit of the periodic sentence in favour of an open form with an almost infinite capacity for addition and reduplication" ("Aspects of Language in *Under the Volcano*," in *The Art of Malcolm Lowry*, 78).

[5] All further references are to the 1968 edition of *Dark as the Grave Wherein My Friend Is Laid* and are included in the text as *DAG*.

[6] These are Mrs. Lowry's words quoting Lowry.

[7] In his essay "Malcolm Lowry as Modernist," from *Possibilities: Essays on the State of the Novel* (London: Oxford University Press, 1973), Bradbury remarks that "there lies, behind the experimental and modernist spirit, a deep vein of romanticism .... Lowry's essential assumptions about art thus tend to be purist romantic ones" (184). Lowry cannot be called an "anti-realist" even though he uses parody and explores the boundaries of fiction and life in "Ghostkeeper" and "Through the Panama." In "Notes on the Rhetoric of Anti-Realist Fiction," Albert Guerard suggests some useful distinctions between American anti-realist fiction and fiction that imitates life and uses inherited forms.

[8] All further references are to the 1970 edition of *October Ferry to Gabriola* and are included in the text as *OF*.

[9] Lowry's first oblique reference to the "Voyage" comes in a late 1939 letter to Conrad Aiken. Lowry closes thus: "Do send me news of you both and news too of the voyage that never ends'" (*SC* I, 249). Very likely Lowry and Aiken had already discussed the idea of never-ending voyage.

[10] Lowry always believed that he had lost all of "In Ballast" in this fire, but in a private conversation in the 1990s Jan Gabrial told me that an early, much shorter version of the manuscript had been left with her mother in New York in 1936 and was now in her possession. I did not see this version.

[11] In his article "Lowry's Debt to Nordahl Grieg," Hallvard Dahlie examines the textual similarities of *Ultramarine* and *The Ship Sails On* in detail. It seems likely that Lowry was more impressed by Grieg's life and ideals than by his style. Grieg, an idealistic man from a distinguished family, sailed as a common seaman while young, spent a year at Oxford, and wrote essays, poetry, plays, and fiction. He held strong proletarian sympathies. In 1937 he went to Spain as a correspondent, and during 1936–37 he published the anti-fascist periodical *Vein Friem* (*The Road Ahead*). During World War II he went to England where he read his poems of peace and patriotism for the BBC/Norway Broadcasts, These poems were published after his death as *War Poems of Nordahl Grieg* (1944). The plane he was travelling in as a reporter was shot down near Berlin in 1943. Grieg was a restless, committed man of action and deep feeling, and he may well have provided the model for the best qualities that Lowry gave Hugh in *Under the Volcano*.

[12] This outline appears on the title page of the statement. Further references to "Work in Progress" are included in the text as "WP," followed by the page number. David Miller's short monograph, *Malcolm Lowry and the Voyage That Never Ends* confuses the order of the sequence.

[13] *Malcolm Lowry*, 419. Day goes on to suggest that Lowry began the "Ordeal" after the accident, but soon lost interest. This seems unlikely since the 1951 "Work in Progress" emphasizes its importance, and Lowry refers to the "Ordeal" later in a 1954 letter to David Markson (*SC* II, 720).

[14] In *Malcolm Lowry: His Art and Early Life*, 113–17, Muriel Bradbrook discusses the background and fictional transformation of the Fitte episode. She emphasizes the importance of Lowry's early years to his life's work. For further discussion of Lowry's part in the inquest into Fitte's death see the correspondence in the *Times Literary Supplement* for 26 April and 10, 13, 17, and 24 May 1974.

[15] By this point in 1951, *October Ferry* had not developed into a major novel, and "La Mordida" completed the sequence. Sigbjørn's fears about his wife's scepticism parallel Margerie's reaction to Lowry's version of his back injury. She lost patience with his ramblings. As Lowry suggests, the "Ordeal" was to end much like the story, "The Forest Path to the Spring."

16 See *Toward a Philosophy of History* (113). Ortega's ideas were most congenial to Lowry. A staunch Heraclitean, Ortega praised the dynamic of creativity and maintained that through memory man accumulates, possesses, and must use his past in order to create the future. This belief in memory and the past is a constant hope of the Lowry protagonist.

[17] In "Malcolm Lowry's Metafiction," Wood offers a refreshing and important argument for re-evaluating Lowry's later fiction as metafiction instead of as failed novels. He is quite right in seeing "Ghostkeeper" as a paradigm of Lowry's intention and method, and I would agree with his speculation that the "Voyage" would have been metafictional.

[18] Lowry describes the convoluted plot of "In Ballast" to David Markson in an August 1951 letter (*SC* II, 417–20).

[19] In an important unpublished letter to Albert Erskine dated December 1953, Lowry repeats this idea of the dead man forced to follow the live one. See my discussion of this letter in chapter five of *The Voyage That Never Ends*.

[20] I discuss the genesis of *October Ferry* in detail in the third essay of this collection: "Beginning Yet Again."

[21] In *Mythology in the Modern Novel* (8), John White speaks of *Under the Volcano* and *Finnegans Wake* as "seeking to create a new myth." Lowry's myth is best understood in the terms of Robert Scholes and Robert Kellogg. They define *mythos* as "traditional story" which can be retold or recreated; see "The Narrative Tradition."

2

Outward Bound

In 1927, aged eighteen, Malcolm Lowry travelled to the Far East as a cabin boy aboard the *Pyrrhus*. Some time after his return to England six months later he began work on a novel, his first, which was to be called *Ultramarine*. With Conrad Aiken's *Blue Voyage* and Nordahl Grieg's *The Ship Sails On* as models, Lowry slowly put together his story of a young man's initiation into life aboard a cargo freighter. The young hero, Dana Hilliot, rejects the present realities of sea-life and a hostile crew by persistently escaping into memories of the past until events onboard force him to choose between a continued destructive withdrawal into self and a dangerous but creative acceptance of life. This initiatory voyage came to represent the logical starting point in Lowry's projected *The Voyage That Never Ends* which was to comprise all of his inter-related and major works, including *Under the Volcano*.

Ultramarine, however, partly due to its derivativeness and partly due to the over-shadowing fact of *Under the Volcano*, has been consistently neglected by readers and critics alike. That the continued neglect of Lowry's first novel is unwarranted is the basic assumption of this study. George Woodcock, in his "Introduction" to *Malcolm Lowry: The Man and his Work*, emphasizes *Ultramarine*'s importance:

> [M]uch of the matter of his early novel finds its way, transformed, into *Under the Volcano*, and its experiments with time and memory, with the reality of the past making the present unreal, will be repeated in all the major novels. A reading of it is indispensable to a full understanding of Lowry.[1]

Ultramarine, originally published in 1933, was reprinted with some of Lowry's later revisions in 1963. According to Margerie Lowry's "Introductory Note," it was intended to be "in its rewritten form, the first volume in … *The Voyage That Never Ends*."[2] With this purpose in view, Lowry changed the name of Dana's ship to the *Oedipus Tyrannus* and made other links with the *Volcano*. Although the book obviously remains a first novel and is certainly not of the stature of *Under the Volcano*, *Ultramarine* is seldom, if ever, given its due. For the most part, critics are content to point out the novel's debt to Aiken's *Blue Voyage* and Grieg's *The Ship Sails On*.[3] Lowry himself was ashamed of the book.

In spite of weaknesses, the structure of the book illustrates the tremendous control which Lowry was developing over his materials. As with the *Volcano* and *Dark as the Grave*, in *Ultramarine* Lowry expands a short period of time, approximately forty-eight hours, into the months and years enfolded in Dana's consciousness. Nineteen years are contained within the small circle of two days passed in one place.

The structure of *Ultramarine* is circular. Beginning in Dana's mind, the narrative circles repeatedly from external action and dialogue back into Dana's consciousness until the final line of the book places the reader within the hero's mind once more. The book is crowded with images of circles and encircling—the engines, wheeling birds, eyes, Dana's lost compasses—even the ship, the harbour of Tsjang-Tsjang, and the sea, function as further layers of encircling reality.

Within the first four chapters, Lowry counterpoints two geographical and spiritual points along the circumference of the superimposed circles of the voyage and Dana's consciousness. The first geographical and spiritual point is the ship's departure for the East which Dana remembers as the book opens. It is essential to emphasize that *Ultramarine* begins as the *Oedipus Tyrannus* is nearing the port of Tsjang-Tsjang, the furthest point of her voyage. In Dana's mind, however, the ship is still preparing to leave Liverpool. During the course of the first four chapters, Dana moves deeper into his past before gradually circling his way back again, in chapter four, to the time of his departure from home. His memory transcribes an enormous circle until it catches itself up at the crucial moment of severance, the sailing of his ship. This point in time haunts him because it symbolizes severance from his youth and initiation into life. Furthermore, it is just this initiation or birth, this breaking out of the womb-like circle of his past, from which he shrinks in dread.

The second geographical and spiritual point of Dana's vicious circle is the furthest point of the voyage, the harbour of Tsjang-Tsjang and the abyss of the present self. While the ship is idle at the dock, Dana, his mind and soul in an analogous static state, plumbs the depths of his private hell. This hell, projected upon external reality by his distorted vision, results from his constant re-living of the past in the present and his persistent refusal to welcome life. Transfixed, like a "tinfoil Jesus," between these two points, Dana must first learn to recognize the self-inflicted hell for what it is and then to move out of his closed circle of time and space.

By the end of chapter one with the boat docked and night falling, Dana, who has refused to enter life by going ashore, retreats to his bunk and his memories of the past. The visions which he has as he falls asleep highlight his spiritual crisis. Dana is so entirely enclosed in self that he cannot consciously articulate his problem until the end of the book, while readers, drawn into the maelstrom of Dana's mind, experience the claustrophobia of a consciousness closed in upon itself. Believing that the ship "had a manifold security: she was his harbour; he would lie in the arms of the ship" (*U*, 43), Dana glides into a sleep immediately filled with wheeling screaming horror:

> Above, the moon soared and galloped through a dark, tempestuous sky. All at once, every lamp in the street exploded, their globes flew out, darted into the sky, and the street became alive with eyes; eyes greatly dilated, dripping dry scurf, or glued with viscid gum: eyes which held eternity in the fixedness of their stare: eyes which wavered, and spread, and, diminishing rapidly, were catapulted east and west; eyes that were the gutted windows of a cathedral, blackened, emptiness of the brain, through which bats and ravens wheeled enormously .... (*U*, 44)

Significantly, the vision is one of movement and the breaking of enclosing circles: lamps explode, their "globes" flying into the sky, eyes waver, and "diminishing" are "catapulted east and west"; even the enclosing glass of windows is shattered allowing bats and ravens to "wheel enormously" through their empty frames. This is a vision of the chaotic flux which Dana must accept. At this point in his voyage he is only capable of seeing this chaos as nightmarish horror. The closest he comes here to confronting his true position is suggested in the final sensation of the dream and the chapter—without his compasses (to draw continual circles or to locate his own centre) he is "Lost. Lost. Lost." (*U*, 45).

In chapter two, the ship static in the harbour parallels Dana's increasing withdrawal into an abyss of self. Dana escapes the reality of present time and space by dredging up time past and pre-voyage places until they form a hard shell of encrusted memory around his timorous psyche. The climax of his descent into self comes, when, with perception inverted and distorted, he envisions the *Oxenstjerna*, a symbol of movement, life, and a positive growing past, the ox-star "that shines above the lives of men," grounded and oozing death:

> It is the *Oxenstjerna* they are talking about, the *Oxenstjerna* that has gone aground. It is the *Oxenstjerna* which now turns over and sinks into the sand, while the oil spreads a mucous film over the Mersey; and now the white sea gulls ... known by name to the dockers, are dying by the score. (*U*, 74)

With the virtuosity that characterizes *Under the Volcano*, Lowry forges here a most striking image of stasis and enveloping death which functions like a magnet within the heart of the book. In one brief passage he enfolds the cluster of motifs surrounding the *Oxenstjerna* with the various bird motifs in the novel and even with the haunting motif of eyes; "a mucous film" (like all the eye imagery, drawn from Lowry's personal sufferings) recalls the vision of eyes in chapter one, and fuses with the general theme of Dana's spiritual blindness. Lowry's technique, in a miniature example such as this image of the *Oxenstjerna*, as well as in larger structural units, is one of enfolding and encircling. The image is superficially quite simple, but it vibrates with a plentitude of centripetal meaning. In addition to embodying several motifs, motifs which can only be fully understood when viewed within the totality of the book, the *Oxenstjerna* passage symbolizes Dana's consciousness. Like the ship he has gone aground and "now turns over and sinks into the sand" (*U*, 74).

The lowest point of Dana's descent occurs in chapter three as he stumbles about Tsjang-Tsjang in a drunken nightmare. This lowest point, however, fully in keeping with Lowry's concept of the fusion of opposites, marks the beginning of his ascent; Dana grapples with the recognition and articulation of his position. His self-analysis is still typically exaggerated and maudlin but he at least admits to these aspects of his nature. Enclosed within the rhetoric of his self-portrait is the further realization that he alone creates his heaven or hell:

> Tinfoil Jesus, crucified homunculus (who is also the cross), spitted on the hook of an imaginary Galilee! Who is the crown of thorns dripping red blossoms and the red-blue nails, the flails and the bloody wounds. The tears, but also the lips cupped to embrace them as they fall; the whips, but also the flesh crawling to them. The net and the silver writhing in the mesh, and all the fish that swim in the sea.—The centre of the Charing Cross, ABCD, the Cambridge Circle, the Cambridge Circus, is Hilliot—but every night, unseen, he climbs down and returns to his hotel—while the two great shafts, the propeller shafts, the shafts of wit, laced with blood, AB, CD are the diameters. Now with his navel as centre and half CD as radius, describe a vicious circle! (*U*, 98–99)

Amidst a geometrician's paradise of circles, Dana sees himself as a cheap poseur, a Christ who climbs down from his self-inflicted cross to seek the shelter of his bed in a hotel room. The image of Dana as the centre of a circle with the four circumference points making a cross, ABCD, crystallizes his physical and spiritual dilemma; the points are fixed, the radius is given, the circle is closed, vicious.

Questioning his entire purpose for this voyage, Dana explains his failure in the very terms which will help him break out of his calcified circle of time and space. Challenging Janet's belief in him he cries,

> could you still believe in me, still believe in the notion that my voyage is something Columbian and magnificent? Still believe in my taking a self-inflicted penance; in this business of placing myself within impenetrable and terrible boundaries in order that a slow process of justification to your self may go on. (*U*, 99)

Naming the names and saying the words is always magic with Lowry. Dana will soon break out of the seemingly "impenetrable and terrible boundaries" of his self-created hell. As centre to his circle he will move and in moving transcribe an ever new circumference.

By chapter four, Dana's agonized attempts to re-inhabit the past have brought him circling back to the point at which the book opened, the departure from England of the *Oedipus Tyrannus*. In the flashback of his return to Liverpool after the farewell with Janet, the Mersey strikes him as "like a vast camera film slowly and inexorably winding. Soon he will be entangled in her celluloid meshes, and wound out to the open sea" (*U*, 142). In a sense, Dana has encircled in memory his own position (much as he does later with Andy); he has come full circle. Now is the time to strike out anew. The challenge to Andy represents his first decisive action of the voyage. He does not grasp the profound truth, however, that this intense moment which gathers up all his anger and frustration is, in fact, a *punctum indifferens*. Life cannot be seized and frozen in this way for it flows on, forever eluding the grasp. As the card players remark upon returning to their game after Dana's interruption, "—pass—" "—pass—" "—pass—" (*U*, 153).

The ship sails on or, at least in chapter five, it prepares to leave port. Prior to the ship's departure, the culminating crisis of the book occurs. Norman's pet pigeon (with consequences that recall the Ancient Mariner's albatross) escapes from its cage and drowns. Dana and the crew stand by helplessly watching it die while a nearby motor boat "its occupant spinning the easy wheel while it circled around gaily ... turned on itself and rolled in its own swell" (*U*, 162). The last moments of the ship's stasis at the dock parallels Dana's inability to save the bird. Suddenly, amidst rolling winches and coiling ropes, "the windlass clanking and racing around gladly" and the tiger "moulding its body to the shape of his cage" (*U*, 166), Dana remembers Norman's grief at the loss of his pet and sees the truth:

> No, such things couldn't happen really. But Norman's words made a sort of incantation in his brain. "Time!" Of course there would have been time. Time wouldn't have mattered if you'd been a man." (*U*, 166)

This truth is useless, however, unless one knows how to use it, and Dana is still uncertain. With the renewed peace of the vessel under sail, he contemplates the roaring fires in the "pulsating and throbbing" engine room:

> Why was it his brain could not accept the dissonance as simply as a harmony, could not make order emerge from this chaos? ... Chaos and disunion, then, he told himself, not law and order, were the principles of life which sustained all things, in the mind of man as well as on the ship. (*U*, 169)

Being unable to accept chaos as good is Dana's great sin. In his effort to order and contain reality, he has only succeeded in stifling himself, and life, within a tightly sealed tomb of time and space.

Now that he has admitted the priority of chaos, he is ready to move on to a reconciliation with Andy who symbolizes the forces of life into which Dana must be initiated. With the meaning of the maelstrom and "a reason for his voyages" clearly perceived, Dana looks down into the engine room once more. There he sees Nikolai, the fireman, serving the source of energy and chaos:

.The iron tools blistered his hands, his chest heaved like a giant swimmer's, his eyes tingled in parched sockets, but still he worked on, he would never stop— this was what it was to exist— (*U*, 171)

Never to stop in the journey of life, this is Dana's discovery. Life is flux, chaos, energy, while death, like a ship gone aground, like a fixed, transcribed circle ABCD, is stasis. Paradoxically, life exists in the fiery abyss of the ship and Dana cherishes his discovery while "somewhere," as if warning that this point of rest is a *punctum indifferens*, "a lantern clanged with eternal, pitiless movement" (*U*, 172).

Significantly, *Ultramarine* does not end on this pinnacle of insight. Although the narrative rhythm reaches completion by the end of chapter five, the novel continues, mirroring in its structure what Dana has still to learn. In this sense *Ultramarine* was an ideal prologue for Lowry's intended voyage that never ends. Dana Hilliot, prefiguring the restless voyaging of subsequent Lowry heroes, realizes that he has "surrounded Andy's position" and must move on; life is a continual movement of centre and circumference:

(There is ... a stormflood within, as my heart beats with the beating of the engine, as I go out with the ship towards the eternal summers. A storm is thundering out there, there is the glow of tropical fire! Bad, or good, as it happens to be, that is what it is to exist! ... It is as though I have been silent and fuddled with sleep all my life .... I know now that at least it is better to go always towards the summer .... Then at last again to be outward bound, always outward, always onward, to be fighting always for the dreamt-of-harbour ... —) (*U*, 201)

Then, lest this solution of life's mystery appear too simple, Lowry charts the next stage in Dana's initiation. A fireman is ill and Dana is chosen to replace him; he must descend into the abyss of life which he earlier contemplated with acute insight. During his last moments on deck, a strange craft drifts through the night mist morseing her name: *Oxenstjerna*. Like a voice from his past this ship calls to him, reminding him that on the point of creating a new circle into the future he must take the past with him—as comfort and as threat. If he again makes the profound mistake of withdrawing into a hard shell of time and space, he will destroy his world. For life is perpetual activity "always outward, always onward."

Certainly *Ultramarine* is not an *Under the Volcano,* but then few books are. That it is a worthwhile book in its own right is equally clear. In his first novel, Lowry explored the problems of time and space and of self-enclosed perception which distinguish his fiction. The structure of the book, prefiguring in its involutions the structure of the *Volcano,* supports Lowry's vision of a mind so turned in upon itself, so obsessed with the past, that only a series of shocks can free it. For such an individual (for life itself Lowry would have us believe) the achievement of equilibrium is temporary; beyond one hurdle lies the next, a worse one; "that is what it is to exist." As a member of Lowry's *Voyage* cycle and precursor to *Under the Volcano* or as an independent novel, *Ultramarine* succeeds in its portrayal of initiation; the voyage has begun, the ship is outward bound.

(1976)

Notes

[1] Woodcock was one of the first Canadian critics to appreciate the significance of Lowry's work in general, and I was grateful, as a young scholar, that he was so quick to accept this essay on *Ultramarine* for *Canadian Literature*. For his own comments on the novel, see *Malcolm Lowry: The Man and his Work* (5).

[2] *Ultramarine*, 7. All further references are to the 1963 edition and are included in the text.

[3] See, for example, the first two chapters of Richard Hauer Costa's *Malcolm Lowry*. By far the best discussion of *Ultramarine* to date is chapter two of Tony Kilgallin's *Lowry*; Kilgallin reveals many further influences on or allusions in the novel. Lowry's anxiety over his propensity to borrow from other writers lasted his entire life and I discuss this issue in several of the essays that follow but especially in "Respecting Plagiarism."

3

Beginning Yet Again: October Ferry to Gabriola

October Ferry to Gabriola represents Margerie Lowry's editing of a work-in-progress, but although the text is unfinished and there are undeveloped aspects of the writing, *October Ferry* is by no means a raw effort. The novel functions very well and is a rich, often moving work which, together with "The Forest Path to the Spring," presents Lowry's most sustained vision of paradise.[1]

Lowry began work on the *October Ferry* theme shortly after a 1946 trip to the British Columbia gulf island of Gabriola when he and Margerie joined forces to write a short story based on the trip (20:1). Dissatisfied, Lowry put the story aside, but interestingly enough, the twenty-eight-page story contains the narrative scaffolding of the novel to come. The bus, the level-crossing, the bastion hiding the Gabriola ferry, the beer parlour, Mrs. Neiman, and the return to the dock—each element is present in miniature. Most notably, the twilight approach to the island, with its hopeful swinging lantern and welcoming voice, persists from this first attempt through later reworkings of the material.

Lowry began working in earnest on the Gabriola theme in 1950 (*SC* II, 302), and by late 1951 he believed the novella to be "a hell of a fine thing." By 1953 he was obsessed and delighted by *October Ferry*, which was threatening to become a novel, though still closely related to companion stories in *Hear us O Lord*. As the novel grew it severed its close relationship with the stories in *Hear us O Lord*; however, both books deal with the return from withdrawal to a state of balance. Along with "The Bravest Boat," "Present Estate of Pompeii," "Gin and Goldenrod," and "The Forest Path to the Spring," *October Ferry* grows out of Lowry's profound, almost symbiotic, relationship with the British Columbia coast. In December 1956, Lowry wrote to David Markson that he was "working like absolute sin on *Gabriola* with which I have completely fallen in love" (*SC* II, 866). Lowry's destructive love affair with the novel arose perhaps, as he himself suggested, from some "fanatical narcissism or other that makes me set the touchstone impossibly high, as a result of which I am now writing a huge and sad novel about Burrard Inlet called *October Ferry to Gabriola*" (*SC* II, 866).

October Ferry to Gabriola is the superficially simple story of the search by a husband and wife for a new house because they face eviction from a much beloved fore-shore cabin on Eridanus Inlet; however, what Lowry means by eviction, secular and divine, not to mention the significance of the new house (their fourth), is not simple. The theme of eviction and the search for a new house, combined with the protagonist's problems of guilt, fear, and hatred, become increasingly important as the book proceeds. The story covers approximately twelve hours of the day on which Ethan Llewelyn (a semi-retired lawyer whose name means "of strength unknown") and Jacqueline travel from Victoria to Nanaimo by bus, wait in Nanaimo for the Gabriola ferry, and then leave on the ferry for the gulf island. This simple immediate level, however, acquires increasing complexity and significance through the consciousness of Ethan, who spends the first part of the day reliving his past, including his boyhood in England, his courtship and marriage in Ontario, the burning of a second house in Niagara-on-the-Lake, and the finding of a third home in British Columbia. Using Ethan's memory, Lowry condenses considerable time and space into the present three or four hours spent on the bus and thereby incorporates the necessary background exposition and, more important, dramatizes the presentness of the past.

Two insufficiently developed subjects counterpoint the main theme of eviction and search. Throughout, Ethan suffers paralysing guilt over the suicide of a university friend, Peter Cordwainer—a subject which had long haunted Lowry himself, as is clear from his plans for the "Ordeal" and *Lunar Caustic*. Lowry has Cordwainer follow Ethan from England to British Columbia in the guise of billboards advertising the Cordwainer Industries' product: "Mother Gettle's Kettle Simmered Soups." In addition, Ethan is tormented by the case of a fifteen-year-old Vancouver boy sentenced to hang for murder. Despite his disgust with society's condemnation, Ethan finds that he is unable to defend the Chapman boy.

October Ferry portrays the ordeal of life in terms of the usual Lowry predicament. Ethan, who has withdrawn from civilization, is in danger lest his "retreat" become totally atavistic. During the long bus ride, which occupies two-thirds of the book, he withdraws simultaneously into his own guilt-ridden consciousness and into his past. His perception of reality, like the Consul's, grows increasingly distorted; the landscape bristles with symbols, signs threaten, snatches of overheard conversation are strange messages for him, and films appear to mirror and comment upon his life. Ethan has been a sailor and a musician, and like similar Lowry heroes, he is also divided against himself. Thus, Lowry refers to Poe and to the film *The Student of Prague* in order to suggest the disturbing presence of a *Doppelgänger* in Ethan's life, and even the opening quote from George Eliot reminds the reader that when men sell their souls to the devil, "there is a dark shadow beside them for evermore" (epigraph, np). Again, as in the previous novels, the Lowry protagonist is outward bound: "beginning: beginning: beginning again; beginning yet again" (5), and *October Ferry* can best be understood, thematically and technically, in terms of Lowry's obsession with movement and growth. Eridanus represents the past and the necessity to move on, to begin again; Gabriola symbolizes the future.

Although there is no magnificent "Apologia" for *October Ferry* as there is for *Under the Volcano*, Lowry did write Albert Erskine about his plans. This letter of 27 December 1953 (*SC* II, no. 598) contains his most detailed extant analysis of the book. He wrote the letter to Erskine shortly before departing on a visit to his friends, the Neilsons, on Bowen Island—"a December Ferry to Bowen Island"—and his comments are typically wayward and amusing. At this point, he was nearing completion of a final draft, but if Day's interpretation of the following months is accurate (see Day, 431–37), Erskine was far from reassured by his claims. Lowry, however, was optimistic:

> As for where the story's going there is an excellent and sinister reason for its apparent inability to move into the future: it turns out that both characters are potential suicides. Each has also become afraid that in a fit of hysteria or drunkenness one may murder the other. Thus the difficulty of the future taking any shape at all, as of the present having any meaning for the protagonists, is really the whole plot. They have more trouble getting to Gabriola than K to the castle though Gabriola is not a castellan symbol; it is, finally, the future. (*SC* II, 697)

Lowry found writing *October Ferry* especially difficult: "[I]t has cost me more pains than all the *Volcano* put together" (*SC* II, 659), and toward the end of his life he felt that it had become a "challenge" to his personal salvation. The published letters, especially from 1953, contain many references to his plans for the book. For example, in another letter to Erskine, he compares the form of the novel to a triangle:

> You will be wondering at the length of this first chapter too … so I will expound thus far the magic of Dr. Lowry's dialectical-Hegelian-spiritualism-Cabbalistic-Swedenborgian-conservative-Christian-anarchism for ailing paranoiacs: the first chapter … is as the base to a triangle or a triad (and/or a radical having a valence of three): viz

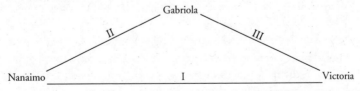

Which is meant to illustrate no more than that Chapter I might be 180 pages long, Chapters II and III each half that length, without its form being overbalanced—to the contrary. (*SC* II, 687–88)

This concept of a "triangle or a triad" is crucial to an understanding of the novel's structure as well as to an appreciation of the Cabbalistic ordeal of the protagonist, which is discussed further below. Lowry goes on to assure Erskine that the repetitions of the first part of the narrative are meant "to give the effect of the man *caught*, washed to and fro in the tides of his mind, unable to escape."

In the December 1953 letter to Erskine, Lowry again explains the structure of this book. The three chapters of *October Ferry* have now become three "parts":

> However I'm only equipped to write all this: not to describe it. I believe it to be bloody good and that it gets better. But it's not intended to fall into any particular category or obey any of the normal rules of a novel. The second part of the book concerns their difficulty in finding the ferry and takes place in Nanaimo, mostly in a pub, where Ethan gets pretty tight; there are powerful dramatic scenes (though I sez it) in Nanaimo both in the present and the past: a scene of lyrical beauty is balanced against a Grand Guignol horror that takes place on the scaffold. (A waiter turns out to be a man Ethan's saved). The third part is on board the ferry itself. (*SC* II, 697)

The triangle or triad represents the structure of *October Ferry* to the same extent that the circle denotes the *Volcano*. The number three appears throughout the text: the Llewelyns have had three houses, and with Tommy they form a family of three. The three parts of the book correspond to the three temporal dimensions (past, present, and future) as well as to the elements of fire, earth, and water. During the bus ride Ethan broods about fire, in Nanaimo he is on *terra firma*, and on the ferry he is surrounded by water. The fourth element, air, is present throughout—rushing past the bus and ferry, through Ethan's soul, and through his own personal "Cave of Winds." The protagonist sits, talks, and thinks within three specific spaces—the bus, the Ocean Spray Bar, and the ferry. There are three bars in the book, and in the third Ethan reflects upon the way the partitions can be moved in order to expand the men's side:

> These partitions were usually movable, for at crowded hours the Men's side was much fuller than the Ladies and Escorts: the partition would thus often be found slowly moving in on the territory of the latter, producing, sometimes, if you were obliged to leave your lady for several minutes, on your return a certain eerie feeling of perichoresis. An isolation that was, at the same time, begotten by an interpretation. (251)

"Perichoresis" literally means the act of going around, rotation, and there is a great deal of literal perichoresis in *October Ferry*. However, it is also a theological term for the unity of the divine trinity through interpenetration,[2] a point Ethan notes when, catching sight of the astrological magazines by the Nanaimo dock, he contemplates "the duplication of the cube, or the trisection of the right angle, not to say the Symbol of the Divine Trinity in Unity" (233). Lowry delighted in unusual words like this which hold such different meanings and belong in such different contexts but at the same time can be forced, as in this passage, to *mean* both things at the same time. Here Ethan's immediate context of "movable" partitions and an "isolation" which is paradoxically "interpenetration" contribute to Lowry's particular sense of "perichoresis" as a spiritual unity somehow discoverable in circular movement.

Lowry found the triangle a useful structural paradigm for *October Ferry* because of its versatility and all-inclusiveness. Geographically, it represents the Llewelyn's voyage: "For they had been traveling as it were along the upended base of a triangle of which Eridanus itself on the mainland could roughly be considered the apex" (153). Spiritually, it indicates the result of their voyage; not only may they find the Divine Trinity in Unity, but they may also anneal their little secular family of three and achieve the social unity that William Plantagenet and Geoffrey Firmin lack. Most important, the triangle or triad is, together with the circle, the main structural element of Achad's Tree of Life. According to Achad, the Tree of Life is composed of a "Trinity of Triads," with the second and third triads derived from the first by reflection to form a balance.

The Cabbala is far from the only influence upon Lowry's novel, but it is significant that Achad's *Q.B.L.* was one of the few books that Lowry asked specially to have sent to him in 1956 (*SC* II, 798).[3] The Cabbala with its "method of thought" is important to the epistemology of the book, and in addition to the figure of the McCandless, who is a Cabbalist, the text contains many images drawn from Achad's studies. The noteworthy point about the "Trinity of Triads" in *Q.B.L.* is that it represents a path or a way, a method, in fact, for the adept to achieve balance. By progressing from one triad or level to the next, the adept gradually attains inner balance, wisdom, harmony, or, if you will, God. The three triads are contained in the fourth level of the Tree, the tenth *Sephira* called "Malkuth," or "The Kingdom":

> Finally, this TRINITY OF TRIADS being in itself a UNITY is Symbolized by the TENTH SEPHIRA called MALKUTH, THE KINGDOM, a SINGLE SPHERE pendant to the above and summing up in itself all the foregoing qualities which it MANIFESTS according to the Creative Plan. All these qualities may be said to be Potentially inherent in KETHER The Crown—with which MALKUTH is, in a certain Mystical sense, ONE, as it is written: "Kether is in Malkuth and Malkuth is in Kether but after another manner." (*Q.B.L.*, 8–9.)[4]

As Lowry himself emphasizes, there are three parts to *October Ferry*, and the Llewelyns are searching for their fourth home on Gabriola, which represents their salvation. Without forcing the novel into a constraining mould, it is possible to see the three parts of *October Ferry* as parallel with the "Trinity of Triads" in Achad's Tree of Life. The fourth house on Gabriola, which they have such difficulty in reaching, parallels "Malkuth," "The Kingdom"—the Divine Trinity in Unity. Each of the three stages of the journey on bus, land, and ferry represents a stage in the ordeal, and the arrival at Gabriola symbolizes Ethan's attainment of balance, his self-unification.

Certainly, Achad's system offers rich metaphoric possibilities. His Tree of Life embodies constant movement and expansion and is thus an image of time as flowing and creative, and of space as never enclosing or stopping this flow of life. In *The Anatomy of the Body of God*, for example, Achad explains that the Tree of Life is "not a fixed design but capable of indefinite progression towards the Infinitely Small or the Infinitely Great. For it can be so drawn that it appears with all its details and properties, repeating themselves in every direction of Space to Infinity" (12). Similarly, the three parts of *October Ferry* flow and expand, each mirroring and reflecting the other through Lowry's brilliant use of image, motif, and allusion, and equally important, Ethan perceives the nature of reality in precisely Achad's terms:

> All at once, without knowing why, he felt as if he were seated at the center of the infinite itself, then, that this was indeed true, that the center of the infinite was everywhere, just as its circumference must be nowhere. Everything seemed part of a miraculous plan, in which nothing stood still, everything good was capable of infinite development, everything evil must inevitably deteriorate. (224)

Although the entire time span of *October Ferry's* tripartite structure is approximately twelve hours, Lowry expands the few hours on the bus to include the thirty-nine years of Ethan's life through a further structural division of the first part of the text into another triad. Thus, part one of *October Ferry* presents three distinct time loops within Ethan's mind: the first loop includes chapters one to ten, the second chapters eleven to twenty-one, and the third chapters twenty-two to twenty-seven.

Each of these loops develops a period from the past that Ethan is, in fact, reliving. The first loop consists of Jacqueline's and Ethan's earlier years, as well as their courtship and marriage. Here Lowry introduces details of Jacqueline's birth, her mother's suicide, her father's beliefs, and important information from Ethan's past. The Cordwainer theme is also initiated and the significance of the films, especially *Outward Bound*, is dramatically established.

In the second time loop, Ethan's mind travels over the early years of his marriage, the birth of his son Tommy, and, most important, the burning of his second home. As Ethan moves closer to the surface of the present, he plunges deeper into despair and fear. Fire and loss, which threaten the sanity of both characters, as well as their marriage, dominate the Niagara-on-the-Lake period. In this time loop, Lowry counterpoints a film of Temple Thurston's *The Wandering Jew*, with an account of Thurston's death by fire in order to explore the interpenetration of reality and illusion, life and art. Horrified by the intuition that life and art are contained in each other or that both are contained in some larger dimension of a serial universe, Ethan experiences a hellish "St. Paul's vision upside down" arising from "an almost complete and mysterious identification of subject with object" (146):

> Yet this [vision] seemed the home also of more conscious mental abortions and aberrations; of disastrous yet unfinished thoughts, half hopes and half inten- tions, and where precepts, long abandoned, stumbled on. Or the home of a

half-burned man, himself an imperfect visualization, at the stake; this place
where neither death nor suicide could ever be a solution, since nothing here had
been sufficiently realized ever to possess life. (146)

Ethan's predicament parallels the Consul's. As he sits in this bar, he gradually loses
all sense of separate identity or even reality.

The third time loop of the first part of *October Ferry* brings Ethan's consciousness
to the most recent past, his life at Eridanus and the threat of eviction. Peter Cordwainer continues to haunt him as he becomes more and more certain that his life
has been one long penance for Peter's death. Ethan, "bound to these thoughts like
Ixion to his wheel" (192), sinks deeper and deeper into despair. To make matters
worse, the apartment house where he and Jacqueline have stayed while searching for
their fourth house turns out to have been an abortionist's clinic. As Ethan points out,
they seem to be living in the world of Sartre's *No Exit* (198). The descent into the
abyss of self reaches its climax as Ethan, his mind surfacing to a present in which he
feels "strapped into his seat" (208), confronts his image, or perhaps his *Doppelgänger*,
in the rear-view mirror of the bus:

> The face in the mirror, a half face, a mask, looked at him approvingly, smiling,
> but with a kind of half terror. Its lips silently formed the one word:
>
> Murderer! (216)

This expressionistic touch recalls Ethan's earlier memory of "the face of a sort of
devil" that had confronted him in the mirror of a Niagara-on-the-Lake bar (47).

In each of his works Lowry employs complicated temporal involutions, and in
October Ferry, as in *Dark as the Grave*, they intensify the protagonists' struggle to
break free from the tentacles of the past. A sense of psychological time is suggested
by these narrative loops, which contrast ironically with the relentless unilinear movement of the bus and of clock time. In this way, Lowry establishes the crucial rhythm
of "the man *caught*, washed to and fro in the tides of his mind, unable to escape"
(*SC* II, 688). In each time loop Ethan's consciousness flows back and forth between
present reality on the bus and the greater reality of his past. Lowry's intention was
to suggest the flux and reflux of the tides, so that in chapter thirteen, "The Tides of
Eridanus," Ethan would become aware of a "slow, stealthy, despairing *deepening* of
the medium of his thoughts [which is] like a tide of Eridanus coming in" (76). With
the steady advance of the second loop into the past, Ethan faces greater and more
dangerous "snags":

> Now there was only this tide of his mind still rising, and deepening, reaching
> out toward those other grislier, more menacing timbers that were fears,
> anxieties, obsessions, horrors, it had not yet set afloat. (81)

In addition to establishing this tidal rhythm of the mind and introducing
terrifying "snags" from the past, the temporal loops of this part of the narrative
create the rhythm of withdrawal and return within *October Ferry*, as well as

contributing to the larger pattern of the "Voyage" cycle. With each loop Ethan's thoughts are swept from brightness to a state of darkness, from communication with others to utter isolation, and with each, Ethan must begin again to confront the meaning of his past by moving deeper into an inner hell.

The second phase of *October Ferry* takes place in the present, beginning with the arrival of Jacqueline and Ethan in Nanaimo in chapter twenty-eight, "Wheel of Fire." The bus follows a hearse into the town, and this chapter, enclosed within the fiery wheel of Ethan's consciousness, prefigures his symbolic death and descent into hell in the Ocean Spray Bar. The bar in chapter thirty-one, "Twilight of the Raven," with its "columns of mirrors, carefully designed to look broken, under a ceiling of dried blood," its light that turns the "denizens of the place into corpses," and its view-destroying glass of "a thick corrugated verdigris green" (25) portrays a closed, static hell:

> Though its boundaries seemed yet to be determined, if the purpose were not
> to leave them flexible as now, this newly renovated Men's section proper of the
> beer parlour appeared to be finished to the satisfaction of whatever inverted
> genius had created it. Finished. It was the end. (258)

The reality of present time and the sense of temporal flow fade as Ethan, trapped within the bar and his own tormented mind, presents his statement for the defence—the defence of Chapman and his self-defence. Chapter thirty-one, in many ways the most powerful and extraordinary chapter in the novel, is reminiscent in its complicated richness and temporal stasis of chapter ten in *Under the Volcano* and is discussed in greater detail below.

The third and final phase of the narrative begins with chapter thirty-three as Ethan and Jacqueline board the little ferry outward bound for Gabriola. At last, time regains reality as the ferry, not without a final setback, approaches the island amidst "a *boundless sense of space*, cleanliness, speed, light, and rocketing white gulls" (329 [italics added]). The boundlessness of space is crucial because, in Lowry's view, space with rigid bounds constricts and destroys. Only when boundaries are flexible and open to the flow of time are life and creativity possible. Although the return to Nanaimo threatens to cancel their hopes of reaching Gabriola, it proves to be a good omen. Someone throws the evening newspaper on board, and they learn of the reprieve from eviction which is essential to their victory in the future because it frees them from restrictions and entanglements in the past.

The novel closes with Ethan's vision of the approaching evening when he will walk along the shore of Gabriola with Jacqueline in "the moonlit, meteor-bright night" (331). This vision of the stars and moon, consistent Lowry symbols of life and hope, gives way to the present reality of Gabriola with its "sheltered valley that sloped down to a silent, calm harbour" (33). For the moment, Lowry's protagonist has achieved wisdom, balance, and a temporary point of rest.

Lowry establishes the conflict between motion and stasis, or time and space, in the opening paragraphs of the book where the prose reflects the poles of Ethan's experience: on the one hand, Ethan moves swiftly with the bus; on the other, he is immobilized, bound by his ticket. Lowry first accentuates the flow of his narrative before sharply disrupting this rhythm—but a long passage is necessary to illustrate his method:

> The October morning sunlight filled the swift bus, the Greyhound, sailing through the forest branches, singing straight out to sea, roaring toward the mountains, circling sudden precipices.
>
> They followed the coastline. To the left was the forest; to the right, the sea, the Gulf.
>
> And the light corruscated brilliantly from the windows in which the travelers saw themselves now on the right hand en-islanded in azure amid the scarlet and gold of mirrored maples, by these now strangely embowered upon the left hand among the islands of the Gulf of Georgia.
>
> At times, when the Greyhound overtook and passed another car, where the road was narrow, the branches of the trees brushed the left-hand windows, and behind, or in the rearview mirror ahead reflecting the road endlessly enfilading in reverse, the foliage could be seen tossing for a while in a troubled gale at their passage. Again, in the distance, he would seem to see dogwood rocketing through the trees in a shower of white stars. And when they slowed down, the fallen leaves in the forest seemed to make even the ground glow and burn with light.
>
> Downhill: and to the right hand beyond the blue sea, beneath the blue sky, the mountains on the British Columbian mainland traversed the horizon, and on that right side too, luminous, majestic, a snowy volcano of another country (it was Mount Baker over in America and ancient Ararat of the Squamish Indians) accompanied them, with a white distant persistence, and at a different speed, like a remote, unanchored Popocatepetl.

Name:	Mr. and Mrs. Ethan Llewelyn	Seat No. 17	
Address:	c/o Mrs. Angela d'Arrivee	Northbound	X
	Gabriola Island, B.C.	Southbound	
	Date: October 7, 1949		
Important: to insure your return space on the Vancouver Island Limited register your ticket upon arrival at your destination.			
Victoria	Duncan		Nanaimo

"Well, damn it," he said, "I don't think I'm going to."

"Not going to what, Ethan sweetheart?"

Ethan and Jacqueline sat, arm in arm, in the two back left-hand seats of the Greyhound and once when he saw their reflections in the window it struck him these were the reflections of some lucky strangers who looked too full of hope and excitement to talk.

"Register our tickets at the depot to insure return space. It seems to be
tempting fate either way you look at it."

Jacqueline smiled at him with affection, absently, patting him on the knee,
while Ethan regarded their ticket again.

Victoria ... Duncan ... Nanaimo hath murdered sleep.

And in Duncan too, the poor old English pensioners, bewhiskered, gaitered,
standing motionless on street corners, dreaming of Mafeking or the fore-top-
gallant studding sail, or sitting motionless in the bankrupt rowing club, each
one a Canute; golfing on the edge of the Gulf, riding to the fall of the pound;
bereaved of their backwaters by rumors of boom. Evicted ... But to be evicted
out of exile: where then?

The bus changed gear, going up a hill: beginning: beginning: beginning
again: beginning yet again: here we go, into the blue morning. (3–5)

The sentences describing the movement of the bus through the trees and
morning light gradually become longer, then slightly shorter as the bus slows.
Participial phrases and temporal clauses accumulate, frequently joined with
conjunctions or adverbs and separated by commas. In this way, the sense of flow is
established. Finally, with "downhill:" and the increased speed of the bus, the
sentence opens out into a sweeping six-line description of sea, sky, and distant
mountains.

Abruptly, this rhythm breaks. Time stops on the space of the printed page as the
reader (and Ethan) confronts the bus ticket. The preceding sentences read beauti-
fully aloud, but it is impossible to capture in spoken words the visual impact of the
ticket with its oblong angular shape, categories, and spacing. The Llewelyns are
objectified, distanced, isolated within the visual bounds of the ticket; their reduc-
tion to names and numbers robs them of individual identity. A major theme of
October Ferry is the search for identity, and here Lowry skillfully introduces the
quest through his style. Who are these people anyway? The black and white fact of
the ticket offers no answer.

After the interruption of the ticket, dialogue begins and the focus narrows to the
present state of the two passengers on the back seat within the bus. The sense of
speed and movement has vanished, although the full irony of Ethan's refusal to
tempt fate by insuring "return space" on the bus awaits future reversals for its full
impact. Even the old pensioners, left behind in Duncan, stand or sit "motionless,"
their limbo projected in the cumulative adjectives and right-branching phrases
which throw the sentence into reverse by drawing the reader back to the subject of
this long sentence fragment. The disjunct verb "Evicted," the ellipsis, and the final
question bring the sentence and the reader's attention to an abrupt halt, and not
until the bus changes gear does the sensation of movement, at first jerky and
tentative then more decisive, recommence.

Chapter thirty-one, "Twilight of the Raven," like chapter ten in *Under the Volcano*, marks the climax of horror in Ethan's struggle for balance as Lowry intensifies themes of eviction, guilt, and social responsibility through the fusion of external and internal reality within Ethan's troubled mind. While he sits in the bar, physical immobility paralleling spiritual paralysis, time seems to stretch and blur until he loses his grip on the present. A close examination of chapter thirty-one reveals how well Lowry uses narrative techniques to achieve his effects.

"Twilight of the Raven" (the title recalling Poe's nightmare poem "The Raven" and Wagner's *Gotterdämmerung*) takes place in the third bar. The fact that Ethan's visions occur in bars is important, for the bar is a place of secular and divine law, a place of judgment and prosecution, a place where the soul sits in judgment upon the excesses of the flesh. Furthermore, to Ethan's eyes, "life was like this bar, from which you could not see out" (263). Ethan's plight is intensified by the fact that he is breaking Canadian law as soon as Jacqueline leaves him sitting unaccompanied in the Ladies and Escorts. The waiter, who has just seen "the goddam inspector" (257), asks him to leave, so that Ethan, evicted from the room with a view, from communion with his wife, must sit in the infernal Men's bar where the "windows were either boarded up, like those of prisoners, he thought, in the citadel of Parma, against the view, or the glass was a thick corrugated verdigris green" (259). Once in the Men's, Ethan is trapped "in a deliberately uncomfortable attitude he could not, for some reason, change" (260). Like Geoffrey, like all Lowry's heroes, Ethan the "misoneist" (199), or hater of change, becomes paralysed. Moreover, the lack of a view in this repulsive bar mirrors his own distorted, self-enclosed, destructive perception, and Ethan, in fact, describes the bar in expressionist terms: "Considered as a painting, as a work of imagination ... a modern master could scarcely have improved on it, for the room seemed to be the perfect outward expression of its own inner soul" (258).

Slowly, as Ethan becomes more and more enclosed by his distorted perception, external reality gives way to inner nightmare. "Sunrise! Twilight of the Dove" (255): the repetition of the phrase (263 and 264) enfolds the opening of the chapter into the inferno of Ethan's thoughts because "Sunrise," as well as signifying beauty and rebirth, is the time for hanging. At this point, rebirth merges with death as the negative associations of sunrise reflect back to cancel Ethan's earlier vision of an Eridanus sunrise. As is typical with Lowry, the interpenetration of a sunrise depends upon point of view and ability to act; therefore, as Ethan's thoughts shift from "the delight of swimming at sunrise" (255) to "a thick morning mist ... creeping out of the hollows into the prison cabbage patch" (264), he seems less and less able to transcend his abyss of self.

The sunrise of the condemned man ushers in one of the most gruesome passages in any of Lowry's works, as Ethan presents, "by prolepsis" (266), his arguments for the defence of young Chapman. Lowry's use of the term "prolepsis" is interesting.

In rhetoric it refers to the anticipation of arguments or the setting forth in brief the details of what is to follow. The word also signifies, in a more literal sense, the taking of a future event as already existing. In this sense, "prolepsis" sums up aptly the temporal stasis of this chapter by suggesting the impossibility of the flow of time into a future that already exists.

With the long quotation from *Demian*, it becomes evident that Ethan is defending himself as much as the Chapman boy. It is Ethan who is the murderer, and it is Ethan who is afraid to leave his "own lost Paradise, his own irrevocable past, in short that of Eridanus itself" (269). At this point accusatory voices take over, embodying simultaneously the most acute distortion of Ethan's consciousness and the truth itself. The chapter concludes with a chorus of past and present voices screaming at Ethan—voices from the bar, voices from the newspaper (Lowry collected newspaper clippings concerning the actual trial of a Vancouver boy), voices from his own divided consciousness:

> "Save him!"
>
> "Oh, shut up!"
>
> "It's no good, this kind of life."
>
> "But you, Ethan Llewelyn, what did you say? What did your able pen do, your pen more able than mine, or your still small voice, the one voice, the one pen still able to save him?"
>
> "Hang him!"
>
> "Hang him!"
>
> "The appeal for clemency of Richard Chapman, the fifteen-year-old rapist has been refused by the Cabinet today. Richard must keep his date with the hangman next December thirteenth."
>
> "Hang him!"
>
> "Hang Ethan Llewelyn!" (271)

It is impossible in a short space to recapture the entire chapter with its many echoes from the rest of the book, its refrains of reprieve, sunrise, scaffold, Dweller on the Threshold, and so on.⁵ The chapter reflects, contains, and develops the two previous nightmare moments in bars. The essential function of the chapter, however, is to serve as a temporary stasis within the flux and reflux of the narrative. It is at this point, in the present, that Ethan experiences his most intense hell, for he is immobilized, trapped and surrounded by his own mind until he loses touch with physical reality. Here the rhythm established in part one—the rhythm symbolized by the rising of the tides—breaks, in preparation for the gradual ebbing and creation of a new rhythm in part three.

Lowry's use of specific techniques in *October Ferry*, if not as refined as in *Under the Volcano*, is nevertheless interesting. In addition to allusions, Lowry uses motifs, filmic devices, signs, newspapers, dialogue, visions, hymns, and several languages to support his expanding edifice. Even chapter headings serve specific purposes, counterpointing or balancing other chapters, commenting ironically upon chapter contents, stating and repeating themes, always forcing the reader to read reflexively.

Lowry's notes for *October Ferry* contain references to "visual Murnau-like" techniques, and he appears to have considered writing in terms of shots and cuts. In fact, films are of considerable significance in the text. Jacqueline and Ethan attend, or see signs for, more than a dozen old films, among them *The Student of Prague* (1926), *Looping the Loop* (1928), and *From Morn till Midnight* (1920). Griffith's *Isn't Life Wonderful* (1924) along with *Outward Bound* (1930) and *The Wandering Jew* (1933) provide three important allusions, and to Ethan, who sees life as "a sort of movie, or series of movies" (42), films are more "realistic" than novels because they create an illusion of motion (61). Lowry goes so far as to have Ethan search for faith in "the Faith Thriller at the Reel Pulpit" (273).

More than once, Ethan reflects on the interpenetration of life and art encountered in film:

> (and ah, the eerie significance of cinemas in our life, Ethan thought, as if they related to the afterlife, as if we knew, after we are dead, we would be conducted to a movie house where, only half to our surprise, is playing a film named: *The Ordeal of Ethan Llewelyn*, with Jacqueline Llewelyn). (26)

This is very much what happened in *Volcano*, chapters two to twelve of which can be seen as Jacques's film, "The Ordeal of Geoffrey Firmin." In a draft for a section of *October Ferry* entitled "Plato's cave," Lowry reflects on the "reality" of films. At first he thinks of cinemas as caves of illusion with the life at Eridanus as real. After leaving his cabin he is not as sure:

> Now it was the other way around. They lived in the cave, they were traveling toward the grave, and yet, if poetry was life, life was art too, what they saw in the film was life …. It was all very odd: two kinds of life perhaps, a life of life and a life of death. It was a continuous performance. (17:13, 4–5)

Road signs and advertisements appear constantly, and in keeping with the camera's ability to endow inanimate objects with meaning, these signs acquire an exaggerated, almost supernatural significance. "Safeside-Suicide," "Mother Gettle's Soup," even the billboards in chapter twenty-eight (221–25), provide external glosses on the action of Ethan's mind.

One of the more complicated instances of a film allusion in *October Ferry* is that of Temple Thurston's *The Wandering Jew*.[6] In chapter twenty, entitled "The Wandering Jew," Ethan sees the film and experiences the terrifying sensation that he *is* the accused Jew (132). Here, as in *Volcano*, the Lowry hero under stress loses all sense of psychological space; he is unable to distinguish the boundaries between self and not-self. Of course, the parallels between Ethan and the Jew are not just fanciful; Ethan is chased from one home to another in his journey through life, and, like Thurston's Jew, he does finally receive grace.

Lowry, however, attempts to make more of the film than simply a thematic parallel for his story, and here the allusion becomes confusing. When Ethan learns of the death-by-fire of Temple Thurston, he perceives a precise parallel between the writer's death and that of the Jew in the film. This coincidence provides him with "a glimpse into the very workings of creation itself" (147). It is as if Thurston "created" his own death on one plane only to re-enact it on another. The film apparently functions as a kind of gate or secret passage into the realm of connection and coincidence that, for Lowry, constitutes reality. Consequently, the film reassures Ethan of the significance of the universe: "Gone was his fright. In its stead was awe" (148). Nevertheless, the meaning of the elaborate Wandering Jew-Temple Thurston complex is less clear than this summary would suggest, and in an amusing marginal note on the manuscript, Lowry spoke for the reader too when he wrote that "its purpose in the book baffles me."

Lowry's use of Griffith's *Isn't Life Wonderful* is also a puzzle in some respects. Ethan's version of the film bears small resemblance to the actual film except for the presence of two lovers in a forest who comment, after being robbed, "Isn't Life Wonderful." In Griffith's film there is no fire and no looting soldiers, and the film ends with the marriage of the lovers as they begin life in a tiny cottage. According to Mrs. Lowry, Lowry would frequently be carried away by an idea, shot, or scene in a film and proceed to create his own version.[7] In subsequent discussions he believed his "creation" to be the actual film. If this is what happened to the Griffith picture, it is not difficult to understand his invention of the fire (especially for chapter fifteen), but it is strange that Lowry overlooked the symbolic parallel of the happy ending. Perhaps the reader is meant to infer that the Llewelyns will have a similar happy ending, for *Isn't Life Wonderful* provides a clear thematic parallel to their story. Like Griffith's lovers, Ethan and Jacqueline are homeless and beleaguered, but they too maintain their love and faith.

October Ferry is as rich in reference, quotation, and literary and filmic parallels as *Under the Volcano*. The most important allusion is to Sutton Vane's play *Outward Bound*, but Lowry also gleaned many references from Eino Railo's *The Haunted Castle*, a study of gothic and romantic literature, and from Charles Fort's books.[8] He uses Blake and Shakespeare to develop themes and refers to such diverse writers as Chaucer, Berkeley, Defoe, Bunyan, Carlyle, Bulwer-Lytton, Coleridge, Clare, Wordsworth, Keats, Emily Brontë, George Eliot, Hardy, Poe, Melville, Dostoevsky, Flaubert, Stendhal, Sartre, and Hesse.

Outward Bound, from which a film was made in 1930, casts the greatest light upon Lowry's intentions. Written in a disarmingly simple style, Vane's play portrays the postmortem voyage of a small group of passengers outward bound for heaven or hell: "It's the same place, you see."[9] The three acts of the play take place in the ship's bar, where the bartender, Scrubby, a kind of Charon, gradually reveals the nature of the voyage. Two of the passengers, Ann and Henry, have committed suicide and are, therefore, "half-ways" who must "go on like this … backwards and forwards—backwards and forwards." In the December 1953 letter to Erskine (mentioned earlier), Lowry describes his plan of making Peter Cordwainer appear to Ethan on the ferry as Scrubby:

> [Ethan] has to face the fact also that he actually is—or has been—next door to
> a murderer and a criminal himself in the case of Cordwainer: though it's time
> he stopped punishing himself—he's had 20 years of penal servitude already—
> and others for it, including Cordwainer himself, who appears in a dream to
> him on the ferry boat (Scrubby the barman in Outward Bound—you might
> expect to find him on a ferry boat) to inform him that in so far as Ethan had
> murdered him, he had saved him from the lot of a suicide in the next world.
> (*SC* II, 698)

In act three of *Outward Bound*, the passengers hold a meeting in the bar—"in view of the shortness of time … and the nature of the harbour we are approaching" (112)—to look over their pasts and to be examined by a clergyman. Each of the passengers receives his sentence except the suicides who remain suspended in limbo. Scrubby reminds Ann that time does not exist in limbo: "A week! A century! A moment! There's no time here" (170).

This lack of time and space—heaven and hell are the same place and time does not exist—is clearly paralleled in parts of *October Ferry*. Lowry has also incorporated the bar as place of judgment and the theme of suicide within his novel. The title *Outward Bound* is important, not only in *October Ferry*, where it provides two chapter headings, but throughout Lowry's "Voyage" cycle. From *Ultramarine* on, the "outward bound" motif recurs as a reminder that the voyage must always begin anew. In fact, Vane's play provides an interesting insight into Lowry's entire concept of the voyage: anyone who commits suicide (as Ethan nearly does in chapter thirty-four) literally or metaphorically, remains trapped, like Ann and Henry, in a limbo where time does not exist and where the voyage cannot go on.

Motifs are important structural techniques in *October Ferry*, and like allusions, they are largely unexplored. Signs—"Safeside-Suicide," notices—"Vous qui passez/ayez pitié," seemingly casual puns such as "called to the bar," phrases like "beginning again," and Luther's hymn "*Ein Festerburg ist unser Gott*" recur throughout the book. The repetition, as Lowry pointed out to Erskine, is purposely "beyond that which you can believe" (*SC* II, 664) because Lowry saw his use of motifs as something new to fiction. In a note to Margerie on the manuscripts, he remarks:

> Leit-motifs go backwards & forwards here as they don't in Wagner, & the whole
> technique & meaning is revolutionary & new to art, I believe, certainly to fiction.
> And it has to be *simple*, unaffected naturalism "au meme temp." (19:24, A)

The motifs serve many functions: they introduce and develop themes, comment ironically upon an event or thought, and generally enrich the meaning of the text. Most important, of course, they disrupt the cause and effect progression of the story by their "backwards & forwards" movement. Just as the closely interwoven texture of the narrative represents the consciousness of the protagonist, so the *leitmotifs* suggest the density of a mind that remembers and interprets everything it perceives.

The words "time" and "life," for example, occur repeatedly in the first part of the novel, but it is not until chapter twenty-four that their significance is sharply focused:

> And down down it was anyhow, what with *Time* and *Life* on the table with their bouncing advertisements of a bouncing life with Big Cousin that never was on land or sea, or if it was, in his opinion shouldn't be .... Christ Jesus how he hated it all. Where had *their* life, their time gone. (181)

"Time" and "life" reflect back upon the preceding chapters. Up to this point Ethan has only been remembering (not living) "*their* life, *their* time."

As the narrative moves into the present, the "time" and "life" motif recurs more frequently. The Llewelyns pass a magazine stand in their search for the Gabriola ferry ticket office, and on the stand appears: "Your weight and your destiny. *Time* and *Life* ... " (234). With each repetition of the words, associations multiply. At this point the motif serves as a subtle reminder of the continuity between past and present, but the interpretation of this link is left uncertain; time and life will either continue to be only a memory *or* the present will become a lived reality. Later that afternoon, as they again make their way down to the ferry, the motif carries some help: "Libra's year ahead. Difficulties of the Fourth House ... *Time* and *Life*" (284). The sign of Libra, with the balance or scales, symbolizes the supposed justice in Ethan's legal profession and suggests that in the year ahead Ethan will achieve balance. "Difficulties of the Fourth House," yet another *leitmotif,* refers to the Llewelyn's trouble in finding their fourth home (Achad's fourth world): until now the stars have been against them, not to mention Ethan's misanthropism; however, with "Libra's year ahead," they will surely have "time" to build a new "life" in the "fourth house."

In the last chapter, "Uberimae Fides" (bountiful faith), Ethan has discovered the faith necessary to go into the future and relinquish the past. The reprieve from eviction reinforces the need for a new life: "No, it was time to leave, however much it hurts. Time to—" (325). Finally, as the ferry approaches Gabriola, the Llewelyns know that now they are moving in time once again: "Well, time and heart enough to find out about everything now ... " (329).

Although *October Ferry* is as rich in symbolism as it is in motif and allusion, there are three symbols which are of particular importance: symbols of place (both Gabriola and Eridanus), the mirror, and once again the circle or wheel with its ambivalent associations of containment and movement. Gabriola and Eridanus symbolize the poles of human experience. Being an island, Gabriola calls to mind the references to Atlantis scattered through Lowry's work as well as the reference to Prospero's island in *October Ferry* (157). Situated in the Gulf of Georgia, the island is in a sense afloat on the gulf ("Golf-gouffre-gulf") that consumed Geoffrey Firmin in *Under the Volcano*. Angela d'Arrivee (the angel of arrival if not of the Annunciation), who lives on Gabriola, is waiting to welcome the Llewelyns, and, as Lowry told Erskine, the island "is, finally, the future." Despite its inaccessibility and mystery, Gabriola is a positive force, but Eridanus is a more ambiguous symbol. It is the name of their inlet and of a ship that ran aground there. It is also the name of a constellation—the river of life and death. More ominous still, the Eridanus is the river that, in the *Aeneid*, "watered the Elysian Fields of the Earthly Paradise" (164). Eridanus is a type of the earthly paradise, "a gift of grace, finally a damnation" (79), and as long as they are able to live there without wanting to possess it, physically or spiritually, the Llewelyns are safe. Ethan, however, has come to wear the cabin "like a shell"; he wants to secure it for himself forever. But in the Cabbala shells signify the *Qliphoth* or world of demons which in turn suggests that Ethan's desire to withdraw into the safety of Eridanus has transformed his paradise into a trap. So obsessed has he become with past happiness there, so terrified is he of losing it, that he is unable to face either the present trip or the future.

In an important sense, *October Ferry* is like a mirror in that many of the chapters are reflections of each other, and the constant repetition of motifs increases the mirror-like quality of the text. Mirror images, of course, are both positive and negative. Broken mirrors occur in each of the bars in which Ethan experiences his hellish visions, and twice he confronts his own face in a mirror (46, 216) only to perceive that he is a "murderer!" These mirrors inevitably recall the distorting and mysterious mirrors in expressionist films. In *The Student of Prague*, for example, young Baldwin sells his soul to the devil by giving him his mirror image, but when he finally frees himself from this satanic mirror image by shooting at it, he kills himself. More positively, the mirror is essential to Achad's theory of the Tree of Life, wherein the reflections will be clear as long as the glass is whole or undistorted. Certainly, for Ethan, who needs the help of Coleridge's *Aids to Reflection*, as well as the Cabbala, in order to achieve balance, the search for a clarity of mind and soul that will perfectly mirror the universe is just another set of parameters for his spiritual and metaphysical quest.

The text itself approximates, in Lowry's eyes, a magic mirror, for it reflects the creative process of God, and Lowry was forever searching for the art form that would be in constant motion and thereby incarnate his belief in change at the same time as it reflected the perpetual motion of the universe. In one of the novel's more striking passages, Ethan, who is sitting in the Ladies and Escorts side of the Ocean Spray (the bar with a view), describes the activity of the bartender:

> The bartender, glancing from time to time out of the window at the scene out-
> side, began to pile *the glasses one within another* in a stack on the counter, a

> dull-seeming occupation, about which, Ethan now understood from the bartender's glances of satisfaction at the stack, the position of which he altered now and then, evidently to suit some aesthetic whim, there was, on the contrary, something almost godlike: *it was a creative process, an act of magic*: for within each glass lay trapped the reflection of the window, within each window the reflected scene outside, extended vertically by the glasses themselves, *the reflected windows flowing upward* in a single *attenuated but unbroken* line in which could be seen a multiplicity of light-houses, seabirds, suns, fishing crafts, passenger boats, Australia-bound colliers, the miniscule coal rushing audibly down the minute chute. (250 [italics added])[10]

The stack of glasses is "a creative process, an act of magic" because it reflects "flowing," "unbroken," "multiplicity." Like Achad's Tree of Life or Dunne's serial universe (viewed positively), the stacked glasses reflect yet control the continuous movement of life. This passage expresses the heart of Lowry's philosophy and aesthetics while, at the same time, reflecting all his novels; glasses, bars, windows, ships, lighthouses, and seabirds echo and reverberate through *Ultramarine, Lunar Caustic, Volcano,* and *Dark as the Grave*. The very word "reflection" appears on practically every page of *October Ferry* to remind the reader of the "Voyage" and to heighten the reflexive nature of the individual text.

The symbol of the wheel or circle functions as dramatically in *October Ferry* as in *Under the Volcano*. Indeed, the narrative creates a kind of "perichoresis" of Ethan, Jacqueline, and Tommy, or, even more accurately, of the trinity of past, present, and future. But wheels and circles are as ambivalent in *October Ferry* as they are in the rest of Lowry's fiction. For example, Ethan is continually enclosed within the circle of his own consciousness, whether he is in a shell-like house, on a bus, in a bar, or on a ferry. (At one point Lowry toyed with the idea of bringing the bus on the ferry). References to Ixion (St. Catharine's College, Cambridge), where Peter died, appear frequently, but the wheel in its negative guise appears most powerfully in chapter twenty-eight, "Wheel of Fire." The phrase "wheel of fire" comes from *King Lear*, where it evokes an Ixion-like torture:

> You do wrong to take me out o' th' grave
> Thou art a soul in bliss; but I am bound
> Upon a wheel of fire, that mine own tears
> Do scald like molten lead.[11]

Ethan, like Lear, must continue to suffer.

Wheels and circles exist on every side—Nanaimo is laid out "like the spokes of a wheel," and as the bus follows a hearse leaving a Catholic church a Latin phrase (perhaps from a tombstone) catches Ethan's attention: "*Circum ipsam auteum libamina omnibus mortuis*" (230). The wheel symbolism reaches its climax at the end of the chapter as Ethan overhears a conversation between two old men, a conversation "addressed mysteriously to Ethan himself; and ... almost every phrase had another meaning, perhaps many meanings, intended for his ears alone" (231). One of the men describes how a blacksmith makes huge coach wheels:

> "—well, they shrink them on. Now the wheelwright has delivered the wheel to the blacksmith, and the blacksmith builds a ring of fire … now they have the iron welded together and they put it in the fire …. Then, when it's ready the blacksmith with his two helpers, they take it out of the fire with tongs, and they force it over the edge of the wooden wheel, and then it smokes *something awful*, it damn nearly sets fire to the wheel. So then they run like mad pouring water on it. Now you understand it has swelled in the fire, and now it shrinks quickly, and now it has clasped the wheel forever—" (231–32)

"Clasped the wheel forever" develops into a refrain that haunts Ethan through the second part of the book (236, 282) because the iron wheel is a terrifying image of Ethan's mind which has been relentlessly clasped by the past. The burning wheel, reminiscent of Blake's tiger, also suggests the plunging of the spirit into the moulding fires of experience, and significantly, the blacksmith builds a "ring of fire" in order to temper the iron. Ethan himself has been plagued by a "ring of fire" at several points in his past life; advertisements for Mother Gettle's soup seem "ringed with hellfire" (47), and the fires in Niagara-on-the-Lake spring up around the Llewelyns so that they are surrounded by an actual "ring of fire" (118). Ethan Llewelyn is being tempered in the fires of his ordeal, which, if they do not destroy him first, will shape him into a better man.

As Ethan moves into the future in part three, the circle changes from a searing static enclosure to a symbol of movement and life. The gliding, "free-wheeling" ferry with the seagulls circling overhead and "great whirlpools and whorls like seashells" (299) in the water beneath, the ferry with its circular lounge and wheel-house in which the skipper twirls the wheel (297), transcribes one last complete circle before finally heading out to Gabriola. This last circle, superficially so full of despair, brings the ferry back to Nanaimo where Ethan learns of the Eridanus reprieve. He realizes then that the day's "multiplicity of signs," indeed the disasters, events, coincidences of his entire life, were full of an interrelated significance that contained this moment. Ethan has overcome the "extremity of motion that was no motion, where past and future were held suspended, and one began thinking of treadmills" (53). He has overcome his fear of change by obeying the Cabbalist command to "fear not CHANGE, but embrace it with open arms for all change is of the nature of love" (*Q.B.L.*, 100). The "free-wheeling" ferry is once again outward bound: "Beginning: beginning again: beginning yet again" (322).

Like *Under the Volcano*, *October Ferry* is a deeply religious novel, and Ethan Llewelyn's voyage is a multi-levelled quest: a search for "life" in every sense of the word. On the social level, the voyage represents Ethan's need to be reunited with mankind. During his three-and-one-half-year retreat at Eridanus, throughout his entire life in fact, he has become more and more withdrawn. Here, the Lowry dilemma of withdrawal and return is re-enacted with Ethan ultimately "received by mankind." In his letter to Erskine, Lowry clarifies this aspect of the quest:

> The ferry reaches Gabriola at dusk, where those meeting the boat are swinging lanterns along the wharf but you have the feeling that Ethan is now being received by mankind, that arms are stretched out to help him, help he now has to and is prepared to accept, as he is prepared to give help to man, whom he had formerly grown to hate so much: thus the characters journey toward their own recovery. (*SC* II, 699)

This social acceptance by mankind includes renewal of Ethan's marriage, which had been under considerable strain, and the finding of a new home for his wife and son.

The psychological level of the quest is perhaps more important, for it is on this level that Ethan must come to terms with his past in order to discover the future. Again, in his letter to Erskine, Lowry goes on to explain that,

> on this plane the whole thing can be read slightly differently and in a sense more hopefully, as a kind of abreaction of his past: I like the word cathexis, too. In some psycho-genetic sense also—if that's the word?—the news of their own reprieve (on this plane) would seem to precipitate Ethan's recovery, in the way that shell-shocked soldiers may recover at the news of the armistice. (*SC* II, 700)

Lowry's use of the term "abreaction," a psychoanalytic term for the release of psychic tension through verbalizing repressed traumatic experience, is important because the highly ratiocinative narrative may well be seen as therapeutic verbalization of the past.

Possessed by past traumas, Ethan is unwilling to relinquish his own youth, hence his guilt over Cordwainer's suicide merges with his reluctance to defend the Vancouver boy and intensifies his torment: not only was he Peter's murderer, but now, through professional inertia, he is also killing Chapman. The significance of both Cordwainer and Chapman crystallizes in his imaginary defence (self-defence) of Chapman when Ethan quotes a long passage from Hesse's *Demian*. According to Hesse, the time of puberty is a profoundly traumatic "sequence of death and rebirth." Loss and loneliness terrify the adolescent, making him long to stay within the comforting world of childhood: "they cling their whole life long painfully to the irrevocable past, to the dream of a lost paradise, the worst and most deadly of all dreams" (268). Because Ethan is unwilling to leave the paradise at Eridanus, which he has polluted with his repressed guilt over Cordwainer and Chapman, reliving the past trauma is the necessary therapy that finally frees him from the past and from his youth (from Eridanus, Cordwainer, and Chapman) and allows him to mature in the future.

Closely connected with the concept of Eridanus as a childhood paradise is the image of the cabin and the physical and spiritual Eden it represents for the Llewelyns. They are Adam and Eve, evicted from paradise, exiled from God, and beginning the soul's long voyage back to God, their harbour and home. William New, in "Gabriola: Malcolm Lowry's Floating Island," suggests that Ethan's voyage might be seen as the neo-Platonic journey of the soul in exile on its way back to God,[12] but the religious quest cannot be reduced to one myth. Ethan is searching for faith and this search continues through the book until, in the last chapter, "Uberimae Fides," he appears to have found it.

The metaphysical quest unites the social, psychological, and religious levels of the narrative. The Llewelyns, Ethan in particular, must come to understand the nature of reality. Significantly, Ethan recognizes that he has been a "misoneist" because the focal point of his voyage, the messenger of *October Ferry*, is that he must learn to accept the protean nature of reality. He has come to want to possess Eridanus, despite the profound truth

> [t]hat impermanence, indeed, the ramshackle tenuity of the life, were part of
> its beauty. The scene, too, that confronted them through their casement
> windows was ever-changing; the mountains, the sea never looked the same two
> minutes on end: why then be afraid of change? (171)

By refusing change, Ethan has attempted to stop time, to enclose and thereby spatialize experience. Through his fear and guilt he has become static, a piece of death. In a fascinating marginal note to a manuscript version of the ferry's approach to Gabriola, Lowry scribbled: "outside time, an ocean of suffering, just as he had seemed outside time in that three years on the beach" (16:11, 77). Only by placing himself within the flow of time, only by crossing the borders of self and escaping from the closed circle of consciousness, can Ethan be "received by mankind," transcend the past, or find the faith to carry him forward into the future.

Finally, the voyage in *October Ferry* is an epistemological quest, and it is on this level, more than on either the metaphysical or the religious, that Achad's interpretation of the Cabbala operates. Not only does it provide an interesting structural model, many images, and at least two important symbols (the numbers three and four), but it is also an epistemological tool for the achievement of harmony or balance. Ethan finds that a book on the Cabbala given him by the McCandless is

> not only extraordinarily interesting but, as a method of thought, profoundly
> helpful. In fact he could sum up no better their life on the beach than to say it
> had been, in a manner, *his* cabbala, in the sense that, if he was not mistaken,
> that system might be regarded on one plane as a means less of accumulating
> than of divesting oneself—by arrangement, balancing them against their
> opposites—of unbalanced ideas: the mind, finally transcending both aspects,
> regains its lost equilibrium. (169)

Achieving equilibrium through balanced opposites has been Lowry's and Ethan's goal throughout, and the reader shares in this epistemological quest by experiencing with Ethan the tortuous exploration of the past which is necessary for the growth of human consciousness.

October Ferry is not as successful as *Under the Volcano*. It is not as polished and interwelded, and some minor inconsistencies persist: for example, the name of the boy accused of murder changes, and the wine becomes gin once Ethan is on the ferry. The son, Tommy, is dismissed from the story so quickly that the reader wonders why, apart from completing the trinity symbolism, he exists at all. These slips are unimportant, however, in comparison to the incomplete portrait of Ethan himself. Lowry had planned to develop Ethan, especially with regard to the reasons for his professional retreat, and the more recently discovered working notes for the novel contain many attempts to expand upon Ethan's drinking problem and his disillusionment with the law.[13] More thorough exposition of Ethan's despair would have lent him greater credibility, but as the novel stands it is hard to believe that Ethan's agony is like Lear's, whereas Geoffrey Firmin's tragic disintegration is totally convincing. The working notes also include long passages on the Cabbala, and Lowry, who was planning to expand the character of the McCandless, may have intended to incorporate more of the Cabbala into the portrait of Jacqueline's magician father.

As Lowry pointed out in his letter to Erskine, *October Ferry* does not "fall into any particular category or obey any of the normal rules of a novel" (*SC* II, 697). But *October Ferry* can be described as a "lyrical novel," at least insofar as it shares the qualities of formal design and a passive, solipsistic protagonist that Ralph Freedman identifies as characteristic of the mode.[14] Furthermore, because the narrative charts the growth of perception in a highly sensitive individual through the intensely personal reliving of past experience, it conforms rather closely to Aiken's definition of the novel as "the novelist's inordinate and copious lyric,"[15] and although there is little lyric tranquility in *October Ferry*, Ethan does achieve a point of temporary rest and insight. As in "The Forest Path to the Spring," which *October Ferry* anticipates, "the characters journey toward their own recovery."

Despite weaknesses, *October Ferry* is successful in its own right. The intricate tripartite structure with its temporal involutions and complex motifs sustains the powerful rhythm of withdrawal and return, and Lowry succeeds wonderfully in his portrayal of eviction and quest with Ethan learning that he must accept change and leave his past in order to embrace the future. As the McCandless points out in his telegram to the Llewelyns after the burning of the Barkerville Arms:

> GREATEST COMMISERATION ON YOUR LOSS BUT CONSIDER SO-CALLED DISASTER CAN BE BEST POSSIBLE THING FOR YOU BOTH STOP I TOLD YOU LONG AGO WHAT PERILS CAN LURK AT THAT GATE OF UNCHANGE. (95)

And in a fascinating marginal note to himself on a draft of Ethan's final vision of the meteors, Lowry underlined the importance of the Llewelyns' search:

> "it must ... be firmly implanted in the drang of the situation and the reader's mind *far more than ever* THEIR NEED for a house they can really call their

own, for even if you feel they're not going to get one perhaps, it is on this continued search ... that the pathos and drama of the situation depends." (19:15, 52)

Not a very comforting proviso, perhaps, but for Lowry it is not the finding but the searching that is important, and *October Ferry* ends with a sense of movement and expectation. Ethan, balance restored, is now ready to resume his multi-levelled voyage into the future.

October Ferry to Gabriola is a triumphant and integral continuation of the "Voyage" theme and, in his letter to Erskine, Lowry leaves no doubt as to *October Ferry's* role: "The end is thus a kind of *Volcano* in reverse and the final theme Faustian, with everything from flights of angels, balls of fire, and Madonnas, to the intervention of grace and the Himmelphart" (*SC* II, 699).[16] With *October Ferry to Gabriola* the Lowry voyager escapes (for the moment) the negative circle of self and distorted perception, and the trap of the past. The luminous wheel moves bringing faith, life, and balance:

> Voyage, the homeward-outward-bound voyage; everybody was on such a voyage, the Ocean Spray, Gabriola, themselves, the barman, the sun, the reflections, the stacked glasses, even the light, the sea outside, now due to an accident of sun and dislimning cloud looking like a luminosity between two darknesses, a space between two immensities, was on such a voyage, to the junction of the two infinities, where it would set out on its way again, had already set out, toward the infinitely small, itself already expanding before you had thought of it, to replenish the limitless light of Chaos— (252)

(1982)

NOTES

[1] All references are to the 1970 edition. In her "Editor's Note," 335–36, Margerie Lowry explains her editorial task, but because the manuscripts of the novel do not fall into easily distinguishable drafts, it is difficult to assess how closely the published text follows Lowry's plans. As a consequence, many critics (for example Day and Cross, 1980) have been reluctant to accept the work as it stands, and *October Ferry* has not been subjected to the kind of serious attention which has opened up *Under the Volcano*. Significant discussion of Lowry's later work began with William New's valuable 1972 article, "Gabriola: Malcolm Lowry's Floating Island" in *Articulating West*, 196–206, and continued in 1974 when Muriel Bradbrook published *Malcolm Lowry: His Art and Early Life*. In her 1978 article, "Intention and Design in *October Ferry to Gabriola*," in *The Art of Malcolm Lowry*, 144–55, Bradbrook offers one of the most sensitive readings of the novel to date. In her discussion she draws upon "Work in Progress" and the manuscripts and arrives at much the same conclusion about the novel's

richness as I do, but where she contrasts the open and unfinished form of *October Ferry* with the more traditional "composite" form of *Hear us O Lord*, I maintain that there is a deliberate, discernible, albeit open, "design" in *October Ferry* as well. Perhaps the most positive assessment of the novel is by Terence Bareham in "After the Volcano: An Assessment of Malcolm Lowry's Posthumous Fiction," in *Malcolm Lowry: The Writer and His Critics*, 235–49. According to Bareham, it is a "remarkable achievement" and its "central integrity is intact," 248.

[2] According to *The New Catholic Encyclopedia*, 2:128, perichoresis is the interpenetration of the three Persons of the Trinity. Greek theology emphasizes the *activity* of union, a kind of "reciprocal irruption;" western theology emphasizes the state of "unicity."

[3] During the forties Lowry had access to Charles Stansfeld-Jones's (Frater Achad) library on the occult, but he was particularly influenced by two of Achad's studies, *Q.B.L. or The Bride's Reception* and *The Anatomy of the Body of God*. References are included in the text.

[4] I have reproduced this diagram from *Q.B.L.* in *The Voyage That Never Ends* (80).

[5] The allusions to "Sunrise" and the mysterious refrain "Dweller on the Threshold" (111, 263, 296) are important. In his drafts of the novel Lowry had planned to incorporate his version of a Blake stanza:

> He who bendeth to himself a green joy
> Doth the winged life destroy
> But he who embraceth the life as it flies
> Doth live in eternity's sunrise. (16:11, 30)

Although the stanza does not appear in the published text, it clarifies Lowry's concern for movement; to possess is to invite death, whereas to "embrace the joy as it flies" is to *live*.

"Dweller on the Threshold" comes from Bulwer-Lytton's mystical romance *Zanoni* mentioned in Eino Railo's *The Haunted Castle* (209). Lowry's notes for *October Ferry* contain many references to and long quotes from *Zanoni*, which portrays the struggle of the Ideal and the Real via a gothic story of Italian passions. In his explanation of the novel, Lytton writes that the "Dweller on the Threshold" is "FEAR (or HORROR)" which may only be dispelled by "defiance and aspiration ... whose Messenger and Instrument of reassurance is Faith" (*Zanoni*, 538). *Zanoni* was important to Lowry, who saw Ethan as tormented by fears like Geoffrey and Sigbjørn but finally achieving faith at the end of his ordeal.

[6] The film that Lowry is referring to was based upon E. Temple Thurston's play *The Wandering Jew* and was made in Britain in 1933, starring the famous expressionist actor, Conrad Veidt.

[7] During my conversations with Mrs. Lowry in June 1975, she recalled Lowry's tendency to make his own films, starting with an unusual shot or interesting detail in a film they were watching; he was later baffled to discover that he had not "seen" the same film as she.

[8] Lowry took much of his information on fires and other "supernatural" happenings from Charles Fort, who rejected rational explanations of the universe and believed that "all existence is a flux and reflux" within a pattern of "infinite serialization"; see Fort's *The Books of Charles Fort* (313). Lowry's copy of *Charles Fort*, now in the Lowry Collection, was given him by Margerie in December 1953. Eino Railo's *The Haunted Castle* is the source for the "Wandering Jew" passages in chapter twenty and the Spenser stanza (155).

[9] See Sutton Vane, *Outward Bound* (63); further references are included in the text. In his "Introduction" to *Mr. Arcularis, A Play* (v–vi), Conrad Aiken remarks with interest that Diana

Hamilton, the Englishwoman who first tried to stage Aiken's story in the forties, was Sutton Vane's widow. The subterranean links between *Mr. Arcularis* and "The Ordeal of Sigbjørn Wilderness" are touched upon in the Appendix to *The Voyage That Never Ends*, and it is entirely possible that Aiken and Lowry were both influenced by Vane's popular play.

[10] In a typescript of this passage Lowry has a marginal note paraphrasing Achad:

> N.B. An image Kether is then the Junction of these two Infinites, that particularly represents the concentration of the Light to a point on its way to the Infinitely Small, while Malkuth,—the 10th Sephira & Sphere of the elements—which the Cabbalists say is one with Kether—is the substance which is ever expanding, &, so to speak, gradually filling up the nothingness of the Ain-Suph-Aur (Limitless Light of Chaos). (16:12, 16)

[11] See *King Lear*, Act 4, sc. 7, 11. 45–48.

[12] New, *Articulating West*. In "Death in Life: Neo-Platonic Elements in 'Through the Panama,'" Geoffrey Durrant sees another of Lowry's voyages as based upon the neo-Platonic myth of the soul's journey through the world of matter on its way back to God. The parallel is interesting for *October Ferry* and "Through the Panama," with the distinction that, unlike the neo-Platonists, Lowry is not concerned about a timeless goal; it is the voyage that is of value.

[13] Three boxes (19, 20, and 21) of *October Ferry* manuscripts now at the University of British Columbia were received from Harold Matson in the spring of 1973.

[14] In his study *The Lyrical Novel*, Ralph Freedman describes such novels as emphasizing formal design instead of event and employing passive characters who mirror a world perceived solipsistically. In addition, the "lyrical novel" usually creates a strong sense of spatial form; details, images, and other aspects are presented in juxtaposition in order to be perceived as a poetic whole. *October Ferry* conforms to Freedman's description of a "lyrical novel" in some ways, but Lowry never aims to present a timeless static poetic unit in his work. As with any effort to categorize Lowry's writing, the term "lyrical" must be applied to *October Ferry* with restraint.

[15] This remark by Aiken is quoted in Jay Martin's study, *Conrad Aiken: A Life of His Art* (76).

[16] Lowry's reference is to the end of Goethe's *Faust*, II. His words, however, are a paraphrase of Santayana's in *Three Philosophical Poets* (193). Lowry knew Santayana's book well, and Santayana's interpretation of *Faust*, as well as his theory of the romantic journey, influenced Lowry's concept of voyage.

4

"The daily crucifixion of the post": Editing and Theorizing the Lowry Letters

I: "La Carte Postale"

In the spring of 1987, I decided to begin the task of editing a collected letters of Malcolm Lowry (1909–57). This decision was not lightly taken because I knew, after many years of work on Lowry's fiction and with the Lowry manuscript collection at the University of British Columbia, that I would face some formidable problems and challenges. The majority of these was not hard to anticipate, but the full extent of others came as a surprise. Would I have taken this plunge had I known the true depth of the water and *all* the Lowry snags awaiting me? … Yes.

To begin with, there is a large number of letters in the archive; some are very long, and many only exist in Lowry's cramped handwriting. In addition to this familiar problem with legibility, some letters only survive in heavily revised drafts. Despite the impressive efforts made by Basil Stuart-Stubbs and Earle Birney in the early sixties to gather as much material for the archive as possible and Anne Yandle's diligent care in adding to it through the seventies and eighties, inevitably letters still exist elsewhere, with other archives and in private hands. So, beyond problems with legibility and copy text, I realized that I would have to go on a hunt for hitherto unknown, extant letters. But this is, perhaps, less a problem than a challenge, indeed, sometimes an exciting process with immediate rewards. To date, I estimate that there are eight hundred Lowry letters to be collected, transcribed, dated, and annotated in what may result in three volumes (the end result is two very large volumes).

However, as with anything Malcolm Lowry ever wrote, the plot only thickens. His letters are often superb texts, richly woven from the words that were his passion into the symbolic, iconic and indexical signs of his life. Therefore, because Lowry's poetics are as evident in his letters as anywhere else in his *oeuvre*, his editor must always be sensitive to their literary textuality, and I quickly recognized (perhaps had always sensed) that there was no absolute difference between the Lowry letter and the Lowry fiction. What this means in practice, in *editorial* practice, however, is another story. What it means for the present is that I must begin with a theoretical question: What *is* a Lowry letter?

Attendant upon this basic question, of course, are others, such as: What rules can guide the editor in what seems (increasingly to me) to be an empirical, provisional, and open-ended enterprise? What, finally, is an editor, where does he or she differ from a literary critic? If D.F. McKenzie is correct in his 1985 Panizzi lectures, *Bibliography and the Sociology of Texts*, there is not only a great deal of flexibility and latitude available to the bibliographic scholar, but that scholar has a responsibility to the "sociology of texts"; she must take cognizance of authorial intentions, readers' uses, historical change, the symbolic function of signs, and the dynamic interrelation of all these factors in the effort to "show the human presence in any recorded text" (20).[1]

In this initial attempt to discuss the Lowry letters, I cannot cover all these bases. For example, a graphological study should be done on Lowry's writing because it changes drastically, depending upon his age, health, state of mind, and sobriety. Moreover, it is possible that an analysis of how he uses, fills up, or attacks the page— a semiotics of the page—will yield fascinating insights into the man and his writing. Perhaps more importantly, given the degree of revision in all Lowry's texts, a diachronic study of a letter using a stemma that reveals the changes Lowry made (through interlineations, over-writing, marginal additions, etc.) might come close to demonstrating the creative process at work.

But first things first. What is a Lowry letter? Why did he write letters? And why did he use them in the ways he did—in his fiction, for example? In what follows, I offer two synchronic models for his letters, one a typology by function, the other by form. Underlying both is my assumption that letters always fall somewhere between living dialogue, on the one hand, and written texts (such as novels), on the other, and that this dual nature makes their form and function especially unstable and fascinating. For reasons which I hope will be clear, my conclusion is cast in the form of a letter, but it functions, nevertheless, as a conclusion.

Here is where my question begins ...

At the end of chapter six of *Under the Volcano*, and at the heart of this complex tale of loss, failure, and mis-communication, lies this quintessential Lowry scene: On their way to Jacques Laruelle's "madhouse" for a drink, the hapless Firmin trio (Geoffrey, Yvonne, and Hugh) are stopped by the local *cartero*, the present postman in a family of postmen. "'There is a letter, a letter, a letter ... a message *por el señor*,' he cries, searching feverishly in his bag, spreading its contents onto the road. 'It must be. Here. No. This is. Then this one. Ei ei ei ei ei ei'" (*UV*, 196). Failing to find it and disappointed, he moves away only to come "trotting back with little yelps of triumph" (*UV*, 196). What he finally hands the Consul is a post card from Yvonne— the very Yvonne who has just returned to him—sent almost one year previously, a few days after she had left him in November 1937. The Consul hands the post card to Hugh and Yvonne's "scrawl" is reproduced for us: "Darling, why did I leave? Why did you let me? Expect to arrive in the U.S. tomorrow, California two days later. Hope to find a word from you there waiting. Love Y." (*UV*, 197).

The reader, of course, already knows that Geoffrey has not written Yvonne since she left him, that is, he has not managed to post anything he has written. Meanwhile this very card, meant to arrive months before, has "wandered far afield." Originally addressed to Mexico City in early November 1937, it has been date-stamped in Paris, Gibraltar and "even Algeciras, in Fascist Spain" (*UV*, 197); it is now early November 1938—the Day of the Dead. In the context of *Under the Volcano*, what could more poignantly, meaningfully, economically convey the fundamental theme of the story which is about loss—loss of love, loss of faith, loss of peace, and loss of life? And yet, this post card surely represents things both more and other than loss; after all, it does arrive, as does Yvonne, as does this day and this chance (however bungled and destroyed) for salvation. And *that* is the point; it is not quite a dead letter; it is not quite returned to sender; it *does* arrive.

This little scene with the *cartero* and the post card is brief, lightly handled, a minor detail in a novel rich in narrative and symbolic texture. If I stress it here, I do so because for all its simplicity it is, in my view, the *mise en abyme* of the story and the reading process in *Under the Volcano*; it contains the seeds—thematic, textual, ideological, and metaphysical—of Lowry's complex universe, a universe that grows from letters in profound and surprising ways. As a post card, this item is both private and public; what matter, then, if Hugh and we read it? Although it necessarily inscribes the epistolary dialogue, the I/you, thereby linking Geoffrey and Yvonne despite, in spite of, their estrangement, it equally signifies their utter failure to communicate, to read/reach each other in time and *in time*. It arrives, ironically, too late and reveals itself, apocalyptically, just before the catastrophic truth it so clearly announces.[2] Reproduced verbatim on the page, it interrupts the narrative flow and the dialogue, erupting out of the diegetic present to remind the reader of the text she is reading, about the activity of reading and, thus, about the nature of messages, texts, communiqués and their importance and power, their fragility and ephemerality.

Now it does not require an editor to point out all the reverberations of this post card scene, but it is essential for the Lowry editor to remember how important letters are in Lowry's work. And there is another dimension to this post card that is, perhaps, especially obvious to an editor. Yvonne's post card may represent (in part or whole) an actual message sent to Lowry by his first wife who left him in Mexico City at the end of 1937.[3] For reasons which I shall describe in a moment, I suspect this card may be a simulacrum of an authentic utterance or a *real* primary speech genre inserted into a secondary and fictional speech genre that is about the urgent need but inability to say, send, listen, read or write effectively, to bridge or close the gap between I/you, here/there, presence/absence. If I am correct in this speculation, then there are a number of messages in this *cartero* scene for the editor as well as the reader. Not only must I puzzle over questions of accurate transcription, copy text, provenance (whose post card is this anyway?), dating (remember, this one carries at least four date stamps!), and verification (where is the original—is there an original?) which proves that Lowry did or did not himself silently edit (as he almost certainly did with Yvonne's letters in chapter twelve which he cut but did not change in the process of chapter revision), not only must I speak to these issues, but I must also address the question of classification: what *is* a Lowry letter?

Clearly, unlike the unsuccessful Prefect of Paris in Poe's "The Purloined Letter," I must heed Dupin's advice and become flexible, even creative, in my detective and editorial methods. *Caveat editorialis*: Beware "postal différance," and remember that "what above all throws [the editor] off the track ... is that the epistolary simulacrum cannot be stabilized, installed in a certain place, and especially that it is not necessarily, and completely, intentional" (Derrida, "Envois," *The Post Card*, 89).

II: "Litterish fragments" or taking it to the letter

Although Lowry wrote hundreds of letters, he composed them in unusual ways and did unorthodox things with them (with both his out-going letters and with some in-coming ones as well). Unfortunately, his previous editors, notably his second wife Margerie Lowry, have done some equally unorthodox, if all too familiar (to editors) things with Lowry's letters. For example, in *Selected Letters*, edited by Margerie with Harvey Breit, a British Lyons is changed to a "teashop," and most references to his first wife are silently deleted, together with a host of other arbitrarily chosen items; letters written as poems are rendered in prose, documents are reproduced only in part; dates are inaccurate and annotations are scarce. But it is wise not to be too harsh because the task facing the Lowry editor is daunting. A few concrete examples will demonstrate some of the difficulties.

After his first wife left him in December 1937, the distraught Lowry travelled to Oaxaca, Mexico, where he drank heavily, spent Christmas in jail, and wrote some of his most abject, desperate letters such as this one to an old Cambridge friend, John Davenport, English author and literary critic, circa December 1937 (*SC* I, 177):

S.O.S.	Sinking fast by both bow and stern
S.O.S.	Worse than both the *Morro Castle*
S.O.S.	and the *Titanic*—
S.O.S.	No ship can think of anything else to do when
S.O.S.	it is in danger
S.O.S.	But to ask its closest friend for help.
C.Q.D.	Even if he cannot come.

> HOTEL FRANCIA
> OAXACA DE OAXACA,
> MEXICO

John:

My first letter to you was impounded by the police here. It contained both congratulations for you and Clem and commiseration for myself.

Better so, because it was a letter nobody should read. Commiseration = Comisario de Policia.

I have now destroyed this letter but with it also myself. This letter might be prettier too.

No words exist either to describe the terrible condition I am in.

I have, since being here, been in prison three times.

No words exist either to describe this. Of course, this is the end of introversion. If you cannot be decent outside you might as well have a shot at being decent in.

Here I succeeded but what shots will be needed now even God would not care to know.

Everywhere I go I am pursued ...

When the holograph is compared with the version printed in *Selected Letters* (11–13), the extent of the editors' interference is dramatically clear: all references to Jan, Lowry's first wife, are cut and the date of 1936 is incorrect; the references cut from the letter are, in fact, the most useful guides to accurate dating which would place this letter as mid to late December 1937 or even early 1938.

In another example, Paul Tiessen, the editor of *The Letters of Malcolm Lowry and Gerald Noxon,* published a short note written to the Noxons in the summer of 1944 as a brief letter (92) without annotations or textual notes. But the holograph draft from which Tiessen worked shows that this letter was composed either as a poem or a telegram. Unfortunately, however, neither a posted holograph nor typescript poem nor a telegram has, as yet, turned up. In such a case, what should the editor do? He or she should begin, at least, by asking the following questions: can one simply trans/prose without describing the copy text? And, more importantly, what is Lowry after here? If this is a poem, does Lowry often draft his letters (or other prose, for that matter) in the form of poetry, and if so, why? If this note or telegram to Noxon (keeping in mind who Noxon was for Lowry) is an isolated instance or an in-joke, may it not also carry more serious connotations? What combined effect of poetry and prose might Lowry be after here? What can be said about the status of poem-letters as text within what McKenzie might describe as the "sociology of [Lowry's] texts"?

The answer to one of these questions is yes; Lowry did write several poem-letters and he often drafted his prose in quasi-poetic forms. Figure 1 shows a poem-letter as it appears in Douglas Day's biography of Lowry and in *Selected Letters*. In both cases it has been trimmed and tidied-up without comment, but the holograph (Figure 2), from which the first editors and the biographer must have worked, tells quite a different story. My responsibility, therefore, is to prepare a faithful transcription with accurate dating as follows:

Albert the good,

Sorry I haven't written.

  Maybe I am a bit herausgeschmissen,

  I don't eat my food,

  and in my bed I have twice geshitten,

  Anyhow I am living here

  in a comparative state of mundial fear—

  Also give my love to my dear Twinbad the bailer

  I mean dear Frank Taylor.

  This is written on the night of April 18th

  Anyway or the other, there is no rhyme

  Unless you can think of one above.

              Save love,

                   Malcolm

Albert the Good,

  Sorry I haven't written.

  Maybe I am a bit berausgeshimmer,

  I don't eat my food and in my bed I have geshitten,

  Anyhow I am living here.

  In a comparative state of mundial fear—

  Also give my love to my dear Twinbad the bailer

  I mean dear Frank Taylor.

  This is written on the night of April 18th

  Anyway or the other, there is no rhyme

  Unless you can think of one above.

              Save love

                 Malcolm

P.S. We encountered a cyclone—four ships lost

      Somewhat tempest tossed.

FIGURE 1: Transcription in Douglas Day, *Malcolm Lowry*, 403, and in *Selected Letters of Malcolm Lowry*, 164.

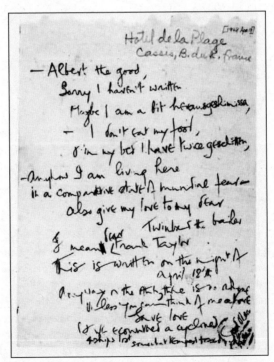

FIGURE 2: Holograph Letter to Albert Erskine. Reproduced with permission of the Malcolm Lowry Estate from the Papers of Albert Erskine (#10280-D), Manuscripts Division, Special Collections Department, University of Virginia Library.

Hotel de la Plage
Cassis, B. du R,
France
[18 April 1948]

– Albert the good,
　　Sorry I haven't written
　　　　Maybe I am a bit herausgeshimissen,
　　　　　– I don't eat my food,
　　　& in my bed I have twice geschitten,
– Anyhow I am living here
in a comparative state of mundial fear –
　　　Also give my love to my dear
　　　　　　　　Twinbad the bailer
　　I mean dear Frank Taylor
　　This is written on the night of
　　　　　April 18th
　　Anyway or the other, there is no rhyme
　　　　Unless you can think of one above
　　　　　　Save love
　(& we encountered a cyclone)
　4 ships lost
　　　　　somewhat tempest tossed.
　　　　God Bless
　　　　from
　　　　Malc
[P.S.] Good heavens, good heavens!
　　—On second thoughts, good lord,
　　　　　　　Good lord—
　Mad one might go but certainly everybody
　　　　Has not jumped overboard. M.

Figure 3: Grace transcription (*SC* II, 121).

Where necessary, some annotation must be included. Here, for example (Figure 3), Lowry's apparent German, "herausgeshimissen," requires comment. Margerie gets it entirely wrong, while Day corrects it, but neither recognizes Lowry's joke or that he is, indeed, joking under the circumstances. Colloquially, *herausgeschmissen* means "to be thrown out" (of the bar, for example) and to be, more generally, cast out, an outcast. The more literal associations of the term suggest a state of being out of pep, verve, or drink (*heraus / Schmiss*). Lowry may not have been a linguist, but he knew only too well what he was saying, and readers of Lowry will appreciate the relevance and poignancy of Lowry's joke. Cumulatively, small touches like these add a great deal to our sense of the writer and the man.

My "Tooloose-Lowrytrek," however, is still only beginning. Each of the three letters just discussed at least *appears* to represent a document that was addressed, signed, and sent to an identifiable addressee, but there are a number of Lowry letters which I very much doubt were ever sent or even intended to be sent; some are addressed to real people, such T.R. Henn, the Director of English Studies at St. Catharine's College, Cambridge, when Lowry was there between 1928 and 1932. From internal evidence, it would appear that Lowry wrote the letter sometime after 14 July 1949, when he injured his back in a fall from his pier, and that he intended to include it in one of his unfinished works-in-progress, "The Ordeal of Sigbjørn Wilderness." Whether or not the editor of Lowry's *Collected Letters* should include it is a question I am leaving open for the time being.[4] What is more important here is the evidence this document provides of the link Lowry saw between his life and fiction, a link that he often forged with letters.

Evidence suggests that Lowry not only drafted *fictive* letters (to real or fictional people) for use in his art, as I am suggesting he did with the Henn letter, but that he used *real* letters—his own and others'—in his fiction. Every "litterish fragment" (*Finnegans Wake*, 66) passed through his postal system on its way to us. It is possible, therefore, to trace the Lowry system by beginning with the fiction, the letter simulacrum, instead of with the life. In time I may be able to prove this with Yvonne's post card in the *Volcano*, but I would like to consider briefly a few other instances.

For example, the penultimate event in the story from *Hear us O Lord from heaven Thy dwelling place*, "Strange Comfort Afforded by the Profession," which is about letters, is a long letter addressed to a Mr. Van Bosch. For biographical and textual reasons, I smell a *real* letter here (as did Douglas Day before me), but what do the manuscripts show? "Strange Comfort" went through many revisions and a version of this letter (at one point addressed to Mr. Van Klett) appears in each of them. From draft to draft we can watch Lowry tinkering with names, dates, and details (such as a reference to Mr. Firmin, a *Volcano*-echo dropped in subsequent drafts). Moving from the manuscripts to notebooks and out-going letters, turns up nothing; there is no extant letter to a Mr. Van Klett (let alone a Van Bosch), but there is some correspondence between Lowry and a Los Angeles attorney, and I suspect that the original of this letter, assuming there was one and that it was actually sent, was destined for him.[5]

The story itself would seem to confirm my hunch because scattered throughout it are verbatim excerpts from letters by Joseph Severn concerning Keats and an excerpt from a 21 February 1832 letter from Poe (one of Lowry's "kindred spirits") to his foster father. Poe writes: "It will however be the last time I ever trouble any human being—I feel I am on a sick bed from which I shall never get up" (*HUOL*, 106). Lowry had carefully copied these passages into one of his notebooks during visits he made to the Poe house in Virginia in February 1947 and the Keats house in Rome in June 1948. I know because I have found the notebooks; I have not found the "Van Bosch"/Benjamin Parks epistle nor am I likely to because I have recently learned that the attorney (Parks) destroyed his files from this period to make room for new ones.

One further example of Lowry raiding his correspondence is worth a closer look. Despite his desperate condition during that hellish Mexican winter of 1937–38, Lowry preserved a holograph letter, dated 6 January 1938, sent to him from his Oaxaquenian friend Juan Fernando "Marquez." Many years later he used this letter verbatim, together with a letter he had written to Juan, in a typescript version of his novel *Dark as the Grave Wherein My Friend Is Laid.* In the posthumously published novel, edited by Margerie and Day, Fernando's letter is reproduced almost verbatim; there are minor layout changes and one significant omission: "Did you keep out of drinking today [*to give that present to your wife on your wedding day*]?" This reference to Jan was there in Lowry's typescript; therefore, it is likely that the cut was made by Margerie during her editing. Indeed, the page proofs show a line through the phrase. Lowry's letter to Juan that follows in his typescript, although included in *Selected Letters* (13–14), is not retained in the published *Dark as the Grave.*[6]

It is now time to pause and reflect upon what tentative conclusions can be made about Lowry's letters *as texts.* How does he use the letter, and why? What types of letter does he write? He uses the letter form in at least four distinct ways: (i) to communicate with a real addressee; (ii) as an intertext in his fiction, whether it is a *real* verbatim letter (that is, written by himself or by another), or an edited facsimile (in Dupin's sense of the word); (iii) as a purely fictive document, an epistolary fiction; and (iv) as a poem-letter, a generic cross which in some ways parallels his use of letters in/as fiction, but which carries both internal differences and some special messages.

If these categories suggest how he used letters, it still remains to ask why he did things this way. First, his ubiquitous use of and experimentation with medium and message are clear signs of Lowry's obsession with textuality which is further manifested in his use of quotations, allusions, clippings, signs, and so forth. Although the term haunted him, plagiarism is an appropriate label for his aesthetic and methodology; Lowry was an inspired plagiarist for whom the entire universe was a book—often open, sometimes terrifyingly closed—and his methods challenge the very notion that we can own words, let alone letters. Second, Lowry's letters create a fascinating leakage. Although they resemble and link up with other aspects of his textuality, they also leak, seep into, fill up the space between presentation and representation. They do this, moreover, neither to lend an air of verisimilitude to his fiction nor to authenticate experience (reading or living), but to conjoin, to connect without blending the two spheres. The leakage, then, creates a kind of doubling, an envelop(ing), or to change the metaphor, it establishes a counterpoint that permits us to hear/see both lines. And what is more, the leakage works both ways: the letters sent as communications to friends and editors develop (into) biographical and literary fictions, while the letters in the fictions carry expository and descriptive information and are always *addressed* (a point I will come back to), thereby reminding us, as Offred says in Margaret Atwood's *The Handmaid's Tale*, that "a story is like a letter" (50). Third, although they are only one skein for/in the textual fabric, his letters (all letters?) stress, underscore, address themselves to the desire for, yet problematics of, presence and absence, of communication, of sending and "getting" (back) the message: *fort/da.*[7] This would be one way, I suppose, of formulating Lowry's central theme: to send and to receive the message—Are you there? Do you hear me? Hear us O Lord! Or, as Lowry said at age twenty-three, after dropping coins on a monastery roof in Granada: "No echoes, no answers— the story of my life."[8]

Letters, of course, can be classified according to their function as documents, texts, artifacts, or to their form within a theory of correspondence governed by the processes (metaphysics) of writing, sending, receiving, and reading. If I think of Lowry's letters functionally, as written texts used as intertexts, as epistolary fictions and so on, then some such synchronic typology as the following suggests itself:

A TYPOLOGY OF THE LOWRY LETTERS AS TEXTS				
A	B	C	D	E
REAL Letters	*UNDECIDABLE* letters	*FICTION* letters	*UNSENT* letters	*POEM/* letters
	– *persona* – *literary* – *philosophical*	– *real to ML* – *edited by ML* – *others' letters*	– *real* – *fictive*	– *real* – *fictive*

Figure 4

By the clumsy term *real* letter (Type A), I mean those documents that the editor or bibliographer can verify as addressed, dated, signed, sent, post-marked, and delivered, documents for which there may be several drafts and which include post cards, telegrams, possibly card greetings, and some inscriptions and public missives such as letters to an editor. The physical and substantive variety of these letters is only as limited as the imagination and personality of the writer. In Lowry's case, they include business and formal courtesy letters, friendly letters with news, literary letters (a wide range here from question and answer to editorial matters to sensitive critical responses and exegesis), political and philosophical letters, personal reminiscences (actual or apocryphal), private cries for money, pleas for help, love letters, and notes. The more personal and literary (or philosophical) the letter, the more it will resemble (in vocabulary, sentence structure, tone, rhetorical strategies—puns, quotations, macaronics, etc.—and style) his fiction.

Type B letters are closely related to Type A. I call them "undecidable" because copy texts for these letters must be derived from drafts (in various stages) for which no A version appears to be extant. (Here is where a diachronic analysis with a stemma would demonstrate Lowry's creative process, a process very similar to that in his fiction). In other respects, they seem to be Type A letters and, as my investigative work continues, some of them may well end up as A, while others may be shifted to D. A majority of these letters falls into the private, literary and philosophical category regarding subject matter, and there is a discernible difference in tone and intention, from many Type A letters, that is determined by the identity of the addressee and Lowry's position as addresser.

Together, Types C, D, and E differ from A and B insofar as their use as text is concerned. What they have in common is the flaunting and foregrounding of their fictionality. Type C letters are Lowry's A and B letters that have been re-cycled in/for his fiction verbatim, complete or in part, with various changes to suit the fictive setting. The "Van Bosch" letter may be one example (Type A). I have also grouped together under Type C all those *real* letters by others that Lowry plundered for his own purposes: the letter from Fernando for *Dark as the Grave*, or the Severn and Poe letters in "Strange Comfort." Type D letters are the most intriguing. Here I have grouped those letters which I do not believe were ever written to be posted. Some ended up in the fiction, however, and may have been composed only as fiction; others were written to an actual addressee, but for one reason or another did not require or receive posting (like the Henn letter).

There are, of course, many questions raised by this re-cycling or fac-simulation process. Some of them are considered below. But the possibility should be at least considered here that all the letters in Lowry's fiction are Type C or D letters. For example, what about Geoffrey's staggering plea in chapter one of *Under the Volcano* on "two sheets of uncommonly thin hotel notepaper ... long but narrow and crammed on both sides with meaningless writing in pencil" (*UV*, 41). Is this a letter? Jacques Laruelle is not sure, but he does recognize "the hand, half crabbed, half generous, and wholly drunken, of the Consul himself, the Greek e's, flying buttresses of d's, the t's like lonely wayside crosses save where they crucified the entire word, the words themselves slanting steeply downhill, though the individual characters seemed as if resisting the descent, braced, climbing the other way. M. Laruelle felt a qualm. For he saw now that the writer undoubtedly had little intention, possibly no capability for the further tactile effort of posting" (*UV*, 41). If Jacques Laruelle thinks he recognizes Geoffrey Firmin's handwriting, Sherrill Grace is sure she recognizes Malcolm Lowry's.[9] But what about the contents of this "letter of sorts"?

" ... Night" it begins. " ... Night: and once again, the nightly grapple with death, the room shaking with demonic orchestras ... " (*UV*, 41). And later—"(Several mescals later.) Since December 1937, and you went, and it is now I hear the spring of 1938, I have been deliberately struggling against my love for you" (*UV*, 43). After five pages, the letter closes with the apocalyptic cry: "come back, come back. I will stop drinking, anything. I am dying without you. For Christ Jesus' sake Yvonne come back to me, hear me, it is a cry, come back to me, Yvonne, if only for a day ... " (*UV*, 46). *Fort/da!*

Everything points to this "litterish fragment" belonging to Type C or D—the familiar handwriting, the biographical details, the style and the tone. Especially noteworthy is the fact that Lowry gets his dating sequence wrong. According to the time scheme of the story, Yvonne would have left sometime around the Day of the Dead, November first or second, but Jan left Lowry in *December* 1937, and Lowry has allowed the real departure time to remain in this letter by the Consul. This may well be another small indication that Lowry was working with/from a real letter; given the importance of the November date to the novel, it is hard to explain the date as a simple error. But, of course, I need the original letter to verify my hunch. Chapter one of *Under the Volcano* closes with Laruelle burning this letter, a poignant yet grim forewarning of the holocaust to come. Did Lowry burn his holograph, or did he send it? If his editor cannot find the original (with his manuscripts? with his first wife?), should she include this printed text (as another "public" letter?) in the *Collected Letters*? Does Laruelle's designation—"it was a letter of sorts"—substantiate or validate my speculations about Type D letters? Or is this one, in the last analysis, a fictive letter?

I have established category E because there are a number of such texts and because I believe Lowry reveals something special in these poem-letters. We know that he thought of himself as a poet, and recent research by Kathleen Scherf suggests that he was a better poet than he, or we, knew.[10] He often drafted prose material in loose poetic form, and most of the poem-letters were written in times of acute emotional and psychological stress. It could be, then, that the poetic form captures the lyric outburst of Lowry's mood or some spontaneous creative outburst. Psychological guesswork aside, however, these poem-letters, like the letters and the prose fiction that incorporates (and, yes, re-cycles!) poems, remind us of the generic boundary between poetry and prose and, thus, of how difficult that boundary is to locate, defend, maintain, of how easy it is to cross over, invade, or set up new lines of communication. Just as Lowry's letters create a linkage across and a leakage into the space between actuality and fictionality, so these poem-letters connect the two spheres of Lowry's art which come back to him and to writing because, as Derrida tells us: "la lettre, l'epître ... n'est pas un genre mais tous les genres, la littérature même" (*La Carte Postale*, 54).

III: Speaking in Letters

Listen! What are the differences among the following letters and what do they have in common?

> Dear old bird:
>
> Have now reached condition of amnesia, breakdown, heartbreak, consumption, cholera, alcoholic poisoning, and God will not like to know what else, if he has to, which is damned doubtful.
>
> [...]
>
> Don't think I can go on. Where I am it is dark. Lost. (*SC* I, 187–88)

> Darling, why did I leave? Why did you let me? Expect to arrive in the U.S. tomorrow, California two days later. Hope to find a word from you there waiting. (*UV*, 197)

> Juan! I am here because there is much hostility in my hotel. I am trying to do some work here but my life is so circumscribed by your detectives [...] that I am rapidly losing my mind. (*DAG*, *TS*, 610, 9:21; *SC* I, 183)

Which one is the *real* letter? Which one was written by Lowry? Which one is the fictional letter? Which one the fictive? All were written by Lowry; one and three were also composed by him, and we have the holograph originals to prove that. The first is a December 1937 letter to Conrad Aiken (in green ink on Hotel Francia letterhead, UBC 1:75); the second, of course, is *la carte postale* addressed to Geoffrey by Yvonne, but written by Lowry into *Under the Volcano*. The third is the letter from Malcolm to his friend, Juan Fernando, which forms part of the epistolary dialogue in the typescript of *Dark as the Grave*. What they have in common is more important than these differences.

They are all letters. They are all addressed, in the sense of spoken to, and as Mikhail Bakhtin tells us in *Problems of Dostoevsky's Poetics*:

> a characteristic feature of the letter is an acute awareness of the interlocutor, the addressee to whom it is directed. The letter, like a rejoinder in a dialogue, is addressed to a specific person, and it takes into account the other's possible reactions, the other's possible reply. (*Problems*, 205)

To set up a typology of written texts according to function, as I did in part two, goes a certain way towards theorizing the Lowry letter, but letters are more than written texts. The letter form must be considered within a theory of correspondence; it is, what Bakhtin calls, a "speech genre," written with the addressee in mind. The letter links across and leaks into that space between interlocutors, yet it cannot exist without that gap between I/you, presence/absence, and on one level the letter is always about that gap. If Bakhtin is correct in asserting that the "reckoning with an absent interlocutor" can be "intensive" with some authors (Dostoevsky is his example, *Problems*, 205), and that epistolary practice is ideally suited to such reckonings, then for a writer like Lowry, who is obsessed with letters, the theory of speech genres may well throw light on aspects of his letters that are obscured by a fictional typology.

Lowry's letters, I would suggest, can be classified as primary and secondary speech genres (see Figure 5): A, B, and some of E are primary; C, D (with some qualifications), and some of E are secondary. Once they have been classified as speech genres, it is possible to consider the discourse itself and whether or not and how a specific letter is single- or double-voiced (see Figure 6). Then, and only then, can the editor talk about the what and the why of a Lowry letter.

A TYPOLOGY OF THE LOWRY LETTERS AS SPEECH GENRE

Primary	*Secondary*
A, B, C, E, and some D	C, D, and some E

FIGURE 5

DIALOGIC RELATIONS IN LETTERS

Primary "Single-voiced"		*Secondary* "Double voiced"
I	II	III
A, B, and E	A, B, C, and D	C (iii, 3—"reflected discourse"), D, and E

FIGURE 6

Bakhtin's theory of speech genres, outlined in *Speech Genres and Other Late Essays*, derives from his translinguistic concept of the utterance "as a unit of speech communion" (written or spoken) within the general human language condition of heteroglossia. Bakhtin articulates his translinguistics in opposition to Saussure and in distinction from von Humboldt and Vossler (see V.N. Voloshinov, *Marxism and the Philosophy of Language*), because he stresses *speech communion* as the fundamental reality of language and consciousness, prior to linguistics, stylistics, speech act theory, or pragmatics. To study verbal language systems from the perspective of utterance is to maintain the vital and necessary link between world and word: "After all, language enters life through concrete utterances (which manifest language) and life enters language through concrete utterances as well" (*Speech Genres*, 63). The utterance, then, is communicative; all utterance (hence human understanding itself) assumes response, "is actively responsive," even when no response is heard, seen or offered, and this quality Bakhtin calls "addressivity" (*Speech Genres*, 99). Addressivity determines and constitutes the features of a speech genre. Other characteristics of the utterance which bear directly on speech genre formation are its "dialogic overtones" (*Speech Genres*, 92) and its boundaries which, unlike sentences, "are determined by a *change of speaking subjects*" (*Speech Genres*, 71) and enable it to form a link in a chain of utterances.[11]

The formation of speech genres provides some degree of finalization (hence of representability) to the utterance, and despite what Bakhtin describes as the extreme heterogeneity of speech genres (written and oral), they are typical forms of utterance (see *Speech Genres*, 60, 87). Speech genres, in general, vary widely in degree of conventionality or freedom, formality or informality; therefore, an individual style (voice) may be virtually erased or intensified depending on the genre. But obvious or not, individual style, according to Bakhtin, cannot be separated from genre or historical process: "where there is style there is genre" (*Speech Genres*, 66). It can, however, be transferred from genre to genre—as we shall see—with important and interesting results.

The model speech genre for Bakhtin is live dialogue which already displays all the qualities of utterance in an almost unlimited array of forms from the simple to the complex, the informal to the formal. According to Bakhtin, primary speech genres are simple, usually oral and unmediated, whereas secondary speech genres are complex, usually written and mediated. "Simple" refers to the fact that the discourse of the primary genres is only directed towards its referential object or objective, while "complex" describes the discourse which is doubly-directed towards its referential object *and* towards another's discourse (as in stylization, parody, and so on) (*Problems*, 185). Primary genres can, therefore, be described as unmediated (that is, using direct presentation), while secondary genres are mediated (*re*presented). Bakhtin's examples of primary speech genres include live dialogue, letters, diaries, minutes, and everyday stories, and of secondary speech genres, artistic, scientific and sociopolitical discourse such as novels (including epistolary novels), scientific papers or articles, the throne speech, an editorial and so on. Two qualities of speech genres make them fascinating but difficult to handle: heterogeneity and transposibility. Because primary genres can be, and always are, in process of being transposed into secondary ones, distinctions between the two types are difficult to stabilize.

This is especially true with the *text* of a letter which, as speech genre, can be primary and secondary. But generic pressures and constraints render the speech forms relatively stable, at least recognizable and learnable. Generic features reflect a conscious or unconscious selection by the speaker/writer of a content, style, grammar, and compositional structure, what Bakhtin calls the speaker's "plan or speech will" (*Speech Genres*, 78). Furthermore, knowledge of the generic form is what enables us to communicate verbally because the generic form elicits and determines (to a degree) the assumed response of the addressee and assists both the finalization of and boundaries to an utterance: "We learn to cast our speech [and writing] in generic forms and, when hearing others' speech, we guess its genre from the very words ... we foresee the end" (*Speech Genres*, 78–79).

Turning back to Lowry's letters, it should now be possible to say more about specific cases (see Figures 4, 5, and 6). Even a straightforward Type A primary speech genre *real* letter by Lowry, such as the "Dear old bird" one to Conrad Aiken, is full of "dialogic overtones." With his slang, colloquialisms, literary and biographical references (and fabrications), Lowry stops just this side of creating a secondary speech genre, which he certainly does do in other letters (for example, to Conrad Aiken, David Markson, or Harvey Burt; see *SC* II nos. 615, 652, and 741) that are heavily interlaced with quotations and very much doubly-directed towards a referential object *and* another's discourse. The letter to Juan exists as a primary speech genre and as an utterance within a secondary speech genre. In its former guise it is much simpler, with fewer "dialogic overtones" than the Aiken one, but in its latter guise it entrains a whole new set of problems.

What happens to the letter itself when it is re-accentuated by being placed with a series of utterances within a very complex secondary speech genre, and what happens to the novel that contains this kind of re-accentuated material? The *real* letter gains a fictive status (purpose, richness) without losing its *real* one, which still exists, and the novel, *Dark as the Grave*, acquires the double-voiced quality "best suited" (according to Bakhtin, *Problems*, 205) to epistolary forms, the quality of "active double-voiced discourse, the reflected discourse of another" (*Problems*, 199). Letters like the post card from "Y." (which is itself re-accentuated in chapter one before we get to read it in chapter six) or the draft letter to "Mr. Henn" (see *SC* II, 848–50) or, for that matter, the Consul's letter in chapter one of *Volcano* all exist as/in secondary genres, and all serve to actively dialogize the discourse by re-presenting the "reflected discourse of another," in these cases, of a character. Do they do so more or less if they cannot be verified to be primary speech genres addressed to or written by a *real* other? Once more I think the question is worth asking because the editor must not only strive to verify and locate, but also to annotate those cases where letters are re-accentuated. This is one major way in which Lowry wrote the letter as a genre into the very warp and woof of his work.

And what about Type D letters, whether they are purely fictive or addressed to a real person? Should they be included in a *Collected Letters*, and if so how? Deciding on the basis of function alone might lead me to say no, but on the basis of form, I think, the answer must be yes, possibly in an appendix, *because* they share so many of the qualities of the letter as speech genre and they create much of the double-voicing of Lowryan discourse. In themselves, they differ from Types A and B on neither the level of genre nor of discourse. Indeed, one could cut across both my textual typology of part II and the speech genre classification outlined above in Figures 5 and 6 to say that Types A, B, and E belong to Bakhtin's metalinguistic. classification of discourse according to dialogic relations as set forth in *Problems of Dostoevsky's Poetics* (185–99). In the first category he places all "single-voiced" discourse that is "direct, unmediated [and] directed exclusively toward its referential object, as an expression of the speaker's ultimate semantic authority." For my purposes, then, Types A, B, and E are such instances of "single-voiced" discourse (see Figure 6). Types A, B, C, and some of D can be classified under II, that is, as examples of "single-voiced" "objectified" discourse of a "represented person." That leaves C, most of D, and some of E classified with III as instances of the most complex form of "double-voiced" "reflected discourse."

These chartings of the letters as speech genres and as discourse throw the following points into relief. The Lowry letter is a highly complex and varied form. It reveals the essentially dialogic nature of his imagination and the central importance of addressivity in and across the spectrum of his writing. For Lowry, as for Bakhtin, the I/you of all dialogic relations, and especially those of the letter, allowed him "to hear voices everywhere" and taught him to reaccentuate his own and others' primary speech genres in the secondary forms of art. But perhaps the most important aspect of Bakhtin's concepts of speech genre and "reflected discourse" is to remind us of the fact that there are no radical linguistic or generic differences between the simplest and most complex letter, between the primary and the secondary speech genres. "Complexly structured and specialized works of various scientific and artistic genres, in spite of all the ways in which they differ from rejoinders in dialogue, are by nature the same kind of units of speech communication" (*Speech Genres*, 75). If that principle is accepted, then *the* Lowry letter must include a very wide range of *real,* "undecidable," fictional, re-accentuated and fictive primary and secondary speech genres. And so too must the *Collected Letters of Malcolm Lowry.*

IV: Fort/da

7 June 1989
Special Collections, UBC,
Vancouver, B.C.

Dear Malc,
For a man who valued communication even more than Dostoevsky's Devushkin, you
sure left behind you some mixed and garbled messages for me to decipher. "No sail, no

mail," *you'd cry in triste tones, while drafting letters, sent or unsent, to anyone who'd listen, scribbled on the versos of your manuscripts, crumpled and smoothed out for interleaving (interlettering!) with the current work-in-progress. "Dear Antonio," you wrote out of some obscure alcoholic premonition in Oaxaca, 1937, "conserve carefully even down to the most cursed piece of newspaper everything in my room [...] I want everything in that drawer as well; it may all possibly have value to me."[12] My God, I feel like "Mrs. Hahn" scratching in an archival dump for your "litterish fragments"! And just what do you expect me to do with all those envois to St. Jude scribbled at the top of your manuscripts? "St. Jude, please help me!" St. Jude, indeed.*

Ah Malcolm, mon semblable, mon frère, I try to keep my patience and my sense of humour because, like so many others, I recognize your genius, your basic humanity, and I can see you there watching all my scratchings for correspondences with a sly grin on your face and a bottle of Bols in your hand. (Anyway, I also know the "daily crucifixion of the post.") And it's true—a fact—your letters, whatever, wherever they are, set up their own echoes and answers. Not hearing the particular voice you always longed for (was it God himself or just your father, that Superaddressee of yours?—more likely your mother, eh?), not hearing that longed for voice, you too heard voices everywhere and transmitted those voices, that contrapuntal babel to us.

But where, you bastard, did you put the letter, the one that was returned to you (fort/da)? I'm haunted by that letter. It's the one that will answer all my questions! The one letter to/for me! Unless you didn't send it after all. Or is it that poem-letter to Scipio Sprague? You know, the one that goes:

> *from Malcolm Lowry*
> *late of the Bowery*
> *whose prose was flowery*
> *if somewhat glowery*
> *who worked nightly*
> *and [drank] daily*
> *and died, playing the ukulele ... ? (SC II, 735)[13]*

I hope, by the way, that you don't expect me to believe in Scipio Sprague!

Or maybe it went missing like that post card? Only this time it became a dead letter destined (post restante), as Melville knew, for the flames. Or was it, and this is worse than the wheels within wheels, than being under Under the Volcano, *was it always already in that shack on the beach at Dollarton on the morning of 7 June 1944? God knows the element followed you around; I hope it's not now following me! (Though earlier today there was a fire alarm in the library and we had to evacuate the archives. And what do you think I was holding when the bells went off? What else but the charred fragments of* "In Ballast to the White Sea"!). *In that June 7th auto da fe perhaps even your unsent letters became dead letters. "On errands of life, these letters speed to death." Ah Lowry! Ah humanity!*

But wait, I don't give up so easily. I want an answer. Did you leave letters behind in that other shack, the last one, that they bull-dozed? Were some of those papers, fluttering around on the beach like lost souls, letters? Mais si, mais si! If they were (St. Jude, help me!), they may have been purloined, and how the hell do you think I'll find them now? And even if I do, will they be real letters or facsimiles?

Never mind, never mind, I don't await your reply: "No echoes, no answers ... " eh! eh? And don't worry. I'll get it all sorted out yet: letters as texts— real, fictional, fictive— and letters as speech genres—primary and secondary. I'll describe your reflected discourse in my own epistolary prologue and I'll trace the correspondences between life and art, of life in art as the "sociology of [your] texts." For all those unresolved letters (you remember—the unsent ones, the lost or dead ones), I'll use an appendix; it's accepted editorial practice and consistent with my dialogic method. These letters demonstrate, better than anything I can say, the capillary links, the permeable membrane you created with the letter to dissolve all our rigid categories. And through it all, I will try to keep in mind the Mene Tekel Peres for editors: Do you like this holograph that you hold? See that you do not mis-read, mis-date or otherwise mis-use it!

No, I don't await your reply, and yet since I have it on your authority that the voyage never ends (which means, I know, that your Collected Letters never can be completely collected), I half expect to hear from you. In fact, I'd love to hear, and I'm sure you must have ways of getting a message through. If so, you can always send it to the above address.

Your Frère Jacques—
S.

P.S. Always remember : "To be means to communicate" (PDP, 287), and the editor's existence, "like the author's is a function of the human communicational system."[14]

(1989)

Notes

*References to *Under the Volcano* are to the 1963 Penguin edition.

[1] In my preparation to take up the challenge of editing Lowry's letters, I was indebted to Professor McKenzie's splendid lectures: *Bibliography and the Sociology of Texts*. I would also like to thank my colleagues at the 1989 Conference on Editorial Problems at the University of Toronto for their stimulating comments and suggestions. Marilyn Randall's astute questions have kept me thinking about a theory of correspondence.

[2] See Derrida's, "Of an apocalyptic tone recently adopted in philosophy," 63–97. The "apocalyptic tone" running through Lowry's writing—his stress on revelation, unveiling,

emasculation and presence, and his play with the number seven, the word "Come" and the universal principle of femininity (in *Volcano* denied)—is a topic for further study.

[3] For biographical details, see Day's *Malcolm Lowry;* Gordon Bowker's *Malcolm Lowry Remembered* and *Pursued by Furies;* Sheryl Salloum's *Malcolm Lowry: Vancouver Days;* and Jan Gabrial's *Inside the Volcano.* The extensive correspondence between Lowry and his first wife has not yet been made public, but a version of the post card, as well as Yvonne's letters in chapter twelve, are present from early drafts of *Volcano.* The 1940 version of this card reads: "Darling ... such a lot of foolish squabbles! Expect to arrive in U.S. tomorrow, or early Sunday. Miss you terribly, I think of our trip down, I may buy a small car and come back down if you decide to stay and we can return together." I would like to thank my colleague, Rick Asals, for his comments on this post card and on other aspects of this paper.

[4] I did include this letter but in Appendix 3, not with the main sequence of letters; see *SC* II, 948–50.

[5] For Day's description of this unhappy period, see *Malcolm Lowry* 249–54. Of the Van Bosch letter, Day concludes: "it is obviously something that Lowry himself had written in 1938–39 to Benjamin Parks" (453). Biographical details plus Lowry's descriptions of his life at this time in other letters seem to confirm this conclusion and suggest a date sometime between 24 July and 29 August 1939. To date I have located two letters to his German publisher whose name was Klett, but neither bears any resemblance to the letter in "Strange Comfort."

[6] A holograph draft of Lowry's letter, two pages (both sides) in pencil and unsigned, is in The University of British Columbia Lowry Archive 1:76. For the complete letter, see *Sursum Corda!* I, 176).

[7] See Derrida's commentary on the *fort/da* in "To Speculate—On 'Freud'" in *The Post Card* 313–22. What is the Lowry legacy?

[8] This typical Lowry remark is quoted in Clarissa Lorenz's "Call It Misadventure," from *Malcolm Lowry Remembered* (85).

[9] Rick Asals has discussed with me an early draft of *Volcano* where Lowry is working on this letter, and he describes the marginalia as examples of Lowry modifying his own hand to mimic the Consul's. He also points out that, like many other things in *Volcano,* this letter went through a number of changes, some substantive, whereas Yvonne's letters in twelve change comparatively little over the years of drafting.

[10] Kathleen Scherf has published an edition of the complete poems with annotations by Chris Ackerley; see *The Collected Poetry of Malcolm Lowry.*

[11] In "The Problem of Speech Genres" from *Speech Genres and Other Late Essays,* Bakhtin examines the distinction between the sentence and the utterance at length; see pages 81–86.

[12] I am quoting here from Lowry's holograph letter (UBC Lowry Archive 1:75) to his Mexican friend. For the reader not familiar with Lowry's biography, it will help to know that Lowry's shack on the beach at Dollarton, British Columbia, burned to the ground on 7 June 1944. Many of his papers and manuscripts were lost, including a major work-in-progress called "In Ballast to the White Sea," a few charred fragments of which are held in the Lowry Archive. The number seven, not to mention the 7th of June, were of great significance to Lowry. My letter can be seen as a parody of Lowry, using Dostoevsky, Poe, Melville, Joyce, Derrida, Bakhtin, McKenzie, T.S. Eliot, and the Bible, or as a secondary speech genre manifesting "reflected discourse."

[13] This poem appears in a 1 June 1954 letter to Arthur A. Sprague (*SC* II, 735), where Lowry writes "and sometimes daily," but see the more familiar version of the poem in *Selected Poems*.

[14] See Morse Peckham, "Reflections on the Foundations of Modern Textual Editing" (144).

5

"A Sound of Singing":
Polyphony and Narrative Decentring in Malcolm Lowry's Hear us O Lord

I

"Hear us, O Lord, from heaven Thy dwelling place." The five bars and two verses of this Manx fishermen's hymn (sung to the tune of "Peel Castle") occupy, like a prefacing quotation, the first page of Malcolm Lowry's posthumously published *Hear us O Lord from heaven Thy dwelling place.*[1] At first glance, this extraordinary text seems to be a mere collection of seven stories, with two of novella length. But as Lowry knew and as that hymn on the first page suggests, *Hear us O Lord* is both more and other than a collection of stories—*more* because it is "a strange assembly of apparently incongruous parts" (31) comprising a unique whole, and *other than* because this text is a celebration and articulation of a vision of reality within a semiotic system that breaks conventional generic bounds and opens up narrative discourse and structure to heterogeneity, multiplicity, and *différance.*[2] *Hear us O Lord*, moreover, is a key text in the Lowry *oeuvre*. Even in *Under the Volcano*, which comes closer to fitting accepted notions of modernist fiction, Lowry's approach to character, language, and structure can raise eyebrows because he is not sympathetic to realist notions of character, or to the so-called classical unities, or to the controlling strategies of myth, symbol, and metaphor exploited by other modernists. Like all of Lowry's work, *Under the Volcano* can be criticized for its highly ornamental prose, the great wheeling sentences which threaten to run out of control, or the metaphors that proliferate into a catachrestic and destabilized discourse. A careful reading of *Under the Volcano*, however, reveals that Lowry was—even there—not interested in homophonic and centred fiction. His priorities are clearer still in *Hear us O Lord* which announces on its first page that it is a text, a song (words and notation) to be sung by many voices on a multitude of occasions, that it is, in other words, a polyphonic discourse without an identifiable centre—unless that centre is the text itself or those who voice it and hear us. Writing to his editor in 1952, Lowry described it as "a sort of novel of an odd aeolian kind" which "makes a very beautiful sound when taken together" as a whole (*SC* II, 583, 660).

In the following discussion, I can only hint at some of the ways in which *Hear us O Lord* teaches us to reread and rethink Lowry's work because my main focus will be on the collection itself and on the ways in which Lowry generates a textual system that resists conventional notions of fiction and of narrative discourse. The highly reflexive, metafictional nature of the text makes it necessary to begin with a description of the story/ies and, from there, to move on to a consideration of what is involved in homophonic or polyphonic narratives and the ways in which Lowry creates something other than a homophonic, centred text.

II

After the page of musical notation and text, the reader comes to the first of a sequence of seven stories that chart the voyage of Lowry protagonists from Vancouver to Europe and home again to Vancouver. "The Bravest Boat" recounts a married couple's celebration of the events that brought them together. They discovered each other by means of a short note sent to sea in a toy balsa wood boat, and every year they participate in a ritual repetition of the words in that message. The focus of this almost plotless and characterless sketch is on the note or, more properly, on the words that comprise the note and that bear witness to the almost miraculous nature of human communication. "The Bravest Boat," like the prelude or overture to a musical composition, establishes the tone, pitch, and key of what is to follow.

The next piece, the long novella "Through the Panama," is an experimental *tour de force* with multiple first-person narrators (writers who are being written by their characters), marginalia, and intertexts. Together with the final novella of *Hear us O Lord*, "The Forest Path to the Spring," and *Under the Volcano* it is Lowry's most challenging and successful fiction. It does not, however, have anything diegetic in common with the first story, and yet it clearly belongs with it; here again are the sea, the journey metaphor, a devoted married couple and, above all, the primary concern with words: words in several languages, words spoken, heard or overheard, sung, written and read, words on signs, words as signs, words authored by the writer or appropriated from other writers or speakers.

The next two stories, "Strange Comfort Afforded by the Profession" and "Elephant and Colosseum," are about writers as well, but not necessarily the same writer, although the Sigbjørn Wilderness of "Strange Comfort" may be the same as the Sigbjørn in "Panama" (3). In the first of these two stories, the writer is in Rome on a Guggenheim Fellowship, but unlike the writer in "Panama" he is entirely absorbed by the notes he is taking and the other texts inscribed in his journal. The writer in "Elephant and Colosseum," with the striking Manx name of Kennish Drumgold Cosnahan (in case we had forgotten the opening hymn), is also in Rome, ostensibly to locate his Italian translators. After an anxious day of grappas, letter-writing, negotiating busy streets, doubting his own identity and reality, and misremembering addresses, *he* finds he is *translated*, though not in the way he expected. Lowry thereby reminds us once more of the variety and power of words.

Just when the reader is beginning to think that he or she has found a centre or a connecting thread amongst these stories (surely they are about writing and writers?)—despite the shifting locale and narrative voice—the next two stories introduce further uncertainties into the composition in the form of new voices and new melodic lines. "Present Estate of Pompeii" and "Gin and Goldenrod," while both containing married couples, do not explore the written signs, the textuality, of the writer's world. Instead, each concentrates on the effort to decipher the physical signs in a landscape, the ruins at Pompeii in one, the route to a North Vancouver bootlegger in the other. This interest in signs hearkens back to "Through the Panama," where the actual position report from one of Lowry's own voyages becomes part of the fiction, and points forward to the path in the closing novella "The Forest Path to the Spring."

The novella, however, which Lowry dedicated to his wife and thought of as the coda to his projected cycle of novels, *The Voyage That Never Ends*, is a lyric paeon of love, nature, and harmony told in the first-person voice of a jazz composer. This character, like Lowry himself, finds health, sanity, and creativity in an isolated existence on Burrard Inlet near the city of Vancouver and is in the process of composing a jazz opera called *The Forest Path to the Spring*. It is not until we reach this story that the sense of completion and wholeness implicit (because potential, always already there) throughout the collection begins to come into focus. Here, we rediscover the hymnic mode, the prose rhythms we now recognize as underlying the entire text, the multiplicity of allusions, references, quotations—of intertexts—and the thematizing of various concerns (notably creativity and communication) that have surfaced on earlier pages. Of all the stories in *Hear us O Lord*, this one, with its eight discrete parts, seems to rest in the narrating voice of the "I" who speaks directly to us and connects each separate part.

There are many elements, then, which serve to unify individual units and the multiple texts of *Hear us O Lord*—themes, intertexts, rhythms, patterns of image and sound, the character types (notably the writer and the couple), and most of all the obsessive interest in language. But none of them provides quite the same unifying force as a single, controlling narrative voice, a consistently developing central character or a sequential plot line. Given that this is neither a conventional novel (if a novel at all) nor a disparate collection, why did Lowry use some unifying elements, while clearly rejecting, indeed deconstructing, others? What is involved in his privileging of fragments, his preference for constantly fluctuating discourse and narrative voices, and what kind of text has he created?

By suggesting that Lowry resisted the conventional homophonic and centred text in *Under the Volcano* and finally rejected it in *Hear us O Lord*, I want to draw attention to the polyphonic, decentred nature of the latter work. The term "polyphonic" was introduced into narrative theory by Mikhail Bakhtin,[3] but it derives, of course, from music where polyphonic composition has a single predominating part or melody and implies sameness of sound (in phonetics) or unison of voice. By contrast, a polyphonic composition employs "two or more voices or parts, each with an independent melody, but all harmonizing";[4] it can be contrapuntal, juxtaposing and contrasting individual melodic lines as in a fugue, or it can take the form of jazz with its stress on rhythm, improvisation, greater melodic freedom and soloing.

Within Bakhtin's theory of language and genre, polyphony holds an important position. Speaking of Dostoevsky, for example, he stresses that the "*polyphonic novel is dialogic through and through*" (*Problems*, 40). In order to reach this conclusion, Bakhtin is using the term polyphony metaphorically, and the shift from music to verbal constructs implies a semiotic parallel between the two media; thus, "polyphony [in literature] presumes a plurality of fully valid voices within the limits of a single work—for only then may polyphonic principles be applied to the construction of the whole" (*Problems*, 34). Although he is careful to avoid the claim that Dostoevsky's polyphony is the sign and condition of artistic superiority and progressiveness, Bakhtin nonetheless privileges polyphonic discourse (in a novel or elsewhere) above other forms.

Bakhtin opposes the dialogic to the monologic principle, and he sees these principles at work in all modes of human discourse, or "speech genres," including ideology and social structures as well as works of art.[5] Where the monologic principle operates by repudiating and suppressing all points of view other than, or contrary to, the fixed authorial or authorized one, the dialogic principle facilitates and activates "double-voicing" within utterances; it does not silence, foreclose upon or finalize but, instead, assumes and permits conflicting points of view and acknowledges the "*living, autonomous consciousness*" (*Problems*, 285) of the other. Monologic discourse in fiction, then, is unitary, homogeneous, single-voiced, closed, and authoritative (the author's word, like God's, prevails); it is homophonic. Dialogic discourse is binary (Bakhtin would say "tertiary"),[6] heterogeneous, "double-voiced," open, and interdependent; it is polyphonic.

It follows from this Bakhtinian distinction between monologic and dialogic principles that centring (as it is usually understood in fiction) will be associated with unified narratives organized around a single, predominating focus—in theme, purpose, structural code, character (either the hero or the central consciousness), or in narrative voice. Furthermore, as Bakhtin warns us, monologic and centred fictions have been perceived as aesthetic, hermeneutic, and cognitive models of narrative perfection, and we must learn to resist the homophonic claim to truth or beauty. Decentred fictions, while by no means lacking order, meaning, or clarity, function differently. In the present context, the term *decentred* describes that typically polyphonic Lowryan narrative which achieves its most thorough articulation in *Hear us O Lord* and springs from his refusal, at every level of the text, of monologic discourse: hear *us*, O Lord.

III

In the following discussion, I will concentrate upon three interrelated aspects of the text that contribute significantly to its polyphonic, decentred structure: the metaphor of singing, narrative voice, and the foregrounding of language via letters. The metaphor of singing, established in the collection title and the hymn on the first page, recurs in each story and, thus, seems to provide a central trope or unifying figure for the text. Lowry, however, develops the metaphor in such a way as to avoid fixed or unified tenor/vehicle relations. To begin with, the metaphor itself takes several forms—a ship's engines sing "Frère Jacques" (21, 26, 33, 40, 69, 82, 93, 94, 98, 165, 182, 218), anagnorisis is the "trumpeted '—' of an elephant" (168), the guided tour of Pompeii is a "conducted round" (183). In fact, the metaphor expands and proliferates, as is often the case with Lowry, until we are dealing with catachresis.

A prime example of this destabilization occurs late in "The Bravest Boat" when the narrator contemplates the perilous voyage of the tiny balsa wood craft with its precious message. The paragraph is long, and the main sentence, which extends over thirty lines and is loosely strung together with conjunctions and punctuation, has a catachrestic musical analogy embedded within it:

> and all this time a sound, like a high sound of singing, yet as sustained in harmony as telegraph wires, or like the unbelievably high perpetual sound of the wind [...] or the ghost of the wind in the rigging of ships long lost, and perhaps it was the sound of the wind in its toy rigging. (20)

The sound, presumably the aural accompaniment that the protagonist imagines for his toy boat's ordeal (the source is never precisely identified), is at first like singing, then like telegraph wires or the wind. The analogies, however, serve less to locate and identify the properties of the sound than they do to multiply its possible correspondences and meanings. The paragraph continuing this passage concludes with the "Frère Jacques" of a ship's engines, but that music seems unconnected with the mysterious harmonies of the "high sound of singing."

It is not until the phrase recurs in the final novella, "The Forest Path to the Spring," that the reader is able to situate this singing within the wider musical analogy of the entire text—if, that is, the reader remembers having already "read [it] somewhere":

> Haunted by a line I had read somewhere: "And from the whole world, as it revolved through space, came a sound of singing," and by the passionate desire to express my own happiness with my wife in Eridanus, I composed this opera, built, like our new house, on the charred foundations and fragments of the old work and our old life. (274)

And it is here, in "Forest Path," that the musical analogy is thematized most fully. As the jazz composer/narrator goes on to explain, his opera is "partly in the whole-tone scale, like *Wozzeck*, partly jazz, partly folk songs or songs my wife sang, even old hymns, such as *Hear Us O Lord from Heaven Thy Dwelling Place*. I even used canons like *Frère Jacques*" (274). The title of this opera is *The Forest Path to the Spring* and it is, by analogy (albeit a convoluted, destabilized one), the text we have been reading. What the text shares with the jazz opera—the main way in which they are alike—is its multiplicity. Both are built "on the charred foundations and fragments" of previous texts and earlier life, and both are composed polyphonically, with one story, like one independent melody, counterpointing another, and with all stories recapitulated in "Forest Path."

Hear us O Lord provides a textual composition, modelled on polyphonic musical forms (the fugue, say, or better still, free jazz),[7] which derives from the plurality of narrators across the entire textual system of seven discrete stories and the "double-voicing" of the narrator's discourse within each story. Of course, degrees of plurality and "double-voicing" vary from moment to moment (or story to story) within the system. "Through the Panama" is both "double-voiced" and plural (a point I shall return to), but even in a story like "Elephant and Colosseum" which seems homophonic and centred, Lowry is resisting, in subtle and interesting ways, the centripetal pull of conventional narrative discourse.

The diegesis of "Elephant and Colosseum" is quite straightforward: Cosnahan, in Rome to speak with the Italian translators of his novel, *Ark from Singapore*, sits on a restaurant terrace contemplating his novel's success, the Roman traffic, and his Manx family; he starts a long letter to his absent wife, then sets out to find his way to the publisher's office. When he finally locates the firm, he learns that his translators are in Turin, not Rome, and he wanders off in dismay towards the Rome zoo where he discovers Rosemary, the elephantine heroine of his novel.

This whimsical little story observes all the rules of unity (in time, place, and action) and is firmly grounded in its main character, but conditions for homophony and centredness cannot be taken for granted in a Lowry short story. Who is this Cosnahan after all? Is he Manx or American, a writer or a magician, a success or a failure? Is he really that face on the jacket of his book? What language does he speak—English, Manx, or only fragments of German, Latin, and Italian? And what is his true biography? Cosnahan no longer knows. In fact, it is this uncertainty, not the securely centred voice and identity of the protagonist, that forms the central thrust of the narrative. "What did man know of his own nature," Cosnahan muses:

> How many people went through life thinking they were other than they were? Not even the evidence of his own essential being right under his red nose would convince him. How many lives were necessary to find out? [...]
>
> Yet what did he, Cosnahan, know of himself? Was he a writer? What was a writer? (146)

In this gentle little story, Lowry thematizes the problematics of ontology and epistemology and comes to the conclusion that the "I" or self is heterogeneous, multiple, and polyphonic. When Cosnahan finally finds what he wants—"the kind of recognition no one would suspect [.] A word [...] or not even a word, but some sign" (139)—it comes in the form of Rosemary's trumpeted " '—' " (168) because he speaks to the animal in a double voice: English and Manx Gaelic. In other words, Cosnahan is most himself—the self that persists through time and connects the young man caring for an elephant on a ship with the middle-aged author of the novel about that voyage standing before a cage in the Rome zoo—when he is polyphonic. It is his unique polyphony that the elephant recognizes and that validates him.

"Through the Panama" is Lowry's most thoroughly dialogized text. The narrator, like the space of the page with its double columns of prose, is divided into two counterpointed voices: Sigbjørn Wilderness/Martin Trumbaugh. Sigbjørn, together with his wife, is on a voyage from Vancouver on the west coast of Canada, south, then east, through the Panama Canal, and north-east across the Atlantic to Europe. He is, in fact, writing in his journal rather than narrating a story as such. Thus, it is his private journal that we are reading—or, rather, hearing, over-hearing since his discourse is couched in the form of dialogue with himself or with his eponymous character Martin: "This is the ship's endless song," he writes to/tells Martin, himself, and us, after inscribing a round of "Frère Jacques" on the journal's first page. But the polyphonics of this story only begin with Sigbjørn's dialogic discourse. As the text develops, Martin Trumbaugh acquires his own separate voice with which to answer, challenge, and appeal to Sigbjørn, the ship's Captain, and the reader. At points, Sigbjørn's erstwhile "character" even takes over the primary column of text, thereby pushing his creator into the margins of the discourse.

The polyphony of "Through the Panama," however, is by no means limited to this proliferating "double-voicing" of Sigbjørn and Martin. On almost every page (or most journal entries), other voices can be heard. Predominant among these are Coleridge via his "Ancient Mariner," Helen Nicolay via her book, *The Bridge of Water*, about the building of the canal, and the ship's engines via "Frère Jacques." But the text is a veritable chorus of voices from Rilke and Poe to the "ventilators singing in wild organ harmony: Hear us O Lord, from heaven Thy dwelling place!" (95) and "'the whole earth [from which], as it spins through space, comes a sound of singing'" (97). Despite this apparent chaos and cacophony, however, "Through the Panama" is neither formless nor ugly. Though it lacks a coherent centre in narrative voice or unified character and is an enormously intricate, intertextual composition, difficult to read or listen to, it is nonetheless rewarding if one accepts its atonality and polyphony. It generates a polyphonic system whose very decentredness becomes its principle of organization.

While the polyphony of *Hear us O Lord* can be located in the catachresis of its tropes and the plurality of its narrative voices, it is inextricable from Lowry's language, whether we are considering a single word such as "translate" (in "Elephant and Colosseum"), larger units of discourse like the phrase, or discrete "speech genres" like the letter. Lowry's prose is highly macaronic, rich in puns, and larded with intertextual echoes from other authors or other Lowry texts. At its base is anacrisis— "the provocation of the word by the word"—achieved by a pervasive repetition which contextualizes, recontextualizes, and decontextualizes language.[8]

I have already mentioned Lowry's play with the word "translate," and the phrase "a sound of singing." The source of dialogism that I would like to consider now is the larger discourse unit represented by the letter. Letters can be many things, and function in many ways, in Lowry's fiction; they can vary in length from the shortest note to the inserted complete text; they can be entirely fictional, transcribed from some external, extra-textual source, or their origin and status may be made deliberately ambiguous. They are always, however, important instances of polyphony in and through which Lowry foregrounds language and disrupts the reader's attempt to identify a single, authoritative narrative voice. Lowry's letters dialogize his discourse and occupy the boundaries between so-called world and text, text and text, and writer and reader. As Bakhtin reminds us, a "characteristic feature of the letter is an acute awareness of the interlocutor, the addressee to whom it is directed. […] and it takes into account the other's possible reactions, the other's reply" (*Problems*, 205). "Strange Comfort Afforded the Profession" is a case in point.

This story opens with Sigbjørn Wilderness writing "in a black notebook" (99). He is standing in front of the house in Rome where Keats died, on 24 February 1821, in order to copy the words from the Italian inscription before entering "with a sigh of relief like a man going to bed, the comforting darkness of Keats's house" (100). Once inside, he begins to transcribe the documents displayed in glass cases into his black notebook, and although these documents are bizarre and macabre in this museum context, Sigbjørn derives a strange sort of comfort from reading and transcribing them. The items that particularly move him are two letters from Joseph Severn describing Keats's deterioration and death which Sigbjørn carefully copies, including the lines crossed out by Severn regarding Keats's medical knowledge of his own condition.

From Keats's house Sigbjørn moves to a nearby bar to contemplate the signifi-cance of what he has just seen and written. He opens the black notebook to jot down his thoughts, but is immediately confronted with material he had copied on the previous day from signs in Rome's Mamertine Prison. From this point on, Lowry takes us deeper and deeper into the textual world of Sigbjørn's notebook, with its recorded visits to the shrines of other writers and its shifting contexts for the written word in the form of letters. As Sigbjørn flips through his notebook, he comes to notes on an earlier visit to the Poe house in Richmond, Virginia, and the Valentine Museum with its display of Poe's relics.

Just as he had in the Keats house, Sigbjørn had carefully transcribed Poe's letters, in particular one dated 21 February 1831 (ten years, almost to the day, after Keats died); now it confronts him from two years ago and thousands of miles away on the pages of his own notebook and in his own handwriting. He reads: "'It will however be the last time I ever trouble any human being—I feel I am on a sick bed from which I shall never get up'" (106). Musing on these words and nursing another grappa, Sigbjørn has a type of double—or triple—exposure vision of himself reading in Rome and in the Valentine Museum superimposed upon the image of himself copying and "of poor Poe sitting blackly somewhere writing" (107) to the foster father who received and read these letters before saving them for posterity. Past/present, private/public, writing/reading—all these apparent opposites begin to merge as Sigbjørn realizes that such distinctions are meaningless. Moreover, life and art lose their separate identities in the context(s) of a letter when Sigbjørn suddenly understands that, in writing this anguished letter, Poe (not unlike Keats, perhaps, not to mention Sigbjørn or Malcolm Lowry) "was transcribing the story that was E.A. Poe" (107).

At this point, the narrative pauses as Sigbjørn once more leafs through his notebook re-presenting to the reader's eye key passages from the transcribed letters that we, too, have now already read. Certain words or phrases stand out as if in a kind of scripted chorus of desperate voices: "I am perishing" ... "*adds to his torture*" ... "*The lower is the true prison*" ... "*Warp son of a bitch*" ... "For God's sake pity me" (108). Hear US, O Lord! But "Strange Comfort" does not end until Sigbjørn's own voice is inscribed in this chorus. Turning, by chance, to the opposite end (in fact the first pages) of his notebook, Sigbjørn finds there a draft of a letter composed in July 1939, addressed to a Mr. Van Bosch and "written in the notebook because it was that type of letter possible for him to write only in a bar" (111). The letter is reproduced for the reader who discovers, as Sigbjørn rereads it, that it is an abject plea to a lawyer that he be sent enough money to escape from an utterly miserable existence in Seattle. "I would be better off in a prison," he wrote/reads; "I am dying in this macabre hole and I appeal to you" (113). Appalled by this image of himself and by the sound of his younger voice, Sigbjørn almost rips the pages from the notebook. Instead, he "meticulously" crosses the letter out "line by line" thereby ensuring, as had Severn in the crossed-out lines of his letter describing

Keats's suffering, that the words themselves will continue to exist (to be readable and transcribable), albeit under erasure.

Through his eponymous hero, who in so many ways parallels and recapitulates his own biography, Lowry demonstrates the degree to which boundaries of all kinds are artificial constructs.[9] What is more, he shows the power of the word—here the letter as written, read, and re-read—to dismantle boundaries. Because language is dialogic, the word acquires different meanings in different contexts, depending upon the interlocutor, the addressee, and the reader (who may or may not be the same at any given time), and these meanings cannot be finalized until discourse ends in silence. Sigbjørn Wilderness's black notebook provides the comfort of continuity and interlocution. It inscribes a polyphonic discourse that includes us and the possibility of our reply, of our response to those crossed-out lines, and that finds its centre in a textual process (read and/or written) that connects past with present, one writer with another, one reader with another in a text (story or notebook?) that can be read/written from either end.

IV

How do we interpret the polyphonic, decentred system of Lowry's *Hear us O Lord*? How does it signify, or more importantly, what does it signify? Like Bakhtin, Lowry assumes the existence of/necessity for a "superaddressee";[10] hence, the address in the collection's title. To read *Hear us O Lord* we must begin by accepting the catachresis, the plurality of voices, and the dialogic discourse of the text and, from there, go on to read contrapuntally from story to story, or inside a single story, within the participatory process of its polyphonic system. The text itself repeatedly demonstrates and encodes its own hermeneutic strategies, just as it repeatedly thematizes the ideas that demand a polyphonic, decentred representation. *Hear us O Lord* signifies by foregrounding, contextualizing and recontextualizing the signs of its own heterogeneity. The notation and words of the hymn with which the volume opens remind us of the human continuum connecting language as read, written, spoken, heard, and sung.

This concept of continuum became increasingly important to Lowry the more he came to believe in a protean, dynamic reality as the ontological ground of all being. As a writer, his problem was to create an image of this reality in his work.[11] The challenge led him to formulate his plan for a cycle of novels called *The Voyage That Never Ends* and to develop a polyphonic, decentred fiction which could (at least in theory) be read back and forth in time (like Sigbjørn's notebook in "Strange Comfort"), up and down in space (like "Through the Panama"), and which could never be finalized, closed, or stopped (like the eternally returning tides in "Forest Path"). In *Hear us O Lord from heaven Thy dwelling place*, Lowry presents his most successfully crafted inscription of a reality he saw as an endlessly created, unfolding and seamless texture of identity, consciousness, and language.

Central to Lowry's vision, especially as presented in these stories, is his belief that the text of this world is not a divinely authored one attributable to a monologic (authoritative, homophonic, centred) Logos and merely represented, reinscribed and interpreted by human creators. Lowry's reality is a humanly authored text-in-process that brackets Logos—Hear *Us* {O Lord}—that, at its best, echoes the polyphony of utterance in a protean natural world from which "as it revolve[s] through space, [comes] a sound of singing."[12]

(1990)

NOTES

[1] *Hear us O Lord from heaven Thy dwelling place* was first published in 1961, when it won the Canadian Governor General's Award for Fiction. All references in this study are to the Penguin paperback edition (1969) and are included in the text. Some of the stories in *Hear us O Lord* appeared separately during Lowry's lifetime (1909–57), but he intended the collection to be a carefully orchestrated unit. The collection, with the stories in their published sequence, was close to its final form when he died, but Lowry, who revised his work right up to the galleys, would certainly have made changes. In a 1952 letter, he describes *Hear us O Lord* as having twelve chapters, and the story "Ghostkeeper" (see note 11) might well have been included. For Lowry's comments on *Hear us O Lord*, see *Sursum Corda!* II, nos. 579 and 580.

[2] Jacques Derrida's concept of *différance* comes close to describing Lowry's typical play with language, but Lowry's philosophical position is closer to that of Mikhail Bakhtin who accepts the infinite possibility of interpretation while, at the same time, stressing the constraints of borders and the necessity of limits that make genres possible.

[3] See *Problems of Dostoevsky's Poetics*, chapter one, especially page 22, where Bakhtin describes his use of the term "polyphonic" as a "graphic analogy," and page 32, where he discusses A.V. Lunacharsky's earlier use of the term. All further references to this study appear in the text as *PDP* followed by the page number.

[4] This definition is taken from the Random House Dictionary of the English Language.

[5] By "speech genre," Bakhtin means relatively stable forms (types) of utterance. See "The Problem of Speech Genres" in *Speech Genres and Other Late Essays*. Dialogism is discussed at length in *Problems of Dostoevsky's Poetics* and in "The Problem of the Text" in *Speech Genres and Other Late Essays*. For Bakhtin, dialogism signifies those active relations between and amongst utterances, such as the "relationships between rejoinders in a dialogue" (*PDP*, 183), that are the proper study of metalinguistics. For a careful analysis of Bakhtin's dialogism, see Julia Kristeva, Σημειωτική / *Recherches pour une sémanalyse*.

[6] The term "binary" is slightly misleading with reference to Bakhtin for whom discourse (all utterances, even a single word) is constituted of a trio of relations (dialogized word-author/speaker-addressee/listener) and presupposes a fourth element in the form of a "superaddressee." See "The Problem of the Text" (121).

[7] For the best discussion to date of Lowry and jazz, see Graham Collier's "Lowry, Jazz and the 'Day of the Dead,'" in *Swinging the Maelstrom*, edited by Sherrill Grace, 243–48.

[8] The twin devices of Socratic dialogue were syncrisis and anacrisis, and Bakhtin argues that together they "dialogize thought, they carry it into the open, turn it into a rejoinder, attach it to dialogic intercourse among people." See *Problems of Dostoevsky's Poetics* (110).

[9] This "fictional" letter to Van Bosch describes Lowry's own situation in 1939 when he was obliged to live in Vancouver, apart from Margerie Bonner, who would soon be his second wife, and was sent remittances from his father through a Los Angeles lawyer.

[10] See note 7. Bakhtin's "superaddressee" could be thought of as God, Truth, the people, science, etc., but however we think of this "higher instancing of responsive understanding," it is a "constitutive aspect" of an utterance. "For the word (and, consequently, for a human being)," says Bakhtin, "there is nothing more terrible than *a lack of response.*" "The Problem of the Text," 126. Lowry's *Hear us O Lord* addresses itself to precisely this concern.

[11] His protagonists discuss the aesthetic problems for the writer in *Dark As the Grave Wherein My Friend Is Laid* (154), and in the story "Ghostkeeper" in *Malcolm Lowry: Psalms and Songs*, 202–27.

[12] It should be noted that this phrase, which Lowry uses on three occasions (pages 20, 97, and 274) in three different stories is, in fact, a quotation from Conrad Aiken, the American poet and novelist whom Lowry chose as his artistic model and close friend from the age of nineteen. When Lowry uses the Aiken passage in "Through the Panama" (97), where it occurs as an inscription in Sigbjørn's (possibly also Martin's) journal, it appears thus: "'And from the whole earth, as it spins through space, comes a sound of singing.' (C.A.)." Each time Lowry borrows Aiken's words, he reaccentuates and recontextualizes them, thereby dialogizing the utterance, addressing himself to Aiken, and establishing Aiken as one of many voices to be heard by us.

6

Respecting Plagiarism: Tradition, Guilt, and Malcolm Lowry's "Pelagiarist Pen"

> *Who can say how many pseudostylic shamiana, how few or how many of the most venerated public impostures, how very many piously forged palimpsests slipped in the first place by this morbid process from his pelagiarist pen?*
>
> (Joyce)[1]

I

> *Frankly, I think I have no gift for writing. I started by being a plagiarist. Then I became a drunkard. Then I became a hard worker, as one might say, a novelist. Now I am a drunkard again. But what I always wanted to be, was a poet.*
>
> (Lowry)[2]

It is no exaggeration to describe Malcolm Lowry as obsessed with, haunted by, yet thoroughly devoted to, the idea of plagiarism. The irresistible temptation to plagiarize, the terror of being discovered, the complex mixture of shame and fascination associated in his mind with his predilection for and sensitivity to the words of another writer, are everywhere apparent in his work, from his earliest surviving letters and fiction to his mature fiction, his poetry, and his late correspondence. To recognize these facts, however, is only to begin what should be a careful consideration of the parameters, motivation, and final result of Lowry's life-long preoccupation with language and with a developing poetics that had as its central characteristic his belief in a shared inheritance of words—a belief sincerely held despite the discomfort, guilt, and insecurity it caused him. To the direct question—was Lowry a plagiarist?—I would answer no. But was he afraid of being charged with plagiarism and found guilty? Was he ever so accused? Was he at times uncertain about the status of his own authorship and originality? To all these questions the answer is: yes.

Surprisingly little study has been made of plagiarism or the plagiarist, but a great deal has been written about theories of textuality and discourse, and these theories provide crucial insight into the nature of plagiarism and the domain of the word. I will turn to a theoretical discussion of the problem later. In order to understand Lowry's position, and his ambivalent feeling (never amounting to a conviction) that no one could claim exclusive ownership of language, it is first essential to assemble the evidence, to trace some key influences, to uncover his developing philosophy of language and his poetics from his many comments on the subject. For this evidence I will turn primarily to his letters, because I know them well and because Lowry reveals himself in them. Moreover, for reasons that I hope will become clear, I see no theoretical need to make an absolute distinction between Lowry's letters and his fictions.

Lowry's susceptibility to the published words of other writers is evident in some of his earliest surviving letters. At age seventeen, as a public school boy, Lowry was already reading voraciously, writing his own fiction, and fictionalizing his own life *as a writer.* Perhaps none of these activities is especially remarkable, for, after all, what young writer does not read and attempt to emulate and imitate what he or she finds appealing? With Lowry, however, the period of apprenticeship seems to have been peculiarly profound, long-lasting, and complex. Beginning with Richard Connell, an American writer who is now totally forgotten, and moving on to other writers who are better known, such as Nordahl Grieg and Conrad Aiken, Lowry's *identification* with a particular writer and that writer's work left crucial marks on his psyche, on his choice of subject matter for his fiction and poetry, and on his style and poetics.

This phenomenon of identification is not entirely encompassed by what Lowry himself described as his "aggregate daemon," although there is a certain overlap, of course, between the "daemon" and his identifications ("Thoughts to be Erased from my Destiny," *Collected Poetry,* 218). That "aggregate daemon" comprised a very wide range of fellow writers (his "kindred spirits") whose work could be said to have influenced and inspired him—from the plays of Eugene O'Neill, the novels of Julien Green, and the poetry of T.S. Eliot, to Melville, Poe, Henry James, James Joyce, philosophers like Bergson and Ortega y Gasset, and mystics like Swedenborg, Ouspensky, and Dunne. Lowry's extreme sensitivity to everything he read or saw, whether serious literature, films and plays, or newspapers, notices, and signs, menus and other ephemera, and his amazing ability to remember these texts and use them in his own work, has been discussed by biographers and literary critics alike.[3] What has not been given sufficient attention is the scope and literary consequences of Lowry's capacity not only to read, remember, and reinscribe everything from images and headlines to whole passages of complex poetry and prose, but also to develop such an intense identification with the work of a particular writer that he, in a sense, took on that person's identity—at least for his own creative purposes. It is the larger phenomenon of identification, including Lowry's "aggregate daemon," that I am calling his "pelagiarist pen."

Lowry's "pelagiarist pen" began its work as early as 1926, after he discovered the short stories of Richard Connell (1893–1949). During the spring and summer of 1926 Lowry was writing regularly to a young woman with whom he fancied himself to be in love. He was seventeen and studying at The Leys School in Cambridge; she was a year older and studying art in Liverpool. Lowry's letters to her comprise a sort of courtship, naïve and clumsy, perhaps, but also touching, funny, and very revealing; in them we have our earliest portrait of Lowry as a young artist. In his efforts to impress Carol Brown, Lowry parades his knowledge of literature, the arts, and current hits on the London stage. Moreover, he advises her on her art, and describes the stories he is trying to write and sell to publishers. Then, in one important letter, dated 14 May 1926—written at about mid-point in his imagined romance—he claims that a story he has sent her, called "The D Box," which was published in the English monthly *20-Story Magazine*, was in fact *"written by Clarence Malcolm Lowry in the flesh."*[4] He goes on to explain that, although the story is attributed to one Richard Connell, *he* is the real author, and that he undertook to allow the attribution as a favour to Connell, who, so he says, is a fellow student at The Leys. School records show no trace of a contemporary of Lowry's called "Richard Connell," but Lowry paints a most elaborate portrait of this apocryphal fellow student and rival writer in colours that cannot help but strike the Lowry critic as all too familiar. "I am not the money making Richard Connell who has cultivated quite a fruity sort of market," says Lowry—

> He is "Carl." He is also the biggest liar, the biggest coward, the bravest man, the most immoral and the most puritanical man, the most insipid drunkard, and the worst and best friend alternately that I hope to have. He drinks to inspire himself, and he goes to church to think out a story about dopes. He is, of course, quite mad—having in that respect a very similar temperament to myself. He is small, insignificant, and brushes his hair like a fifth rate pawn-broker's assistant [and] he is the biggest crook journalist that ever sent three of the same stories to three different editors. (*SC* I, 29)

I have traced the progress of Lowry's "Richard Connell" *Doppelgänger* in volume one of the *Collected Letters* (*SC* I, 15–17, 29–32, 34–35). Suffice it to say here that in a subsequent letter to Miss Brown dated 23 May 1926 Lowry confesses to "qualms of conscience" over his deception and asks her to "bury Connell and never mention his name again." What appears to have happened is that the young Lowry, carried away by both his enthusiasm for Connell's stories and his desire to impress this young woman, has fabricated an alter ego for himself in the name of the then successful American short story writer, Richard Connell, whose work was appearing regularly in the *20-Story Magazine*, as well as other publications, and was praised by E.J. O'Brien. Judging from the surviving evidence, Lowry's identification with Connell centred primarily on the American writer's portrayal of somewhat pathetic men who indulge strange fantasies about other men whom they imagine as leading exciting, successful lives the very opposite to their own, and on at least two occasions Lowry copied out and claimed as his own stories already published by Connell.[5] It is possible to see in this early and short-lived identification with Connell the first sign of tendencies that would become characteristic of Malcolm Lowry the writer: the need for a *Doppelgänger* figure and the consequent attraction to themes of fraternal rivalry, betrayal, and hero-worship, the complete absorption of another's literary identity, or, conversely, the conflation of his own authorial persona with that of another writer or that writer's creations, and the belief that the written text of another was, in fact, of his own composition. This is the pattern that would emerge most dramatically in his twenties with both Nordahl Grieg and Conrad Aiken.

Lowry's letters to Carol Brown, all written during 1926, bear many traces of Lowry's fascination with the work of other writers (P.G. Wodehouse, Walter de la Mare, Rudyard Kipling, W.W. Jacobs, Pirandello, Rabelais, Joseph Conrad, and others) and his growing awareness of his own propensity to *borrow* from them. However, his next crucial period of "hysterical identification" (as he called it) came in 1928–29, when he discovered Conrad Aiken, and 1930–31, when he discovered Nordahl Grieg. Lowry's relationship with these writers, both biographical and literary, is now well-known, so I will not reiterate all the facts or recapitulate the pros and cons of literary influence. Aiken himself commented upon the degree to which he felt Lowry had lifted material from him for *Ultramarine* and *Under the Volcano*.[6] To date, no evidence has surfaced to suggest that Grieg took any notice of Lowry or *Ultramarine*, and he did not live to know about *Under the Volcano*. There is, however, one important letter that Lowry wrote to Grieg that I want to examine closely, but before I turn to it there are several other examples of the "pelagiarist pen" at work that merit brief attention. These range from Lowry's treatment of the theme of plagiarism and his parodic play with others' texts to his comments upon the practice and his various admissions, anxieties, demurrals, and qualified apologies (qualified because, even when apologizing, Lowry felt unable to resist his "aggregate daemon" and felt artistically justified in following it).

One of the earliest and most sustained examples of his parodic play with plagiarism comes at the expense of a fellow writer, the American poet Richard Eberhart, whose attendance at Cambridge University overlapped with Lowry's. Sometime during the early thirties (probably October 1930) Lowry concocted an elaborate drunken "explication" of Eberhart's poem "Caravan of Silence" for his close friend and "boozem companion" John Davenport.[7] Though it is brief—a mere two-page holograph—Lowry's letter-cum-explication manages to combine out-of-context quotations from Eberhart's "Caravan of Silence" with cheeky paraphrase of that poem and unmarked passages from another Eberhart poem. The pastiche from Eberhart's work is further elaborated with unacknowledged passages from Aiken's poetry and fiction. To say that Lowry's intention or final effect is merely to "send up" Eberhart, however, would be to miss at least part of the point, because the poems Lowry parodies (and the Aiken passages) reflect ironically on Lowry's own status as a young writer trying to say something new while drawing on personal experience. If Richard Eberhart could be accused of self-indulgence and second-rate, derivative writing, so could Malcolm Lowry, and, as Lowry makes clear in his 7 February 1940 letter to Aiken, he remained well aware of the similarities between himself and Eberhart.[8]

Although the parody of Eberhart constitutes a type of playful handling of a sensitive subject, only a few years later Lowry found himself forced to confront the spectre of his own plagiarism in the shape of an outraged writer. The work in question was *Ultramarine* (1933) and the outraged writer was another American— Burton Rascoe. Quite by chance Burton Rascoe was sent a copy of *Ultramarine* in 1935 by Harold Matson, Lowry's literary agent, who was asking Rascoe to read the manuscript of "In Ballast to the White Sea," and thought the published novel would help to introduce Lowry, of whom Rascoe had not heard. Rascoe later claimed that he immediately recognized "whole paragraphs" in *Ultramarine* stolen "word for word" from a story of his called "What is Love?" He accused Lowry of plagiarism, but agreed not to proceed further with the charge when Lowry deposited a signed confession, witnessed by Harold Matson, with his New York literary agent Ann Watkins. This signed confession does not appear to have survived (if, indeed, it ever existed), but in a 19 May 1940 unpublished letter to Rascoe, Lowry acknowledged Rascoe's earlier "kindnesses and forebearances" about "the Latin Quotations, which, I assure you again, was not deliberate plagiarism on my part, but it might as well have been for indeed that whole book was hopelessly derivative." According to Victor Doyen, who has compared Rascoe's story with *Ultramarine*, Rascoe's charge was "preposterous"; Lowry used only brief Latin quotations also found in Rascoe's story, not Rascoe's own words (46–47).[9] The really significant borrowings in *Ultramarine* are, of course, from Aiken and Grieg, with a good many echoes of T.S. Eliot; however, the psychological scars from the Burton Rascoe affair would plague Lowry's conscience (and consciousness) for the rest of his life, causing him to refuse to allow *Ultramarine* to be translated or even read by such close friends as his editor, Albert Erskine, his French translator, Clarisse Francillon, and fellow writer David Markson.[10]

Because so little is known about "In Ballast to the White Sea," which Lowry started in the early thirties, one can only speculate about its contents on the basis of a long, complicated letter he wrote to David Markson in 1951. But from at least the mid-thirties, the theme of plagiarism would provide a *leitmotif* in Lowry's letters to editors and friends and in his work, striking dissonant notes in the fiction and poetry and causing him to become acutely sensitive, almost paranoid, about the slightest echo in his fiction. During the editing of *Under the Volcano*, for example, Lowry constantly pestered Albert Erskine to check what he thought were lines he had taken from other writers. He was especially troubled by echoes of William Faulkner's novel *The Wild Palms* (1939), even after his patient editor had re-read that novel and assured Lowry that he had not taken anything from it. His utter dread at being thought to have copied Charles Jackson's undistinguished 1944 story about a drunk called *The Lost Weekend* now seems quite ludicrous, but it was never so to Lowry. Indeed, this anxiety was later worked into chapter seven of *Dark as the Grave Wherein My Friend Is Laid*, when Eddy the barman asks if Sigbjørn's novel "The Valley of the Shadow of Death" (*Under the Volcano*) is not a "plagiarism" of something—that something, of course, being "Drunkard's Rigadoon" (*The Lost Weekend*). This idea of the Lowry artist as plagiarist surfaces in *Under the Volcano* with Hugh's music, in *Dark as the Grave* as a central concern, in the draft of "The Ordeal of Sigbjørn Wilderness" as ghostly accusations, in several of his short stories, and in the poetry; his poem "The Plagiarist" is a poignant reminder of Lowry's anxiety:

> Crawling on hands and sinews to the grave
> I found certain pamphlets on the way.
> Said they were mine. For they explained a pilgrimage
> That otherwise was meaningless as day. (*CP*, 205)

Of the short stories, "Strange Comfort Afforded by the Profession" is the most important and interesting in the present context. Like so much of Lowry's fiction, its main protagonist, Sigbjørn Wilderness, is a writer haunted by the past and tormented by his problems with writing. Indeed the figure of the artist that emerges in the story is of a man trapped by the fiction of his own life and looking to the example of John Keats and Edgar Allan Poe (whose story "The Purloined Letter" is a splendid dramatization of his own obsession with plagiarism) for guidance. On different occasions he has visited the Poe house in Virginia and Keats's house in Rome (visits that Lowry made himself), and while there copied information on the dead writers and the texts of documents on display. Now when he opens the notebook he carries with him he finds his transcriptions, which are both the raw material for his own work and the "strange comfort afforded by the profession" that he so desperately needs. The fact that some of these documents are actual letters highlights another aspect of Lowry's art, because his practice in all his fiction was to reinscribe the texts of, as it were, *real* letters in his fiction—letters by other writers, letters from his friends, and his own letters to other people—at most changing the names or dates to make the letters consistent with the narrative (see "'The daily crucifixion of the post'").

Whether this use of letters is plagiarism or not is a moot point, for these letters have much the same status within a Lowry text as the many other documents that he loved to use. The intertextuality of Lowry's writing is famous, and it is inextricably linked to the plagiarism question, as we shall see. But plagiarism in quite a precise sense raised its ugly head from amidst the documents in "Strange Comfort" nonetheless. In his 29 May 1953 letter to Arabel Porter, the editor of *New World Writing*, which first published the story, Lowry tangles himself up in a bizarre apology-cum-explanation of how *his* story happens to use a key idea also found in an article called "The Gratuitous Art," by Howard Griffin, that first appeared in the December 1949 issue of a magazine called *Twelfth Street*.[11] At first Lowry told Porter he could not remember ever having seen the piece until "the other day," when the magazine somehow managed to "tumble out from behind his shelves" (*SC* II, 647). Then he wondered how the magazine got into the house in the first place, and speculated that a writer friend, Earle Birney, might have left it there. But because this is not quite the point, he goes on to wonder if he has not, in fact, read the article and then put it away hoping not to be influenced. Finally, he comes to the reason for writing Porter:

> The real object of this letter with its considerable much ado about nothing was merely to tell you that had I consciously known of or remembered that existence of Griffin's article at the time you took Strange Comfort I would have mentioned it to *you* or even to it in a footnote, if you thought that advisable. (*SC* II, 649)

Here again we have Malcolm Lowry looking over his shoulder, fearing another Burton Rascoe affair, doubting his own originality, and, in a very real sense, calling into question his own creative method. In a rather superfluous gesture, he asked Arabel Porter to assure Griffin (whom she knew) that he "wasn't consciously treading on his toes," as indeed he was not, for the "death cult" idea that Griffin wrote about was present in "Strange Comfort" from its very beginning (*as a story*) in 1948. And yet, the final impression created by Lowry in this letter to Arabel Porter is that ideas, even words, are not the exclusive property of anyone. Griffin, he points out, appears to have "profited ... by some ideas of mine, in so far as they are mine, in *Under the Volcano*" (*SC* II, 649). Disingenuousness? Self-justification? Possibly. But also another indication of Lowry's own attitude to language and texts that were there, as it were, for the *taking*, and, as we shall see, this belief has a history and tradition much older than the modern concept of plagiarism.

In an undated, possibly unsent, letter to Nordahl Grieg written in Los Angeles sometime during 1938, Lowry confessed that "much of *Ultramarine* is paraphrase, plagiarism, or pastiche from you" (*SC* I, 192). Lowry may have been thinking here not only of *Ultramarine* but also of "In Ballast to the White Sea," which centred upon Lowry's complex identification with Grieg, the man and writer, and his fictional creations. Without the manuscript of this "lost" novel, however, it is impossible to say how much of a role aesthetics, literary influence, and plagiarism (whether in practice or as theme—or both) would have played in the narrative of "In Ballast." But there are two surviving letters that shed light on Lowry's fascination with the Norwegian writer and the extremely complex imaginative relationship Lowry wove around the figure of Nordahl Grieg. One of these letters, the 25 August 1951 one to David Markson, is well-known to Lowryans; the other, his 8 September 1931 letter to Grieg, is new. The letter to Markson sets forth Lowry's plans for "In Ballast" as he remembers the opus, almost a decade after its loss. Interesting as it is, it is very much after the fact; the 1931 letter to Grieg himself, however, reveals a great deal more about Lowry as a writer at a crucial period in his development.

II

[A]ny text is constructed as a mosaic of quotations; any text is the absorption and transformation of another.

(Kristeva 1980, 66)

"Nordahl Grieg, I greet you!" is an autograph letter of four pages, dated 8 September 1931, with the inside address of the Hotell Parkheimen, Drammensveien 2, Oslo, Norway. It was discovered with the Grieg papers by Hallvard Dahlie, and my annotated transcription of it was first published in *Swinging the Maelstrom* (43–51) and then in *Sursum Corda!* (*SC* I, no. 35). The letter is ostensibly a continuation of the conversation Lowry had just had with Grieg in an Oslo nightclub about the English poet Rupert Brooke, on whom Grieg was doing research for a book.[12] Because Lowry fears that they may never meet again or that Grieg might not be able to visit Cambridge, where Brooke had studied and lived, he is anxious to share some particular information about Brooke that, he believes, Grieg might not otherwise find. His "detail about Rupert Brooke" is Brooke's knowledge of Elizabethan drama, but Lowry's interpretation, development, and emphasis of Brooke's theories serve to focus his own aesthetic concerns and to provide an image of his literary context.

This image emerges from Lowry's use of several intertexts, including three texts by Brooke: two reviews of H.J.C. Grierson's 1913 two-volume edition of Donne's *Poetical Works*, and his major, posthumously published study, *John Webster & the Elizabethan Drama* (1916). Although Lowry does not have the reviews or the book with him in Norway (he says he does not own a copy of the book, which was out of print), he nevertheless proceeds to quote at length and verbatim from one of the reviews and from the book. Moreover, he argues for a reassessment of Brooke based upon that poet's insights into the plays of both John Marston and John Webster, which, he insists, are "indicative of some sort of identity between the two [Brooke and Marston], which Rupert Brooke somehow felt tremendously." In other words,

Lowry claims that there is an identity between Brooke and Marston that reveals "the more terrible and bloody side" of Brooke, a side the poet died too soon to explore or reveal in his verse. Such a claim for spiritual identity between writers, like Marston and Brooke, who appear to be opposites in every way, is a familiar refrain with Lowry. By 1931 Lowry had discovered his Marston in Conrad Aiken, and he was rapidly forging similar psychological, aesthetic, and metaphysical ties with Grieg. Indeed, this very letter is an articulation of the intellectual and spiritual bond he created, in his own mind, with his Norwegian mentor and *Doppelgänger*. That Grieg was unaware of this bond does not matter; this letter is the enactment through inscription, through epistolary dialogue, that gave the reality of utterance to Lowry's relationship with Grieg and with Rupert Brooke. It was—this verbal act—all Lowry needed.

The letter is a palimpsest showing the traces of T.S. Eliot (writing on Webster), Webster and Marston, with glimpses of Shakespeare, Donne, Keats, Chatterton, Swinburne, Strindberg, Kaiser, O'Neill, Sassoon, Aiken, Joyce, and Proust, through a layer of Rupert Brooke and against a ground of Grieg and Lowry. Or, to put the matter another way, the letter is an echo-chamber of voices, real and fictional, from more than three hundred years of literary history; it bears polyphonic witness to a tradition, a context, and a discourse (including a narrative) that defines as it gives utterance to the writer, Malcolm Lowry.

After a brief preamble in which Lowry explains why he is writing—to provide Grieg with the vital detail concerning Brooke, of course, but more important to continue a conversation—he launches into a lengthy, serious, and highly perceptive discussion of Rupert Brooke, which, he hopes, may help Grieg in his appreciation of the English poet. Instead of reading Brooke through his poetry, let alone through the nostalgia that had already fixed Brooke's reputation in the popular imagination, Lowry presents a Brooke seen through his study of Elizabethan drama. Sitting alone in Oslo with neither Brooke's articles nor his book, Lowry draws upon his remarkable memory to produce several exact quotations that support his argument that Brooke, a *poète maudit manqué*, was drawn, irresistibly, to "old bloody minded Marston," and that it was this "identity ... which Rupert Brooke somehow felt tremendously" that led him to his original insights into the importance and contribution of Marston. Moreover, had Brooke survived World War One, Lowry argues, he would have developed his "Dark Self that Wants to Die," possibly through the medium of drama.

Lowry pauses briefly in this lively discussion of Brooke, embellished with numerous asides about the blood, lust, and general misanthropy of Marston and Webster, to develop three points. At the first pause he quotes verbatim eight lines from T.S. Eliot's Webster poem, "Whispers of Immortality" (1920), which allows him to link Eliot and Brooke through Webster and to remind his reader (Grieg and us) that Brooke was among the first twentieth-century critics to reassess these plays and playwrights. This link also facilitates the parallel structure that Lowry is building: as Brooke was to Marston, so Eliot is to Webster; as you—Grieg—are to Brooke, so I—Lowry—am to you (and to Eliot, Webster, Marston).

When Lowry pauses next, it is to introduce Keats, or, more precisely, "a *Keatsian predicament*," by which he means a crisis point of self-doubt and poetic paralysis, such as Keats experienced before his death, but that Brooke, so Lowry speculates, did not quite reach. This "predicament" was, of course, an abyss that fascinated Lowry, and one that he could explore vicariously simply by invoking this list of names: Marston, Webster, Keats, Chatterton, Swinburne, Brooke ... each of whom had gazed into the depths before Lowry arrived on the scene. The digression on Keats leads Lowry into his third confabulation, and introduces new voices into the letter. These are voices from the Great War, his brother Stuart Lowry, an anonymous soldier, and then, once more, Brooke, who, Lowry argues, "died *consciously*," his death, like Chatterton's (if not also Keats's), "the consummation of his own poetic theory." At this point Lowry abruptly concludes that Grieg is the perfect man to write about Brooke, to "surround his position" (*SC* I, 106).

But as Grieg is to Brooke, so Lowry is to Grieg: the implications of Lowry's associations, parallels, quotations, paraphrases, and digressions is that the "consummation" of a "poetic theory" will entail the literal death of one poet or the surrounding of his position (an engulfing? an erasure?) by another. Given what we know about Lowry's own life and writing, it is possible to see in this letter to Grieg the earliest seeds of "In Ballast to the White Sea." Moreover, this letter outlines the "poetic theory" that informed that work and everything else that Lowry wrote. "In Ballast" represents Lowry's surrounding of Grieg's position as author (the creator of Benjamin Hall in *The Ship Sails On*, the character with whom Lowry identified so intensely) by literally (literarily) incorporating Grieg's text, Grieg's conversation, Lowry's letters to Grieg—and hence Lowry's construction of his relationship with Grieg—into his own text.[13]

Rupert Brooke's position in this elaborately constructed relationship with Grieg is that of bridge, and this position is both complex and essential. To appreciate it fully it is necessary to return to the studies Lowry quotes from, in particular Brooke's *John Webster & the Elizabethan Drama*.[14] By the time Lowry discovered Brooke as literary critic (probably after he went up to Cambridge in 1929 and while he was reading Elizabethan drama for the English tripos), Brooke's theories about Elizabethan drama and dramatists had been reiterated and developed by (among others) T.S. Eliot. Lowry's quotation from Eliot's "Whispers of Immortality" confirms his awareness of Eliot's contribution, but also that Brooke's prior claim as critic had been surrounded by Eliot and further supplanted by Brooke's gilded image as the romantic young poet sacrificed in a bloody war. There was, however, a great deal of value and of interest in Brooke's book, especially to an attentive and responsive reader like Lowry. After a lively discussion of Webster's most famous plays, *The

Duchess of Malfi (which had played at the ADC Theatre in Cambridge while Lowry was there)[15] and *The White Devil* (with particular attention to the rhetoric of Flamineo), Brooke moves on, in his final chapter, to consider some of Webster's characteristics, and this chapter is the one of greatest interest in connection with Lowry.

Webster, Brooke maintains, was a plagiarist; he "reset other people's jewels and redoubled their lustre" (147). Brooke confronts this question of Webster's borrowings directly and without apology, finding in the practice evidence not only of a Renaissance view of literature and originality quite different from out modern one, but also the very mark of Webster's genius and the traces of his compositional method. Webster, so Brooke argues (143–44), must have kept extensive notebooks in which he recorded his observations and his reading. When working on his own texts (Brooke hypothesizes), he would consult these notebooks, sometimes copying entire passages verbatim into his work in progress, sometimes altering them to suit his needs. The end result of this adoption/adaptation is a better or, at least, other text, and Brooke is emphatic in his defence of this method: "The Elizabethans had for the most part healthy and sensible views on the subject [of plagiarism]. They practiced and encouraged the habit" (146). Then, shifting almost imperceptibly from a commentary on Webster's and Elizabethan practice to a more general statement of his own views, Brooke announces that "'Originality' is only plagiarism from a great many" (147). He is not, however, oblivious to the dangers of the notebook or of the acute memory as sources of inspiration, because either may lead a writer to "commit the most terrible sin of plagiarism ... without knowing it" (154). Although he does not develop the idea, he does note that the ubiquitous use of notebooks (and, thus, of copying from them) is less a sign of merit than it is of psychology, and, in a remark that could easily apply to Lowry, he concludes that "Webster ... belongs to the caddis-worm school of writers, who do not become their complete selves until they are incrusted with a thousand orts and chips and fragments from the world around them" (156).

What emerges from chapter five of Brooke's *John Webster & the Elizabethan Drama* is, in fact, a perceptive contribution to our understanding of the interrelations among language, writing, and the psychology and aesthetics of plagiarism that foreshadows some of the most recent work on the subject. Moreover, Brooke's remarks are such an uncannily accurate gloss on the methods, preoccupations, and psychology of Lowry that it is not hard to imagine how Lowry (plagued by his fear of plagiarism from his teens) must have felt while reading them, or why he would privilege Brooke the interpreter of Marston and Webster over Brooke the cult poet, and see in the former a vital link between himself and Grieg or between himself and the great Elizabethan tradition of English literature. When he told Jonathan Cape, in 1946, that in *Under the Volcano* he was trying "to strike a blow" for "another Renaissance" (*SC* I, 520) by writing with the passion and depth of the Elizabethans, he was remembering Brooke and Webster.

Oddly enough, Lowry's 1931 letter to Grieg ends with his vivid recollection of himself and Grieg "speaking in whispers." The image is striking. It evokes suggestions of sharing, intimacy, collusion, connection; of secrets, confessions, or promises. In the context of Lowry's letter it sends the reader back to "Eliot on Webster" and to the lines from "Whispers of Immortality," which, in turn, evoke Brooke, whose very name becomes the whispered sign of an immortality created through shared words. By validating—or seeking validation of—Webster's plagiarism as a method of composition, Brooke becomes a validating sign for Lowry.

III

C'est surtout en poésie qu'on se permet souvent le plagiat, et c'est assurément de tous les larcins le moins dangereux pour la société.
(Voltaire, 224)

Whether or not Lowry should be called a plagiarist (let alone *charged* with being one), it is clear that his work resonates with allusions, references, citations, and borrowings from innumerable other texts. In this he closely resembles Conrad Aiken, who, together with Grieg, profoundly influenced him and was quick to accuse him of plagiarism. Tracing Lowry's sources, however, and fleshing out the contexts and associations of these borrowings, are only the first steps in a larger project of coming to grips with Lowry's poetics. That poetics can best be approached through a synchronic analysis of the text using Gérard Genette's theory of "transtextuality," followed by a consideration of the letter in the light of Mikhail Bakhtin's dialogic theory of utterance, which demonstrates how a Lowry text functions as epistolary discourse.

At the beginning of *Palimpsestes: La littérature au second degré*, Gérard Genette sets forth his basic theory of "les relations transtextuelles." He locates five types or aspects of transtextuality—intertext, paratext, metatext, hypertext, and architext—which comprise what he calls the palimpsest that is literature. While each of these five aspects could be fruitfully explored with Lowry, two, intertext and hypertext, are of particular interest to the structure of this letter to Grieg, and I want to apply Genette's terms to Lowry's text in some detail.

By intertext (intertextuality) Genette means the relations between two or more texts that co-exist within one work. The most literal way of inserting one text within another is by citing it with quotation marks and often with a reference, but intertexts are also created through plagiarism, through a fairly close but unacknowledged repetition of material, and through the least explicit means of allusion, which relies on the writer's/reader's "perception d'un rapport entre lui et un autre" (8, "perception of a link between the one and the other"). Once citation is abandoned, however, the line between plagiarism and allusion can become difficult to draw, let alone maintain. Genette's term "hypertexte" must be understood in relation to its (in some senses) mirror image: "hypotexte" (11–12). The hypotext is the original one (insofar as its status as originary can be proven or is traditionally accepted), while the hypertext is the text "au second degré," a transformation of the hypotext. And, within Genette's system, hypertextuality includes any and all relations that link or unite the hypertext with its hypotext.

The complex intertextuality of Lowry's letter to Grieg (like that of everything he wrote) is obvious; I have identified twenty-one references to other writers and/or texts in my annotations to the letter, and there may well be others. Distinctions can be made, however, in the classification of these intertexts. The quotation from "Whispers of Immortality" is a citation (albeit incomplete), and several other works are cited, together with the names of their authors, but there is also an example of plagiarism in the lengthy unmarked verbatim passage from *John Webster & the Elizabethan Drama* (67–68). Allusions, of course, abound, from references to shared places (the Red Mill) and experiences (looking at the Viking ship) to shared literature (including Grieg's own novel *The Ship Sails On*).

These classifications, however, should not be allowed to obscure the complex nature of shifting boundaries between citation and plagiarism; plagiarism and allusion; citation and allusion. What, for example, should be done with this remark of Lowry's: "While Webster, as Swinburne said, took the last step into the darkness—Well!" Although attributing the remark to Swinburne, Lowry does not use quotation marks here; therefore, is this citation or allusion?[16] Toward the end of the letter, Lowry writes: "Well: I hope we may meet again before the worms pierce our winding sheet & before the spider makes a thin curtain for our epitaph." Is this allusion or is it plagiarism from Webster's play *The White Devil*? (Brooke does not quote this passage, so Lowry has taken it directly from the play). Where does our (Grieg's) responsibility to catch on, to "get it," end and Lowry's duty to specify begin? Like a palimpsest, a Lowry text presents a shifting figure-ground relationship, and the points of greatest textual interest are often the most unstable and the most multi-layered.

The intertextuality of this letter leads naturally to questions of its hypertextuality. To begin, it must be clear to any reader that this letter is a highly self-conscious, carefully structured, calculatedly informal text. Its writer is acutely aware of his addressee/reader who is posed as an interlocutor whispering with him, and he is intensely aware of the image he wants to create. While greeting Nordahl Grieg, Malcolm Lowry is also genuflecting in what he hopes will be the right context-establishing directions; he is, in short, Harold Bloom's "ephebe" looking over his shoulder at those who have gone before, and he is trying both to enlist the aid and validation of these distinguished precursors and to outdo them with his own wit and insight. Whether he succeeds or not is irrelevant (although he probably failed to impress Grieg), but it is important to determine which text(s) he thinks he is drawing upon for validation, borrowing from for authority, and re-setting in order to gain a "redoubled ... lustre."

Since there are so many citations of poetry and drama, plagiarisms of prose (critical and fictional), and allusions to texts and genres here, no single hypotext comes easily to mind. Nevertheless, two possibilities should be seriously considered—the particular discourse of literary criticism and the general discourse of conversation. Lowry is writing to Grieg, as I mentioned in part I, in order to impart information regarding Rupert Brooke that he had failed to do when he and Grieg met in the Red Mill. Grieg's interest in Brooke is that of literary critic; he is working on a book about English poets who died young. Therefore, Lowry, in the effort to impress and, let it be said, in a sincere enthusiasm for Grieg, Brooke, and poetry, puts on his literary critic's cap and offers what proves to be (for its time and coming from an undergraduate) an original, convincing reading of Brooke, based upon Brooke's own literary criticism. Literary criticism, then, is the first identifiable hypotext—or layer of hypotext—for this letter, but beyond, behind, holding that in place, is the hypotext of dialogue, what Bakhtin would call "speech genre." And in the immediate case of this letter, the dialogue took shape in the conversation that Lowry and Grieg may have had, one that the younger man wants to prolong— perhaps in a series of letters—into a correspondence. Through the hypotext of conversation, which with Lowry so typically takes the form of monologue, Lowry the writer extends an event—the original (possibly imaginary) live dialogue—into a fiction, a text that is fiction. To use Genette's terms, Lowry has transformed (a simple transformation [14]) the hypotext of conversation into the hypertext of this letter, which, even as it is being written, is on its way to becoming a hypotext (through indirect transformation or imitation) for the larger fiction of "In Ballast to the White Sea."

Insofar as Lowry's hypotext for this letter is dialogue (a conversation), then what Bakhtin tells us about speech genres, utterance, addressivity, and dialogic relations, in his important essay "The Problem of Speech Genres" becomes immediately relevant, not only to our understanding of the poetics of this particular letter, but also to the whole vexed question of Lowry's plagiarism. For example, in his explanation of the theoretical assumption underlying the concept of speech genres, Bakhtin stresses his view of "unique speech experience" as interactive:

> Our speech, that is, all our utterances (including creative works), is filled with others' words, varying degrees of otherness or varying degrees of "our-own-ness," varying degrees of awareness and detachment. These words of others carry with them their own expression, their own evaluative tone, which we assimilate, rework, and re-accentuate. (89)

According to Bakhtin's speech genre model, this letter is an example of a "secondary speech genre" (61–62), that is, a discourse directed toward its referential object/objective (communication with Grieg) and toward another's discourse (both Grieg's and Brooke's, if not also Marston's and Webster's). Because the letter is an utterance, a "unit of speech communion" (Bakhtin, 71) within the human language condition that Bakhtin calls "heteroglossia," it necessarily functions through the active role of the other (the immediate addressee), who must share the language (words and speech genre) of the utterance if communication is to occur. As Bakhtin also points out in *Problems of Dostoevsky's Poetics*, a letter is characterized by a particularly "acute awareness of the interlocutor" (205), and this "awareness" consists in a very wide range of shared words and anticipated verbal responses. The utterance, therefore, in its very origin, is common, shared, and active or participatory: no one owns or can claim discourse; speech genres grow from language that exists in dialogue, dialogistically.

In the case of this letter to Grieg, Lowry has written a highly dialogic text, one that incorporates a whole range of intertexts (as Genette uses the term) and assimilates, re-works, and re-accentuates (in Bakhtin's terms) the voices of others to such a degree that Lowry's own voice (his-own-ness) becomes at times that of a speaker in a dialogue and at others a problematic, blurred chord within the polyphony of "double-voiced" and "reflected discourse" (199). At the same time, of course, the voice of a particular other (most notably, here, Brooke) is subsumed within the voice of the speaker/writer who has signed himself "Malcolm Lowry." Indeed, I would go so far as to say that what I called earlier Lowry's characteristic monologue style is actually inseparable from this multiplicity of voices, this intertextual fabric of citation, allusion, and plagiarism. What this letter to Grieg demonstrates so dramatically is Lowry's early (perhaps earliest) attempt to "surround his [Grieg's, Aiken's, any other writer's] position," to seek validation for a poetic theory that he had already embraced—or could not avoid.[17]

IV

Pas un écrivain qui ne tremble d'être dit plagiaire; c'est qu'aucun ne doute d'en être un.

(Schneider, 93)

Two recent studies of plagiarism go a long way toward defining the act and describing its history, and they do so from diametrically opposed theoretical and methodological positions. Thomas Mallon, in *Stolen Words: Forays into the Origins and Ravages of Plagiarism*, assumes that words can belong to an originator, and can, therefore, be stolen. Moreover, through example after example from British and American literature, he chastises both those who plagiarize and those who attempt to exonerate such crimes. His list of infamous literary thieves includes Sterne, Coleridge, and Charles Reade. Mallon, however, fails to accord sufficient weight to the comparatively recent meaning and usage of the term that he is using. In the narrowly litigious sense in which he applies it, it grew out of eighteenth-century notions of language, authorship, originality, and, hence, of copyright, which are still being sharpened today. What Mallon does usefully underscore is the tradition of plagiarism in English literature since the Renaissance and the practical difficulty of identifying and dealing with it. Michel Schneider's *Voleurs de mots: Essai sur le plagiat, le psychanalyse et la pensée* is an altogether more profound exploration of plagiarism, and one that begins by questioning the foundations of the modern obsession with originality, and by arguing (after Genette) that writing is always "au second degré."

As far as Schneider is concerned, Lowry was not a plagiarist so much as a writer utterly obsessed, even destroyed, by his terror of being found to be one (93). But the literary and psychological profile of the plagiarist that emerges from Mallon's and Schneider's studies so closely resembles Lowry that it warrants careful attention here. Drawn largely from the history of French literature, Schneider's composite picture depicts the plagiarist as a man (no mention here of female plagiarists) who develops intense, even hysterical, identifications with other writers and with their characters. Such a writer's memory for what he reads is excellent but indiscriminate. Often, according to Mallon, he relies heavily upon assiduously kept notebooks for inspiration and material, and in these notebooks he copies entire passages from any other text that catches his attention, and he records all types of observations and experiences. In some cases, such as that of Flaubert, the writer fills up the margins of the book he is reading with annotations until the book becomes a mixture of the reader's and writer's words. Both Mallon and Schneider describe the plagiarist as a man obsessed with his own guilt and as self-conscious and extremely sensitive to the charge of plagiarism. At the same time he is a man who is trapped in the anguished desire to say something new.

Schneider, however, pursues the psychology of plagiarism much further, arguing that the self-styled plagiarist suffers from a persecution complex and is terrified by the thought that his life is always already written, that he is nothing more than someone else's creation. Following Freud's theory of transference and Lacan's concept of the Father, Schneider associates plagiarism with orality and with difficult relations between the writer and his mother-tongue, and between the writer and his father, who always precedes him. He argues that plagiarism, while not itself a psychological structure, is a symptom or syndrome of a neurosis, or even a psychosis, that signals the inability of the writer to separate himself from the other (213–14):

> Le plagiaire en apparence prend l'autre en soi. Il fait comme si l'autre était lui-même. Mais en fait il projette sa proper créativité dans l'auteur-source. (The

> plagiarist appears to assimilate the other into himself. He acts as if the other is
> himself. But in fact he projects his own creativity into the source-author.) (275)

There can be little doubt, I think, that Lowry's fears, creative methods, practices, and psychology correspond very closely to this profile of the plagiarist. If ever there was a writer determined to assimilate, re-work, and re-accentuate others' words, and his own, from notebooks, margins, and letters, from clippings and documents of all kinds, it was Lowry. He most certainly belongs to Rupert Brooke's "caddis-worm school of writers, who do not become their complete selves" until they are "incrusted" with the fragments of this world. What is equally clear is that he belongs to a particular line of writers, which would include Herodotus, Sophocles, Euripides, Virgil, Webster, Shakespeare, Montaigne, Molière, Pascal, Sterne, Voltaire, Rousseau, Milton, Coleridge, Stendhal, Lautréamont, Reade, Aiken, and Joyce, writers for whom to plagiarize is to steal what does not belong to anyone.

Throughout his life, Lowry tried to understand and reconcile himself to his propensity for assimilating other writers, and he sought to control his caddis-worm tendencies by shaping them into a method that would validate his art. In both his fiction and his letters, he wrote about "la littérature au second degré" as an attempt to work through his fear of being written, his identifications with other writers, and his acute sense of guilt over his borrowings. But it is not necessary to reach for Freud and Lacan to understand Lowry's obsessive concern with plagiarism. Living in this century, constrained by modern ideas about authorship, copyright, and what Harold Bloom has so aptly called "the anxiety of influence," what could he do but feel guilt and the constant need to explain?

Only two letters written by Lowry to Grieg appear to have survived. The first is the one discussed here. The second, an incoherent draft written from Los Angeles in the spring of 1939 and probably never posted, picks up the dialogue with Grieg where it left off in the fall of 1931. "Thanks for your letter of 7 years ago," he writes:

> How did your book on Rupert Brooke go?
> I wish I could tell you all the extraordinary coincidences which led up to our meeting. One day I shall. My identity with *Benjamin* eventually led me into mental trouble. Much of *Ultramarine* is paraphrase, plagiarism, or pastiche from you. (*SC* I, 191–92)

Clearly Lowry saw himself as haunted by the hypotext of literature, yet driven, because of his need to contribute to the dialogue, to use the only poetic theory he could (the only one available to him)—the agonistic one of the inspired plagiarist who resets the family jewels and redoubles their lustre.

But whether or not one accepts this romantic picture of Lowry as the doomed and haunted artist (a self-image he did much to promote) in a tradition with Marston, Webster, Chatterton, Keats, and even, perhaps, Brooke, the 1931 letter to Grieg establishes beyond a doubt that he saw himself as belonging to such a line of poets. It demonstrates as well just how he went about forging the links (real or imagined—it scarcely matters) to validate his poetic and his art. More to the point, his theory enabled him to write the monumental *Under the Volcano* (1947) and the brilliant *Hear us O Lord from heaven Thy dwelling place* (1961) before demanding its Keatsian consummation.

(1992)

Notes

[1] The word "pelagiarist" (*Finnegans Wake*, 181–82) warrants a brief comment. In addition to playing on "plagiarist" and "pelagian," Joyce is also echoing the name of Pelagius, the heretic, and possibly an Irish plagiarist, who gave his name to the Pelagian heresy. *Finnegans Wake*, of course, is the plagiarist's nightmare, an "epical forged cheque" (181) composed *of* "litterish fragments."

[2] Lowry kept his "Haitian Notebook" during his January to February 1947 visit to Haiti en route to New York for the publication in February of *Under the Volcano*.

[3] Although many critics of Lowry have commented upon his sources and influences, a few of particular importance should be mentioned here: Kilgallin lists his "kindred spirits"; Costa considers Lowry's connection with Aiken and Joyce; Dahlie examines Lowry's debt to Grieg; and Cowan sees Lowry's response to his precursors as a sign of imbalance, sickness, and error.

[4] Lowry's sequence of seventeen hitherto unpublished letters to Carol Brown are in *Sursum Corda!* I.

[5] Richard Connell's short story "The D Box," which Lowry claimed as his own, first appeared in the American magazine *Red Book* (November 1925), and then in the English magazine *The 20-Story Magazine* (1926). It is the latter publication that Lowry claimed as his own. Surviving evidence from his 1926 correspondence with Miss Brown suggests that he also claimed to have written Connell's "The Yes-And-No Man," which appeared in *The 20-Story Magazine* (1926).

[6] In a 1 February 1967 letter to the editor of the *Times Literary Supplement*, Aiken claimed that *Ultramarine* was largely derived from his *Blue Voyage* and that Lowry had at one point intended to insert an entire page of Aiken's novel *Great Circle* into *Ultramarine* until Aiken stopped him. Aiken frequently made this sort of claim; see Aiken, *Selected Letters*, 239, 323–24.

[7] Lowry's holograph letter to John Davenport is held in the Houghton Library at Harvard University. I have described it at length in "Thoughts towards the Archeology of Editing: 'Caravan of Silence'"; see also *SC* I, no. 25.

[8] In this letter to Aiken Lowry writes: "Dick Eberhart was at Cambridge a little before my time .... I had many strange doppelgänger like remote contacts with him" (*SC* I, 284). Lowry goes on to describe Eberhart's work and to recall a piece of Cambridge gossip involving the American poet and I.A. Richards.

[9] Victor Doyen has examined Rascoe's charge in his thesis "Fighting the Albatross of Self: A Genetic Study of the Literary Work of Malcolm Lowry," 46–47. Lowry's 19 May 1940 letter to Rascoe is with the Burton Rascoe Papers at the Van Pelt Library, University of Pennsylvania, and in 1954 Rascoe added explanatory notes to it in which he reiterated his charges. See *SC* I, no. 141.

[10] In his 27 July 1940 letter to his friend and literary agent Harold Matson, the same agent who had witnessed the embarrassment with Burton Rascoe, Lowry provides interesting "insight" into his obsession with plagiarism. Speaking of his recently revised 1940 version of *Under the Volcano*, he adds the following proleptic apology: "It is 'original' if you fear for past Websterian, not to say Miltonian, minor lacks of ethics on my part, nor is it drunkenly translated with a handpump out of the original Latvian. It is as much my own as I know of" (*SC* I, 342). For the significance of the Webster reference, see part II of this discussion.

[11] A copy of Lowry's letter to Porter is held in the Lowry Collection at UBC, and it is published in *Sursum Corda!* II, no. 576.

[12] Grieg, who had studied English literature at Oxford, was working on a book of essays about English poets who had died young: Byron, Keats, Shelley, and three war poets, Rupert Brooke, Charles Sorley, and Wilfrid Owen. *De unge døde (They Died Young)* was published in 1932.

[13] Grieg's 1927 novel *The Ship Sails On* (*Skibet gaar videre*, 1924) had a profound and lasting effect on Lowry. For discussion of the Grieg influence see Douglas Day and Hallvard Dahlie. Lowry's manuscript of "In Ballast to the White Sea" was destroyed in a fire on 7 June 1944 (however, see note 10, page 36), but Lowry had begun working on the novel in the early thirties after his trip to Norway. For a description of this convoluted plot and the connection with Grieg, see Lowry's 25 August 1951 letter to David Markson (*SC* II, no. 467). Lowry's comment that "when he [Lowry] meets X [Grieg] ... X is on the point of going to *Cambridge* ... to do some research on Elizabethan drama" (418) overlaps with the events and information in the 8 September 1931 letter to Grieg, and this overlap suggests the continued importance of the Marston-Webster/Brooke/Grieg link for Lowry.

[14] Brooke's book, originally written in 1911–12 as a dissertation at Cambridge University, was prepared for publication by his friend Edward Marsh in 1916. Brooke was familiar with the nineteenth century's view of Elizabethan drama, in particular Swinburne's studies, but he went far beyond Swinburne in his critical analysis of texts and his general theories about the drama. Although consideration of the early twentieth-century interest in the period is beyond the scope of this essay, it is worth pointing out that T.S. Eliot's essays on Elizabethan dramatists date from the 1920s (the one on Marston from 1934), and that, if he knew Brooke's book, he does not cite it. Brooke's study contains discussion, ten appendices on Webster's plays, and a bibliography. The five chapters of discussion and interpretation begin with a theoretical statement about drama, in which Brooke demonstrates his awareness of German aesthetics and articulates his preference for the theatrical values of "emotional continuity" (13) and "cumulative effect" (14), which can be achieved by unrealistic as well as realistic means. This opening chapter is an interesting prelude to what, today, would be called a semiotic study of Webster. The second chapter provides some standard, requisite literary history and context, and in the third, Brooke charts the "stream" that joins Marston, Tourneur, and Webster. Lowry takes most of his quotations from this chapter.

[15] Among the various fragments and notebook draft material for "In Ballast to the White Sea" that survived the fire is the draft of a scene in which two Cambridge undergraduates stop at "the little ADC Theatre" to listen to a rehearsal of Webster's play *The Duchess of Malfi* (Lowry Collection, 12:15); the scene, with its speeches from the play, appears to hold symbolic value for Lowry's embryonic novel.

[16] Lowry, in fact, has re-accentuated Swinburne's exact words in his own sentence: "The last step into the darkness remained to be taken by 'the most tragic' of all English poets [Webster]" (Swinburne, Vol. 11, 293).

[17] Most critics (Cowan, Day, and Schneider, for example) view Lowry's plagiarism—or his obsession with it—as a weakness, a failing, even a neurosis, but in my view this is an overly narrow and misleading statement of Lowry's case. As Brooke argues in his book, plagiarism was a common and accepted procedure in the Renaissance, and Lowry was identifying himself with that tradition. For a thorough discussion of that tradition see White. Toward the end of his 8 September 1931 letter to Grieg, Lowry describes Grieg as the best man to "surround Brooke's position" (*SC* I, 106).

7

Ut Pictura Poesis: From Alberto Gironella to Malcolm Lowry

Mais si, sans se laisser charmer,
Ton oeil sait plonger dans les gouffres,
Lis-moi, pour apprendre à m'aimer.

(Baudelaire)

The book is written on numerous planes with provision made, it
was my fond hope, for almost every kind of reader.

(Lowry)

Few readers of Malcolm Lowry's *Under the Volcano* are better versed in the novel's "poetic cases" than the contemporary Mexican artist Alberto Gironella.[1] And few readers can teach us so much about *Under the Volcano*. In *El Vía Crucis del Cónsul* (*The Consul's Way of the Cross*), Gironella has taken up Baudelaire's challenge: to teach us how to read—and to love—Lowry's book.

What I propose to do here is to read Gironella's reading of Lowry and, in the process, to identify the ways in which their texts instruct and control a reader who dares to follow the textual signs in a search for meaning in the complex semiotics of Lowry's, Gironella's, and our contemporary world. My approach to this semiotics rests on basic assumptions that it is best to note at the start because it is at this very point of departure that readers and readings will differ.

Despite all that must be said about textuality, discursive formations, and post-modernism, I believe that Lowry and Gironella intend to create artistic meaning that can be grasped by a reader and that this meaning, in addition to the language, form, and system in which it exists, can enrich our lives. This is a fundamentally romantic view of the artist and of artistic intention that is unfashionable in post-structuralist criticism. It takes us back to Baudelaire—that avatar, "kindred spirit," and fellow traveller of Lowry and Gironella—and back to an allegorical habit of mind in which correspondences are sought between our semiotic systems and a reality that is believed to lie both in and somewhere beyond the surface play of signifiers. The *search* for that paradise where semiotics and reality (be it existential or transcendental) are one is, for the romantic artist, a voyage that never ends; arrival is endlessly deferred and the desire for meaning (call it *correspondance*, presence, Logos) provides the impetus for creative acts that ease the twentieth-century's sense of loss, or what Lyotard calls "nostalgia for the unattainable."[2]

In my reading of Gironella's and Lowry's creative acts, I will employ the tools of the archeologist, as Foucault outlines them in *The Archeology of Knowledge*, to uncover and compare the homologies and differences that allow me to describe the novel and the art as constituting an "interdiscursive configuration" within the discursive practices of romantic, western humanism.[3] But I will also move beyond Foucauldian archeology by insisting upon interpretation.

***

> *The twelve chapters should be considered as twelve blocks … Each chapter is a unity in itself and all are related and interrelated.*
>
> (Lowry)

Both *Under the Volcano* and *The Consul's Way of the Cross* defy summary and confound first impressions. Constructed, like a churrigueresque cathedral, in an "overloaded style" on many levels that duplicate and mirror each other, *Under the Volcano* proliferates images, symbols, signs, intertexts, and meanings in a bewilderingly complex, yet meticulously balanced, system. Taking its cues from the novel, *The Consul's Way of the Cross* reconstructs that system in a multi-media, pictorial language that interpolates itself into the novel *and* stands outside it in an autonomous installation where it mirrors and comments on the Consul's story and the novel's discourse.

***

> *The allegory is that of the Garden of Eden, the Garden representing the world, from which we ourselves run perhaps slightly more danger of being ejected than when I wrote the book.*
>
> (Lowry)

The story, or diegetic core, of *Under the Volcano* is familiar and simple. It is a tale of the collapse and disintegration of a marriage and of the couple whose love could not prevail over the internal and external forces undermining them. Lowry lifts this bathetic story from the level of soap-opera cliché to the level of tragedy and allegory through his discourse: the husband becomes a figure of Adam, Faust, and a cabbalist;

his wife becomes a figure of Eve, Marguerite, and the feminine principle of the Cabbala; the failure of their marriage signifies our failure to remain in the Garden of Eden, which in turn signifies western civilization's failure (in two wars) to preserve the earthly garden of this world. Religious and political allegory expand the simple story into a discursive formation that, as Foucault reminds us, inscribes a "system of dispersion" (37) through "a schema of correspondence" between narrative events and other, extra-narrative "series of events" (74), between the discursive formation of a novel and the "non-discursive domains" (162) of political, social, and cultural events.

***

Aunque el pintor se sirve de los ojos y el poeta de la lengua, ojos y lengua obedecen a la misma potencia: la imaginaci n.

(Paz)

Alberto Gironella's *The Consul's Way of the Cross* exists in three forms: as illustrations in a sumptuous new edition of *Bajo el Volcán*; as an exhibition catalogue containing a critical essay by Lowry scholar Carmen Virgili, with photographs, drawings, a set of testimonials, and reproductions of selected pieces from the exhibition; and as the exhibition itself. In each of these forms the work comprises a complex juxtaposition of visual and verbal texts that comment upon and address each other in a discourse ranging from agonistic celebration to comic parody and from dizzying narcissism to ironic objectivity. To say that *Under the Volcano* inspired *The Consul's Way of the Cross*, or to argue that Lowry's novel provides the model or "hypotext" for Gironella's art is to miss the point by over-simplifying the nature of each text in itself and of the relationship between them.[4]

Judging from the titles alone, I might say that *The Consul's Way of the Cross* refers to *Under the Volcano* synecdochically, as a part to the larger whole, except that Gironella, like Lowry, has a way of proliferating parts until they take on a generative power all their own. Synecdoche, then, will not help me, and another way into the dialogue must be found.

***

Y las verdaderas obras de arte siempre están más allá de su interpretaci n, se caracterizan por su capacidad de permanecer vivas dentro de ella.

(Ponce)

At the May–June 1994 Gironella exhibition in the Mexican Cultural Centre in Paris, the unsuspecting gallery flaneur enters, literally, a set of rooms opening off one another rather like the rooms of the Farolito in chapter twelve of the *Volcano*. The first of these rooms, however, is hung with text. The wall to the left contains row upon row of books, their dust jackets displaying *Bajo el Volcán* on the front or a yellow altar to Malcolm Lowry on the back.[5] In a glass case near the window lie more volumes, some closed to display their deep blue cover embossed with a large black scorpion, others open to reveal the Spanish text.

The right-hand wall is covered by fifty-four brilliantly coloured images (16 x 24 cm) mounted on black mats and recessed in shallow frames. The visual impact is stunning. On closer inspection one sees that each piece, with its dominant blue, white, red, and black composition, is a collaged surface built from paint, ink, various types of paper and labels, and bottle caps. The letters MEZCAL leap out here and there; a horse with the number "7" surfaces at several points; Tarot cards emerge— "The Fool," "The Wheel of Fortune," "The Hanged Man"; the number "666" suddenly erupts from a corner of an image; maps and labels appear and disappear, announcing and obscuring the Battle of the Ebro, Tequila, Johnnie Walker, Carta Blanca, Alas, ALAS! The closer one looks, the more each collaged surface acquires a dizzying complexity and a paradoxical depth, until one slowly realizes that in the background (the pictorial ground) looms the abstract shape of a volcano.

On the threshold of the inner room are more rows of books, open or closed, displaying their dust jackets. Then, facing the viewer from the rear wall of this inner room is the "Grand Altar to Malcolm Lowry," an installation piece (see Figure 1) constructed of wood painted a vivid, cadmium yellow, the very yellow used for cantinas in Mexico. Dominating the "altar" in the central recessed enclosure, sits a slightly larger than life-sized portrait of Malcolm Lowry (looking uncannily like a younger Alberto Gironella), his hand extended from the recess, as if over the counter of a bar, holding an empty glass: "Mescal .... *mescal, poquito.*"[6] And on the counter lie fragments of the Consul's last day, those objects that acquire such vitality in chapter twelve of *Volcano*: dominoes, a gun, cigarettes, a telephone. The letters "Farolito" flash above his head. Instead of votive candles, further evidence from the Day of the Dead sits in the four altar niches surrounding this central recess: "bottles, bottles, bottles .... Rye, Johnnie Walker, Vieux Whiskey, *blanc* Canadien ... the beautiful bottles of tequila" (*UV*, 294). Beside the bottles are four smaller images, one per niche—an elaborately framed crucifixion here, a miniature portrait of John Donne there. Bizarre advertisements, or icons? Above and between the niches are signs and trays, the familiar appurtenances of a cantina, advertising beverages.

Around the three remaining walls of this inner sanctum hang twelve boxed collages ("cajas-collage," each 83 x 100 x 21cm). These are Gironella's windows opening into *Under the Volcano*. Each glass-covered, yellow box encapsulates and comments upon on one of the twelve chapters of the novel. The "slow progression

FIGURE 1: Alberto Gironella before his altar to Lowry.

of the chapters" (*SC* I, 506) is indicated by the shade of blue used for the ground of the collaged images that constitute the narrative link between boxes and across the gulf (*gouffre*/gulf/golf) that separates them; the blue builds from the pale light of early morning to the intense blue of mid-day to a deeper blue fading to grey before it gives way to the black of night. Arrayed in front of and beside each collage are key objects and verbal/visual signs of the chapter being presented; thus, the box for chapter six features a guitar, and the one for chapter nine contains a crutch and bicycle wheel. And always there are bottles. Just as they do in *Volcano*, these disjunct, inanimate, found objects, standing or affixed to the surface of the box, acquire a disturbing, menacing vitality. As one peers in at them, mesmerized, or follows them from box to box, one plunges deeper and deeper into the proliferating thing-ness of the Consul's world. Each box captures and reduplicates the traces—the outline of a volcano, twelve faint letters (one per box) that spell M-A-L-C-O-L-M-L-O-W-R-Y, labels, words, numbers, *things*—already familiar from the wall of collages in the outer room.

The impact of all this reduplication on the gallery visitor as she moves from outer to inner room and slowly around the boxes to the altar is not unlike the shock received on entering a church/cantina/brothel in a Buñuel film where disjunct fragments of the objective world clamour, threaten, or mutely command attention in revolving iterations and *mises en abyme*. How can one read, and learn to love, such a text?

***

> *Hugh and the Consul are the same person, but within a book*
> *which obeys not the laws of other books, but those it creates as it*
> *goes along.*
>
> (Lowry)

The 1992 deluxe edition of *Bajo el Volcán* is a reprint of the 1964 Spanish translation of *Under the Volcano* by Raúl Ortiz y Ortiz, with a Spanish translation, by Carmen Virgili, of the "Prologue" that Lowry wrote for the 1949 French translation of his novel, and with fifty-six full colour illustrations, a cover and a dust jacket by Gironella. This volume takes its place in a long tradition of emblem literature and illustrated texts in which the relationship between verbal and visual languages is central to the semiotics and aesthetics of the text.

Gironella's illustrations of the novel exist in four forms that together constitute a parallel discourse to the novel: dust jacket, scorpion cover design, twelve small black and white reproductions (5 x 6.5 cm) of the lithographs based on the collages in the boxes, and fifty-six plates (16 x 24 cm) tipped-in strategically, with four at the beginning and end of the novel and four per chapter. First impressions on leafing

FIGURE 2: Alberto Gironella's illustration for chapter 4 of *Under the Volcano*

through the volume are of brilliant colour, visual complexity, and dizzying repetition. One illustration seems to duplicate another, but what is duplicated are elements of composition, colour, words, numbers, and fragments of text. Only two plates are, in fact, repeated. The black and white lithograph reproductions, each one set below its chapter number, appear on the individual, otherwise blank pages that separate the chapters. They provide further reiterations of elements in the colour plates, and while they are less likely to catch the eye, they are subtle visual/verbal *mises en abyme*, for the chapter that follows and for the important breaks (*gouffre*/gulf/golf) between chapters.

Nothing in this intertextual assemblage is accidental. Let me take one example: chapter four. Here, the chapter lithograph announces "C.T.M." (see Figure 2), the Spanish translation of "see tee emma" in Hugh's telegram to the *Daily Globe*, the telegram that opens chapter four and finds its way into Hugh's sports jacket, which the Consul will put on in chapter seven and be wearing in chapter twelve. Behind these bold letters is the faint outline of a large letter "C" (from MALCOLM), holding within its open space the words "CONSUL," "mescal," and traces of words barely discernible on the surface of the original collage. In harmony with Lowry's textuality (allusions, echoes, intertexts, re-presentations, proliferating signs), Gironella duplicates Lowry's methods and, thus, aspects of his meaning: everything is connected, interwoven, interconnected, yet these intertexts and signs are contained, controlled, isolated (like the characters), and *framed.*

Turn the page, and the telegram, in Spanish, with its "CTM confederación trabajadores mex," stares back at you. Half a dozen pages into the chapter sit the four illustrations, the first of which is dominated by the large black capitals: CTM. And because this is Hugh's chapter, a fragment of newspaper headline announces the Battle of the Ebro. The next three illustrations introduce new intertextual elements—Peter Lorre, the white horse with the number "7," "la sepulture" (the pulqueria where Hugh and Yvonne stop during their ride and Yvonne sees the armadillo)—and repeat what is, by chapter four, an already familiar set of signs: the volcano, the bottle caps—blue, yellow, and red—and "mescal." Again, Lowry's method is duplicated in Gironella's pictorial language, so that words and images, novel and pictures, together, constitute an interdiscursive configuration.

***

> *Life is a forest of symbols, as Baudelaire said, but I won't be told*
> *you can't see the wood for the trees here!*
>
> (Lowry)

"Golf=gouffre=gulf," or so Geoffrey Firmin reflects in chapter seven of *Volcano* (206) as he stares through binoculars, past Yvonne, from Jacques's tower to the distant golf course. From such small touches, Lowry establishes the correspondences that work inter- and intra-textually across the discursive formation of the novel. *Gouffre* invokes Baudelaire, and the gulf, of course, is the barranca, the ultimate hell-hole in Geoffrey's botched golf game of life. The play on golf, however, carries Geoffrey into an elaborate, erudite parody of John Donne's "A Hymn to God the Father"— "Who holds the flag while I hole out in three?" (*UV*, 207)—a parody that quickly becomes self-parody laced with self-loathing, self-reproach, self-pity, and with irony, regret, longing, and serious humour. Such rich ambiguity of tone and of self-reflexive parody lies at the heart of *Under the Volcano* and represents both Lowry's strength and his weakness as a writer. Time and again, his narcissism is relieved (just in time) by his irony, his "subjective [...] equipment" (*SC* I, 500) balanced by the objective demands of parody.

For whatever reasons, personal, temperamental, artistic, Gironella celebrates Lowry's subjectivity by placing his construction of the Lowryan artist at the centre of his work. In the catalogue for *The Consul's Way of the Cross*, Gironella is photographed seated before his "Great Altar to Malcolm Lowry," bearded, cane in hand, looking for all the world like the Consul and his creator (see Figure 1). His signature repeats itself on all the images until it becomes an inevitable, unavoidable, integral part of the total composition, until it (he) is written into the ongoing voyage, until the name creates itself by asserting filiation and genealogy.

As with Lowry, Gironella's "subjective [...] equipment" is balanced by irony, parody, and serious humour, perhaps even with a touch of one-up-manship. So you can play golf-gouffre-gulf? Well, just watch me! Or just watch Donne watching you from several vantage points including the lower right niche of my altar. The joke, finally is on the reader/viewer who, dismayed by the extravagant self-reflexivity of Lowry and Gironella, may miss the allusions to precursors (here, to Donne and Baudelaire, but there are many others) that simultaneously mock and validate these romantic altar-egos.

***

> *Esto es gallo'. Es su sello y su juego de viñeta-sello con la
> literatura y la pintura.*
>
> (Ríos)

The Horatian dictum notwithstanding (*ut pictura poesis*, as in painting, so in poetry), the semiotic basis for inter-artistic comparison rests on structural homology, not analogy, let alone artistic temperament. To be fully comparable and complementary, the sister arts must be capable of being discussed in the same terms.[7] Where one might argue that pigment, line, and plastic form, the primary tools of the painter, are at best only analogous to the words and imagery, the sentences, story divisions, and focalization of the novelist, it seems to me that Gironella has grasped, almost literally, the principle of homology through the pictorial language of collage, the narrative genre (which, of course, has a long history in painting), and the concept of installation.

Gironella has created works that function autonomously as visual art, that engage Lowry in dialogue and that, within the covers of *Bajo el Volcán*, show us how to read by staging a reading of the novel. Collage works homologously in this staging by constructing a visual/verbal surface composed of the same fragments that constitute Lowry's verbal world—scraps of actual text, quotations, maps, labels. The syntax of Gironella's surfaces develops cumulatively and paratactically, as do Lowry's sentences, through the embedding of visual and verbal signs. Narrative is an obvious, traditional homology articulated here in the twelve collage boxes that should be read/viewed/studied in sequence and that, like the chapters of the novel with which they correspond, carry one back, repeatedly, to the beginning. This narrative compulsion holds the novel and the series of boxes together as a discursive formation, while permitting each one to function on its own, in its own (temporal) frame and space.

Gironella's use of installation is at once the most daring and problematic of his homologies. It is problematic because it can only work for the gallery visitor with intimate knowledge of *Under the Volcano* and Malcolm Lowry. When it works, however, this homology is possibly the most fruitful one because what Gironella achieves by it is a dramatic staging *of the reading process* that literally places the viewer/reader inside a simulacrum of the text and leads her around and around a virtual reality of potentially endless readings of the text called *El Vía Crucis del Cónsul Under the Volcano.*

***

And I am telling you something new about hell fire.
(Lowry)

To some extent, all works of art attempt to instruct and manipulate their readers/viewers. They all assume an audience. Lowry's and Gironella's work, however, demands a participating audience, one that will accept the Baudelairean challenge to plumb the depths and learn to love. But as the traces of armadillos (literally, the bony plates from their backs) in Gironella's boxes remind us, and as Hugh warned Yvonne, armadillos cannot be tamed and, if you try to tame them, they will pull you into a hole with them. This risk of becoming confused and lost—swallowed up—in the proliferations of *Volcano* and the *Consul's Way*, is only one danger facing a reader/viewer. The other is the risk, as Baudelaire knew, of "se laisser charmer," of succumbing to the self-destructive, romantic myth of the artist as demigod at whose altar we must worship and whose art we must accept as gospel.

To recoil and reject, however, is an extreme and hasty response, for taken singly these works provide a fascinating commentary on the activities of readers, on the creation and consumption of art, and on contemporary life. Taken together they demonstrate the attraction and persistence of the romantic artist as a central figure in the narrative of western humanism: Lowry wants to tell us "something new about hell fire" (*SC* I, 520), and Gironella wants to celebrate that telling. Why?

***

The constant repetition of churrigueresque 'of an overloaded style'
seemed to be a suggestion that the book was satirizing itself.
(Lowry)

Although the hells created by Lowry and Gironella are secular, composed in and of the detritus of this world, the ghosts of religious belief hover over every bottle and behind every sign. Churches, altars, candles, magic, hymns, prayers, and ritual pervade novel and art. And yet, because of the irony and parody in both texts, one must ask just what is being worshipped and what gods invoked. The obvious answers spring to mind from the Judeo-Christian tradition that is so obviously inscribed in both, but it is at this point that an important difference (*gouffre*) opens up between Lowry and Gironella.

Where Lowry wants to warn us about the failure of love and the imminent destruction of the world by the forces of evil within us, Gironella is content to comment upon the frantic consumerism of late twentieth-century life. He does this by displaying the empty bottles, crushed snakes (all that is left of the devil?), armadillo plates, dented bottle caps, used matches, torn labels, discarded boots, broken instruments, faded photographs, in short, the garbage of our lives, in aesthetically pleasing arrangements, side by side with images and fragments of the humanist tradition in art, literature, philosophy, and religion, where it carries equal weight and value with that tradition.

This and this alone—this actual, physical, garbage from the real world—is what we stand in the gallery worshipping. Things. Things consumed and discarded. Gironella nowhere indicates that this is his warning, but he has nevertheless actualized the Consul's tragic realization in chapter twelve of the *Volcano* that the things of this world, down to "the ash and sputum on the filthy floor" (*UV*, 362) correspond to his being, sum up his wasted life.

***

> *You like this garden?*
> *Why is it yours?*
> *We evict those who destroy!*

(Lowry)

Lowry's vision is, finally, a modernist one, and *Under the Volcano* is a modernist text, albeit one that approaches what we now think of as postmodernism. For Lowry, the gods, the unities, the design-governing strategies of art are still operative, even though we have abused them. His novel has the high seriousness of a tragedy in which the fate of an individual soul still matters and the desecration of the garden is a sin punishable by eviction. His post-modern qualities lie in his sense of language as a system of dissemination, in the acute intertextuality of his discourse, in the proliferating signifiers of his semiotic system. Between the modernist story of death, loss, and damnation and the postmodernist discourse of *Volcano* sits Lowry's thematization of the vertigo that accompanies his characters' nostalgia for presence, Logos. If this vertigo is not the "obscene" ecstasy described by Baudrillard as central to postmodernism, it is only because Lowry judges and damns it in the act of communication that is, and points beyond (transcends), *Under the Volcano*.[8]

Gironella's *The Consul's Way of the Cross*, as installation, is a fully post-modernist re-statement of the problem. For Gironella, the world is an aesthetic object and Lowry, like his novel, is a part, albeit a privileged part, of that simulacrum. Gironella takes collage, parody, and intertextuality to their dizzying extremes in order to construct an "obscene" shrine at which we worship, without nostalgia, an always already written text that promises nothing beyond its own virtual reality.

***

> For the book was so designed, counterdesigned and interwelded
> that it could be read an indefinite number of times and still not
> have yielded all its meanings or its drama or its poetry.
>
> (Lowry)

But Gironella's art does not exist only in the installation space of a gallery. Within the dust jacket, cover, and pages of *Bajo el Volcán*, his collages serve to reinforce the meaning of Lowry's text and to instruct us in the way of the cross, of the Consul, of reading. Gironella's homage here is to the wonder of human creativity in the tangible text of Lowry's novel. By illustrating the Spanish translation of the novel, the painter's art supplements the writer's (and translator's) in an interdiscursive configuration that works to reassure us that, regardless of how desperate and hopeless the late twentieth century may be, it is still possible to find meaning, order, beauty, and pleasure in re-presentational art and to find hope in the human capacity to make art.

Finally, one must not forget the humour, seriously parodic though it may be. From the gigantic jakes of this world, Lowry and Gironella have fabricated elaborate, churrigueresque jokes that remind us never to take ourselves too seriously. After all, when you close Gironella's *Bajo el Volcán*, what you see on the back of the dust jacket is the grand yellow altar to Malcolm Lowry.

Ceci n'est pas une pipe. Esto es gallo.

(1994)

Notes

* References to *Under the Volcano* are to the 1963 Penguin edition.

[1] The fourteen quotations that frame and introduce the twelve parts of this paper are from the following sources. Charles Baudelaire, "Épigraphe pour tin livre condamné," 186–87: "But if, remaining free from spells, / Your eyes can plumb the hellish deep, / Read me, and learn to love me well"; for parts I, II, III, VI, VII, IX, X, XI, and XII, they are from Lowry's

2 January 1946 letter to Jonathan Cape (*SC* I, 506, 505–06, 507, 515, 518, 520, 521, 525, 527); all other references to this letter are included in the text. The quotation for part IV is from Octavio Paz's "Testimonial" in *Alberto Gironella: El Via Crucis del Cónsul* (Barcelona: Círculo de Lectores, 1992): "Even though painting and writing exist in separate realms, both are the product of the power of imagination" (43); for part V, from Juan García Ponce's "Testimonial" in *Alberto Gironella*: "great works are those which are always beyond the reach of interpretation and are able to stay alive within it" (44); and for part VIII, from Julián Rios's caption in *Alberto Gironella* explaining the artist's ironic use of a phrase from *Don Quixote* as a type of signature: "'This is a rooster.' It is his seal and an interplay vignette/seal between literature and painting" (22). The closing epigram is a combination of the inscription on René Magritte's 1928–29 surrealist painting of a pipe called *The Treachery of Images* and Gironella's "seal." I would like to thank Pablo Restrepo for his translations from the Spanish in the catalogue *Alberto Gironella: El Via Crucis del Cónsul*. Gironella (1929–99), a leading Mexican artist, had solo exhibitions in Mexico, Spain, and France and was represented in group exhibitions of surrealist and contemporary art across Europe and Latin American and in London and New York. He had a long and intimate interest in literature.

[2] See Jean-François Lyotard's discussion of the nostalgia within modernism and the way it is transformed in postmodernism in *The Postmodern Condition: A Report on Knowledge* (79–81).

[3] Michel Foucault, *The Archeology of Knowledge* (158); all further references are included in the text, but see, in particular, chapter four.

[4] "Hypotext" is Gérard Genette's term for the antecedent text in a set of texts that are closely related through their "hypertextuality": see *Palimpsestes: La littérature au second degré* (11–12).

[5] At the Paris exhibition, the two second-floor rooms of the gallery contained Gironella's lithographs and a display of Lowry artefacts, letters, and manuscripts in a further reduplication of intertextualities.

[6] The Consul whispers this to Cervantes at the beginning of chapter ten of *Under the Volcano*. The new Spanish edition, described in part VI, was published in 1992 by Círculo de Lectores in Barcelona. I would like to thank Dr. Ortiz for sending me a copy and for introducing me to Gironella's work

[7] In *The Colors of Rhetoric* (1–69), Wendy Steiner examines the problems and history of the painting-literature analogy and the process of semiotic comparison.

[8] In "The Ecstasy of Communication," a brief section translated by John Johnston from *Le Système des objets* (1968) for *The Anti-Aesthetic: Essays on Postmodern Culture*, ed. Hal Foster (126–34), Jean Baudrillard outlines his distinction between "scene" and "obscene," between a traditional (and modern) faith in representation, referential meaning, and mystery beyond a visible surface and the postmodern "delirium" produced by simulations of the real in which all things exist as fully visible commodities.

8

Midsummer Madness and the Day of the Dead:
Joyce, Lowry, and Expressionism

Since the publication in 1947 of Malcolm Lowry's masterpiece, *Under the Volcano*, it has been critically de rigueur to call Joyce's *Ulysses* (1922) an influence or even a seminal precursor.[1] After all, the two texts have stunning similarities, not the least of which being that they are both "family romances" that take place in a single day. But *Volcano* also parallels *Ulysses* in details of relationship and event: in each an essentially noble, middle-aged husband (the one a Jew, the other significantly mistaken for a Jew) is betrayed by his wife; in each the hero is haunted by his past sins, failures, and guilts; in each a younger male is involved in the hero's life while pursuing his own independent, rather self-indulgent, goals; and in each the wife is a symbol of eternal woman.

Such thematic parallels only scrape the surface of similarity between *Ulysses* and *Volcano* because both texts are complex, multilayered, polyphonic narratives with a multitude of shared allusions (Dante, Goethe, Shakespeare, and Homer, for example) and motifs (dogs, drink, whores, Good Samaritans, riderless horses, etc.) And both texts create, at once, highly symbolic and self-reflexive textual worlds tenaciously rooted in time and place, in history and myth. Both can be boring and fascinating, sad and funny, and both are elaborate *stagings* (or *re*-stagings), before a reader/spectator/voyeur, of the human imagination, consciousness, or soul. Despite their pervasive similarities, however, *Ulysses* and *Volcano* are very different works, so different that, in the last analysis, influence studies break up and founder on the Scylla and Charybdis of comparison. Stephen Spender summed up the situation precisely in his introduction to the 1965 edition of *Volcano* by concluding that "the aims and methods of Lowry are the opposite of those of Joyce and Eliot" (xii) and that "Lowry has borrowed from Joyce [but] turned his symbolic devices upside down" (xiii).

At the bottom of this difficulty in bringing Lowry into alignment with Joyce is the concept of modernism itself and how we have come to understand and use the term. As long as we think of the modern period as the age of Joyce and of the modernist novel as Joycean (specifically after *Ulysses*), then we narrow unjustifiably our perspective on an enormously complex and varied movement. In the interests of unity and order we take the part, albeit an important part, for the whole. Recent developments in postmodernist art criticism and theory, however, are forcing us to reassess modernism.[2] A crucial element in this reassessment is our increased awareness of the contribution made to modernism by German expressionism and of expressionism's overlap with futurism, vorticism, Dadaism, cubism, and surrealism. It is my contention, in what follows, that the profound difference between Joyce and Lowry *as modernists* can be illuminated by examining the response of each to expressionism. Without doubt there are a number of other ways of approaching the Joyce/Lowry question, but a discussion of the expressionist *Aufbruch* (awakening) in *Ulysses* and *Under the Volcano* throws an interesting light on the matter.

Expressionism flourished in all the arts in Germany between 1905 and the mid-1920s. If literary scholars in the English-speaking world know less about it than they might, this is in part because Hitler made every effort to destroy all traces and artifacts of the movement and in part because the movement came to be seen as exclusively Germanic; with very few exceptions, it did not catch on in France or England. The centres for its activity were Berlin, Munich, and Vienna, with considerable expressionist/Dadaist activity in Zürich during World War One. The expressionist artist was revolutionary in his aesthetics and, to one degree or another, in his politics, and he defined himself against the preceding modes of realism and impressionism on the one hand and against the materialism and dehumanization of an increasingly "bourgeois" patriarchal society on the other.

The result of this ferment and revolt was the intense subjectivity (what Kandinsky called "innere Notwendigkeit" [Kandinsky, 26]) of the expressionist Vision expressed in violent outbursts (*Schrei*) from the suffering or inspired poet/individual that led, in turn, through *Aufbruch* to *Erlösung* (deliverance). The violent outbursts were in the form of highly distorted and abstracted presentations of reality or lurid projections of passionate feelings in externalized, objectified forms. Several pictorial images of this Vision come to mind (from the portraits of Oskar Kokoschka or Ludwig Meidner), but the key icon (and iconic sign) in expressionist semiotics is Edvard Munch's *Geschrei* (*The Scream*, 1893). The screaming face in Munch's painting and lithograph had become a visual cliché by 1930—a point I shall return to—prefiguring its marketing on T-shirts and inflatable plastic "dolls" in the 1990s.

In the theatre, the smooth, hypotactic structures of well-made plays gave way to paratactic forms, staccato language, and the objectification of soul states; the modelling, perspective, and representation of previous painting gave way to violent non-naturalistic colours, a rejection of light modulations in favour of planes of solid pigment, and the distortion of recognizable forms. In expressionism, metaphors were literalized, and the more grotesque they were, the better; hence, Gregor Samsa *becomes ein Ungeziefer* in Kafka's *Die Verwandlung* (*Metamorphosis*), a tree *becomes* a cross in Georg Kaiser's *Von Morgens bis Mitternachts* (*From Morn to Midnight*, 1919), and the jungle *becomes* the primitive Soul of the hero in Eugene O'Neill's *Emperor Jones* (1920). What the expressionist never lost sight of was Man, and even when the artist eschewed any direct political engagement, his *Vision* (as Kaiser called it) embraced the redemption and rejuvenation of humanity. Most expressionists were romantic, anthropocentric, and deeply humanist, even when (as is the case with certain dramatists and fiction writers) they employed heavy irony and satire.[3]

The case for Joyce's or Lowry's knowledge of, let alone affinity with, expressionism is an interesting one. Several critics argue that Joyce was contemporaneous or parallel with expressionism or even, himself, a direct influence on the German expressionist novel.[4] More recently, however, Ira Nadel has suggested that Joyce had firsthand knowledge of expressionism through the paintings and plays of the Austrian Oskar Kokoschka and through his Zurich contacts between 1915 and 1920, when he was working on *Ulysses*. These contacts included Max Reinhardt's famous expressionist production of Georg Buchner's *Dantons Tod* and August Strindberg's *Totentanz*, although, as Richard Ellmann notes, Joyce found Strindberg's plays to be little more than "hysterical raving" (Ellmann, 412).[5]

Moreover, in a brief discussion of Joyce and Conrad Aiken, Charles McMichael and Ted Spivey note Joyce's keen interest in Aiken's *Coming Forth by Day of Osiris Jones* (1931) and describe *Osiris Jones* and *Finnegans Wake* (which Joyce was working on when Aiken's poem was published) as "expressionistic."[6] Although the description of *Finnegans Wake* as expressionistic strikes me as inaccurate, Nadel's more general claims are, I think, conclusive. Nevertheless, it is important to remember that James Joyce was no expressionist. If he used expressionism, he did so in the form of parody—parody that served his larger, and different, purposes.[7]

With Lowry the case is more cut and dried. Not only did Lowry know German expressionism well—from the plays of "Gay-org Kaiser" to the famous Ufa films of Robert Wiene, F.W. Murnau, and Fritz Lang—he was an aficionado of O'Neill's early expressionist plays and continued to speak favourably of expressionism (likening it to jazz) throughout his life.[8] Equally relevant here is the fact that Lowry was profoundly influenced by Aiken and that in his 28 November 1951 letter to Seymour Lawrence (the letter that was written for the special issue of *Wake* devoted to Aiken) he tells the story of Joyce "almost up to the very point that great man died ... looking for, trying everywhere to purchase, expecting to receive indeed, Conrad Aiken's masterly dramatic poem, 'The Coming Forth by Day of Osiris Jones'" (*SC* II, 461). Then, just to make the filiation as clear as possible, Lowry explicitly links Aiken's sensibility "with expressionist painters, such as Munch" (*SC* II, 465). Munch, of course, was no stranger to Lowry, nor was the Munch/ Aiken/Joyce/Lowry nexus a new idea for him in 1951: included with his September 1931 letter to Aiken, written in Oslo, is his sketch (*après* Munch) of "The Shriek!" (see Figure 1 and *SC* I, 111).

Elsewhere I have argued that *Volcano* is a profoundly expressionistic vision of the world (Grace, *Regression and Apocalypse*, 163–84), but for the present purpose it will suffice to concentrate upon a few salient aspects of Lowry's expressionism that highlight his difference from Joyce. If Joyce parodies expressionism and Lowry uses it seriously, how do they do this and, more importantly, why?

Speaking of "Circe" in *The Odyssey of Style* in "Ulysses," Karen Lawrence remarks that here "impressionism [has been] replaced by expressionism .... Whole land-scapes and situations symbolically express feelings and sensations .... Nighttown is both the literal setting of the plot of the chapter and the expressionistic equivalent of the feelings of guilt and trespass that are experienced by the characters" (Lawrence, 148–49). "Circe," in fact, stages, in a heightened and exaggerated form—even for expressionism—almost all the features of expressionist plays. It is set in or near a brothel at midnight and peopled by a collection of grotesques, from *real* prostitutes to dogs, ghosts, hallucinations, and talking, inanimate objects; everything swarms with life and is distorted by a mauve or greenish-yellow light (Joyce listed mauve as the key colour in "Circe," but green is equally strong). The two dominant figures of the play, Bloom and Stephen, are obsessed by their families—unfaithful wives, dead children, unforgiving mothers, chastising fathers—and their own sexuality, but each man moves through an apparent *Aufbruch* (Bloom by besting Bello Cohen, Stephen by smashing the light with his Siegfriedian ashplant) towards an apparent *Erlösung* (signaled by Rudy's appearance at the end).

The rhetorical and structural device for the chapter is parataxis: our sense of logical order or linear sequence is disrupted as one ordeal (of accusation, arrest, trial, haunting, etc.) rapidly follows another without explanation, and conventional dialogue explodes into hectic babble, long monologues, and fragmented, staccato outbursts: "Keep to the right, right, right. If there is a signpost planted by the Touring Club at Stepaside who procured that public boon? I who lost my way and contributed to the columns of the *Irish Cyclist* the letter headed *In darkest Stepaside*. Keep, keep, keep to the right. Rags and bones at midnight. A fence more likely. First place murderer makes for. Wash off his sins of the world" (*Ulysses*, 15.231–36).

All the same features occur in *Under the Volcano*, where, it is safe to say, the entire objective world teems with an appalling, threatening vitality when it is perceived through the Consul's alcohol-inspired eyes. Chapters two through twelve are, indeed, the replaying/restaging, exactly one year after his death on 2 November 1938, of the last twelve hours in Geoffrey Firmin's life.

FIGURE 1: Malcolm Lowry sent this Munch *Geschrei* look-alike drawing with a September 1931 letter to Conrad Aiken. I included it with his letter in *Sursum Corda! I* (111).

There are several expressionistic high points in Lowry's text, from Geoffrey's drunken, hallucinatory search for tequila in his ruined garden of chapter five to his terrifying ride on the Máquina Infernal in chapter seven, where he is literally emptied out, stripped of his identity, to the *excusado* scene in chapter ten, where, as in "Circe," all the voices from earlier in the day (or in the book) babble at Geoffrey as he struggles to wipe himself, to read the schedules and advertisements proliferating on the bathroom walls, and to achieve some understanding of his soul's agony. But the chapter that bears closest comparison with "Circe," and that also brings Geoffrey to his tawdry climax and tragic death, is chapter twelve, which is set in the bordello-cum-bar known as El Farolito, at the foot of Mount Popocatepetl: under the volcano.

Here Geoffrey drinks the fatal mescals, reads Yvonne's lost letters, is seduced by the prostitute María, is harangued, harassed, plucked at, babbled at, insulted, exhorted, mocked, and warned by a host of grotesque figures swarming in the smokey gloom or projected from his own inner state. Finally, he is arrested by the fascist military police, who take him for an anarchist, an Antichrist, a Jew, and a spy. As the clock strikes seven and Geoffrey accuses the police—"You stole that horse"— he is murdered: "'I blow you wide open from your knees up, you Jew chingao,' warned the Chief of Rostrums .... 'I blow you wide open from your knees up, you cabrón ... you pelado'" (*UV*, 373). The Farolito, like Nighttown, functions as the setting for the action, as a symbol of the dark climax towards which the protagonist moves, and as the expressionist projection (or literalized metaphor) of his guilt, terror, lust, and self-loathing.

Several features of "Circe" indicate that here Joyce aims at a parody that repeats *with difference* the familiar features of expressionist drama while moving towards a mockery of expressionism and the expressionist protagonist. In general, the obvious absurdity of the episode, its raucous hilarity and extreme exaggeration—a pulling out of *all* the stops—is typical of parody and of Joyce's parodic efforts elsewhere in *Ulysses*. But more importantly, nothing untoward results from the events in Night-town; nothing is unequivocally destroyed or changed, unless it be Madame Cohen's lamp. Joyce's critics have argued that, at best, Bloom and Stephen are redeemed and prepared to enter the new Bloomusalem of "Nostos," and that, at worst, we cannot be certain about anything in "Circe" except that there is no "recoverable truth."[9] If the latter, more cautious, reading of "Circe" is correct (and it is certainly more consistent with what I see as Joyce's parodic intentions), then why has Joyce created this extravagant spoof?

Before attempting to answer this question, I want to examine one specific example of Joyce's parody at work. Towards the end of "Circe," and just before Private Carr punches Stephen, an apocalyptic note that we have heard before is struck once more:

DISTANT VOICES

Dublin's burning! Dublin's burning! On fire, on fire! [*Ulysses*, 15.4659–60]

This is followed by a long, increasingly scrambled stage instruction describing the apocalypse in a string of the most melodramatic expressionist clichés imaginable: "(*Brimstone fires sprung up. Dense clouds roll past. Heavy Gatling guns boom. Pandemonium. Troops deploy. Gallop of hoofs. Artillery. Hoarse commands. Bells clang. Backers shout. Drunkards bawl. Whores screech. Foghorns hoot. Cries of valour. Shrieks of dying....*)" (*Ulysses*, 15.4661–65). According to the stage instruction, the scene climaxes in a black mass celebration of fertility. When the dialogue reappears, however, instead of any serious, conscious registering of disaster, the damned chant "D-O-G" while the blessed chant "G-O-D" "in strident discord" (*Ulysses*, 15.4717). Nothing of any consequence has happened because of this apocalypse, and it is impossible to place it as merely one character's hallucination or as an event in the plot. And this decentring brings us to the point of Joycean parody in "Circe."

At the same time as he repeats and exaggerates the familiar forms of expression-ist drama (scenes of chaos and violence on a cosmic scale; lurid urban settings; a style replete with fragmentation, parataxis, and synecdoche; tag words such as "cries" and "shrieks"; and the themes of suffering, death, and punishment),[10] Joyce denies the *raison d'être* of such scenes and language—a suffering central consciousness, the source for what the Germans spoke of as the *Ausstrahlungen des Ichs* (emanations of the ego). Moreover, he has stripped the event of any symbolic referent or validating context by refusing to anchor it in the plot or in the otherwise densely realist fabric of the diegesis. Once more Karen Lawrence is on the right track when she notes that the basic paradox of "Circe" "is that we do not move beneath convention to the 'real' original selves of the characters or through the rhetoric to 'sincerity'" (Lawrence, 158–59). What we encounter is convention, the melodramatic conventionality of the unconscious, of the inner passions of the soul acted out, of metaphor literalized—of expressionist drama. What we as readers/spectators are invited to recognize in Joyce's parodic *tour de force* is that there is *no expressive origin* free of all traces of the socially, linguistically, and textually constructed Self. Joyce, I am suggesting, has exposed the "expressive fallacy,"[11] with its metaphysics of presence and its privileging of the inner, subjective reality as Truth, and in so exposing it he ridicules, debunks, and defuses the central expressionist paradox and dilemma, thereby freeing his unheroic, most un-*übermenschlich* twosome for their homecoming and comedic end.

In *Under the Volcano*, by contrast, Lowry portrays the inevitable fate of the expressionist Man in his Consul, who subscribes uncritically to the "expressive fallacy." Geoffrey's agony results from what Hal Foster has described as the typical expressionist double bind of alienation: "Such is the pathos of the expressionist self: alienated, it would be made whole through expression, only to find there another sign of its alienation. For in this sign the subject confronts not its desire [for meaning, identity, psychic wholeness] but its deferral, not its presence [nor that of the Logos] but the recognition that it can never be primary, transcendent, whole" (Foster 1985, 62).

Lowry presents Geoffrey's life as a pathopoesis from which he cannot escape because, to the end, he strives to believe (as Lowry also did) in "a content beyond convention, a reality beyond representation" (Foster, 63). Geoffrey believes that Maria is the literal sign of his damnation because she is not Yvonne, and he is killed for being the Jew, spy, *pelado* that he is not. His life, as he recognizes in a moment of terrible insight, is one of constant deferral and fragmentation: "He was surrounded in delirium by these phantoms of himself, the policemen, Fructuoso Sanabria, that other man who looked like a poet, the luminous skeletons, even the rabbit in the corner and the ash and sputum on the filthy floor—did not each correspond, in a way he couldn't understand yet obscurely recognized, to some fraction of his being?" (*UV*, 361–62).

Like "Circe," chapter twelve of *Volcano* also ends with an apocalyptic vision towards which the narrative has been moving from the start. But the differences from "Circe" are instructive. As the dying Consul is lifted and thrown into the barranca, he hears "the world itself ... bursting, bursting into black spouts of villages catapulted into space, with himself falling through it all, through the inconceivable pandemonium of a million tanks, through the blazing of ten million burning bodies, falling, into a forest, falling—" (*UV*, 375). Even Lowry's use of a single word such as "pandemonium" acquires a different intertextual quality from Joyce's when it occurs within the rhythmic, cumulative repetitions of Lowry's prose, and the power of the word (which is sharply undercut in Joyce's context) is further intensified for us as readers because we know the historical reality of Geoffrey's prophetic vision.

What we also *hear* is the Consul's dying Munch-like *Schrei*, which is presented before us in a typically Lowryan narratological simile—*as if* before our eyes on a huge screen—in sharp contrast to the self-consciously bracketed stage instruction employed by Joyce: "Suddenly he screamed, and it was as though this scream were being tossed from one tree to another, as its echoes returned, then, as though the trees themselves were crowding nearer, huddled together, closing over him, pitying" (*UV*, 375). Here the analogical ambiguity of "it was as though" and "then, as though" creates the pathopoetic blurring of the Consul and his world (much as do the lines around the central head in Munch's lithograph). Lowry's wider point (further stressed by the extra-diegetic warning facing the reader on the last page of the text—*¿Le gusta este jardín?*) is that we must all learn from Geoffrey's example: learn to act, to love, and to resist, if possible, the "expressive fallacy."

One could explain Lowry's darker vision with recourse to biography and temperament, or to the historical moment (*Under the Volcano* was written during World War Two by a man peculiarly sensitive to world history and politics), but such explanations account for little; Joyce was writing *Ulysses*, after all, during World War One and was at least equally sensitive to world affairs. The fact remains, however, that *Ulysses* is a tragic-*comic* text and Bloom's ordeal in "Nighttown" is, as Poldy describes it, "midsummer madness," whereas *Volcano* is a comi-*tragic* text set on the November Day of the Dead and on the eve of the outbreak of a war in a world so heinous that it would die of remorse if it should sober up.

Lowry's modernism is deeply infused with romanticism, the ideals of endless voyaging, of individualism and brotherhood. More particularly, his modernism demonstrates the romantic qualities of expressionism in sharp distinction to the highly objectified, depersonalized (as far as the artist's personality is concerned) modernism of Joyce and Eliot. Where Joyce's vision is ahistorical, synchronic, his stance ironic and his style parodic, Lowry's is deeply historical, diachronic, his stance prophetic and pathopoetic and his style kinetic. Where Joyce's vision is centripetal and comic, Lowry's is centrifugal and tragic; where Joyce stages an expressionist parody of the alienated Self, Lowry anatomizes that Self on the stage of this world.

Where Joyce aspires to myth, Lowry aspires to allegory, and the parameters of the modernist novel, of modernism itself, contain them both. In *Under the Volcano*, Lowry reaches back into the expressionist roots of early modernism to explore the causes of alienation, solipsism, and anguish in his hero, and *perhaps* to exorcise them in himself. In *Ulysses*, Joyce remains *hors de combat*, mocking and exposing the failings of Bloom's uneventful life and of our own expressionistic Self-stagings.

(1997)

NOTES

* References to *Under the Volcano* are to the 1963 Penguin edition.

[1] Among the first of Lowry's critics to address the Joyce/Lowry question were Stephen Spender, in his 1965 introduction to *Under the Volcano*, and David Markson, in *Malcolm Lowry's "Volcano."* Richard Hauer Costa has argued, in *Malcolm Lowry* (28–44), that Lowry absorbed Joyce's influence through the mediation of Conrad Aiken, whose fiction and poetry were a source of direct and important influence and stimulus for Lowry. See also Malcolm Bradbury's useful essay "Lowry as Modernist" in *Possibilities*.

[2] In *The Modes of Modern Writing*, David Lodge explores the variety within the field of modernist fiction. Two especially interesting explorations of the relationship between modernism and postmodernism are those by Andreas Huyssens and Hal Foster, but Ihab Hassan was among the first to tackle the problem.

[3] For a detailed discussion of German expressionism, see Bronner and Kellner, Patterson, Sokel, and Willett. I have discussed Munch's *Geschrei* and contemporary parodies of it in *Regression and Apocalypse* (11, 16, and 60) and also analysed *Volcano* as an example of expressionism in English; see chapter seven, "The Soul in Writhing Anguish: Malcolm Lowry's *Under the Volcano*."

[4] Breon Mitchell argues in "Expressionism in English Drama and Prose Literature" (181–92) that Joyce influenced Alfred Döblin (among others). See also Weisstein's comments in the same volume (15–28, 29–44).

[5] Since Frank Budgen's early disclaimer of any influence on Joyce from the visual arts, critics have tended to dismiss the possibility of such influence, but in *The Ruin of Representation in Modernist Art and Texts*, Jo Anna Isaak makes a convincing case for interartistic comparisons based, in part, on Joyce's awareness of contemporary developments in the arts.

[6] According to McMichael and Spivey, "both works are expressionistic: *Osiris Jones* is the form of expressionistic poetic drama, and *Finnegans Wake* represents probably the height of English expressionistic prose" (65).

[7] Joyce's parody in "Circe" conforms to the conventional understanding of the technique as one of repetition with difference that tends towards mockery rather than tribute (see Linda

Hutcheon), and it provides a fine example of what Gérard Genette classifies in *Palimpsestes* as hypotextuality.

[8] See Lowry's enthusiastic praise for Georg Kaiser in a 1951 letter (*SC* II, 374). In a letter to Robert Giroux of 17 January 1952, Lowry writes that jazz "isn't music perhaps so much as a form of expressionism ... more analogous to literature or poetry, than music" (*SC* II, 504).

[9] In *Joyce's Moraculous Sindbook: A Study of "Ulysses"* (200–202), Suzette Henke argues that by the end of "Circe" there has been a revolutionary alteration in consciousness for Bloom and Stephen. Her argument rests on the claim that Joyce is responsible for the "expressionistic dramas" that expose the shadow selves of Bloom and Stephen. By contrast, Hugh Kenner insists that *Ulysses* is all a surface of style and voice on which it is impossible to distinguish subjectivity from objectivity and that there is no "recoverable truth" (Kenner, 91–93).

[10] The apocalypse passage from "Circe" might be compared with a number of expressionist texts for similarities in image, syntax, punctuation, and general exaggerated effect, but the following outburst from Georg Kaiser's Cashier suggests the parallel Joyce had in mind: "Here I stand. I stand above you. Two are too many. There's space for only one. Loneliness is space; space is loneliness. Coldness is sun. Sun is coldness. The fevered body bleeds. The fevered body shivers. Bare fields. Ice spreading. Who can escape? Where is the way out?" (Kaiser, 72).

[11] In *Recodings*, Hal Foster describes the double bind of what he calls the expressionists' "expressive fallacy" as a "paradox: a type of representation that asserts *presence—of* the artist, of the real" (60).

9

Malcolm Lowry: From the Juvenilia to the Volcano

The earliest extant photograph of Malcolm Lowry shows him, aged about five, seated at a small writing table in his parents' garden (see Figure 1). Scattered on the lawn are what appear to be croquet mallets, but the serious little boy, in his school tie, short pants, and knee socks, sits before an open scribbler and squints at the camera as if interrupted in his writing.

It is tempting to think that, even at this tender age, Lowry knew he would be a writer. Certainly by the time he was sixteen and attending The Leys, a distinguished Methodist public school in Cambridge, where all the Lowry boys were sent, there was no doubt about his fate: he would be a writer, a famous writer. Both in his early letters and in his first published work, Lowry talked about his writing ambitions, boasted about his literary knowledge, and tried out the styles and mannerisms of the writers he admired. He adopted a pen name, drawn from his initials (C.M.L. for Clarence Malcolm Lowry), and signed all his stories in the *Leys Fortnightly*: CAMEL.

In the following remarks, I want to consider these early stories, which CAMEL wrote for his school magazine, and I want to examine one of them, "Satan in a Barrel," in some detail. Like all Lowryans, I have known for years that these stories existed, but I did not pay them any particular attention until a Canadian colleague, Juliet McMaster of the University of Alberta, asked me to prepare a volume on Lowry for her Juvenilia Press series. Having completed ten years of work on the *Collected Letters*, I thought this seemed an easy enough request—although I also knew that nothing written by Malcolm Lowry should be underestimated. To my knowledge, the only scholar who had looked at the *Leys Fortnightly* short stories was Suzanne Kim, and it had been thirty years since she, as it were, discovered these juvenile efforts (see Kim). So the time for another look seemed right. The result is a slim volume containing six stories and a set of annotations, but what was actually involved in preparing the volume and what I learned about Lowry by editing these

FIGURE 1: Photograph of Malcolm Lowry as a boy aged about five years.

stories cannot be measured by the size of *Satan in a Barrel and other early stories* (1999).

Now I take for granted that readers are reasonably familiar with the general outlines of Malcolm Lowry's life and that you know his fiction well—not just *Under the Volcano*, but his other novels, novellas, and stories, and maybe his letters and poetry; therefore, I will not spend much time on these matters. However, I will set the stage a bit—hang the hams in the window, as Lowry would have said—as preparation for my central task, which is to analyse "Satan in a Barrel" and what it might tell us about *Under the Volcano*. Between March 1925 and June 1926, CAMEL published six stories in the *Fortnightly*: "The Light That Failed Not," "Travelling Light," "The Blue Bonnet," "A Rainy Night," "Satan in a Barrel," and "The Repulsive Tragedy of the Incredulous Englishman." Each of these little pieces has its own interest, but I have chosen to privilege "Satan in a Barrel" because it is, in my view, the most substantial of the stories and because it tells us more than any one of the other five about what Lowry the writer was and would be.

But before I get down to business with the story, let me go back to the biography for a moment. All Lowry's early stories are firmly rooted in his life at The Leys and in the period when he was writing them: from the early spring of 1925 to the late spring of 1926. I would suggest that this rootedness is a significant point because it illustrates that, even at the beginning of his career, Lowry used his own immediate experiences for his narratives, wove his daily reading and other activities into his work, and identified intensely with that work.

Lowry would claim in later life that he was never understood by his family, and whatever truth there may be in his claims, he certainly grew apart from his brothers and parents and felt himself to be exiled from home. While overt signs of estrangement cannot be found in the early stories, or in the surviving letters he was writing at the time, both the stories and the letters reveal a young man who held himself somewhat aloof, and was always posing, dramatizing himself, angling for attention ... and writing. Lowry attended the Methodist preparatory school, Caldicote, not far from the family home on the Wirral Peninsula in Cheshire, until 1923, when he followed his three older brothers to The Leys. From all accounts, he cut something of a figure at his public school and managed to survive its rigours quite happily. He played sports, acted in plays, took up the ukulele, and began the drinking for which he would become so famous. Both the stories and his letters from 1925–26 make clear that he had very active interests in theatre, literature, and music. He also participated in the *Leys Fortnightly*; he helped out with the magazine, wrote occasional sports reports for it, published some early poems in its pages, and, on two occasions, he wrote witty letters to the editor—one of which I must say more about. In general then, the picture of Lowry that emerges from the available writing is of a very self-conscious young man, who is already anxious to be taken seriously as a writer, who is reading and borrowing happily from other writers, who is exploring avenues of publication beyond the school magazine, and is flaunting his esoteric knowledge (esoteric, that is, for a public school chap in a school that prided itself on athletics, not the arts).

A few brief examples, in Lowry's own words of course, will suggest to you what I mean. By May of 1926, he had obviously managed to gain a reputation. In a letter to Carol Brown, he tells her that the headmaster (the Reverend Harry Bisseker) had complained about him to the master who edited the *Fortnightly*, W.H. Balgarnie (the model for Mr. Chips in the film *Goodbye, Mr. Chips*). Lowry summarized the complaints about him as follows:

> Bisseker actually phoned Balgarnie for half an hour the other night while I was supping with the latter (via the private master's telephone) telling him the following home truths.
>
> 1 that I was a danger to the school.
>
> 2 that the Fortnightly would be blasted everlastingly if they published my latest excrescence on the snobbishness of prefects singing out of one corner of their mouth in chapel, and giving punishments with the other.

3 that the fortnightly would be blasted everlastingly in the after life, for entertaining such an immoral character as myself on their staff.

4 that my works, fairly smart no-doubt, were viper's productions, cheeseparings and hogwash.

5 that he doubted of late whether they were even smart: that they were mere, braggartly, cynicism.

6 that I had been reading Alec Waugh. (which was quite true, rather a hit, that). that not only had I been reading Alec Waugh, but I had been reading Noel Coward, Michael Arlen, Eugene O'Neill, and Samuel Butler.

7 that I was not original, though I thought I was.

8 that it was rot.

9 That I was a disgrace to the school.

10 That I would continue to be a disgrace to the school.

11 that my works were boa-constricterine and adderesque

12 That they were cheeseparings and hogwash.

(*SC* I, 24–25)

Assuming that the Reverend Bisseker did indeed make such comments, it is somewhat hard now to understand why he would take such exception to Lowry's writing, but the alleged quotation of Bisseker certainly enhances Lowry's importance in his own eyes and in the eyes of the young lady he was trying to impress. But this run-in with the headmaster was not the only or the first time Lowry had caused debate in the pages of the *Fortnightly*. In a letter dated 26 February 1926, "Camel" wrote to the editors of the magazine protesting the views of two fellow students who had criticized "Satan in a Barrel" and some of his sports reports. These two anonymous critical letters and Lowry's reply are worth considering for a moment. Lowry's critics argue that

> The stories over the pen name of "Camel" which have recently been published in the *Fortnightly* have for some time been a source of amazement and disgust to us. But when in your last number we read "Satan in a Barrel" ... we felt that a point had been reached when some protest was surely necessary.

and that,

> the *Fortnightly*['s] stories are written thus ... and thus *** and moreover thus ... And what does the first reporter mean by "fox"; "Pericles"; "torpid"; "Pantagruelian"; and such absurd words? (*SC* I, 5–6)

The budding author replies, at much greater length than his critics and with many witty, erudite (Bisseker might think arrogant and cynical) flourishes. He will not apologise for offending them; instead, he calls them "childish," "immature," and ignorant—the fact that they cannot recognize an allusion to Rabelais being proof of their intellectual poverty. Moreover, he describes their criticisms of his style and material as an insult to the Editor of the *Fortnightly*, whose mature judgement is beyond doubt: "it is throwing mud, not only at myself, but at the escutcheon of the *Fortnightly* Committee, and the escutcheon of the *Fortnightly* Committee, I may say, is so clear that we shave in it every other Saturday morning" (*SC* I, 4). But the criticism that receives the most lively response is the protest over his use of ellipses, or "dots," in both the fiction and the sports reports. Now Lowry would always be defensive about stylistic matters *and* he would always love typographic markers such as dots and dashes—his prose is studded with these features—but here, for the first time, he takes up the cudgels in defence of his stylistic proclivities:

> And dots. I admit (being in a generous mood) on reading through my story, that there were, maybe, just too many of them for some tastes: but this error was partly due to the printers, who are liable to print.. as......... (this with all due respect: no offence taken, and none intended, I'm sure—Tilly of Blooms-bury). [...] Therefore I say, dots to you, Sirs. And I may be permitted to add, having a bad cold, that I shall continue to write as I wish, dotwithstanding. (*SC* I, 5)

Of course, any judgement about Malcolm Lowry's prose style or the significance of his fiction has passed far beyond the views of his public school peers and masters, and it is also not, of course, their views that matter. However, what these letters to Carol Brown and to the *Fortnightly* illustrate about Lowry at sixteen does matter. He was already closely identifying himself with the written word, with writing as his chosen mode of communication, with writers (both popular and serious), and with writing as his chief ambition in life, as, indeed, a *way of life*. When we look at the sequence of letters to Carol Brown (*SC* I, 7–56), we see Lowry posing as a writer, flaunting his abilities as a writer (describing Shakespeare and Zola), peppering his love-letters to her with constant references to magazines that publish short stories, to his reading and his views on writers, and to the stories and plays that he is writing. At one point, he claims to have written a successful short story called "The D Box" (29), and he sends Carol a fragment of a story called "The Yes-and-No Man," which he claims as he own (30). However, these two stories were actually written by an American writer called Richard Connell, whom Lowry describes in his letter to Carol as "the biggest liar, the biggest coward, the bravest man, the most immoral and the most puritanical man, the most insipid drunkard, and the worst and best friend alternately that I hope to have. He drinks to inspire himself [and is ...] quite mad—having in that respect a very similar temperament to myself" (29).

Lowry would retract his claim to these two stories in a subsequent letter to Carol, admitting that he "deceived [her] foully about Richard Connell" (*SC* I, 33) and begging her to "bury Richard Connell quietly in a corner of the garden" (*SC* I, 34), but this business of Richard Connell constitutes the first instance I know, not primarily of plagiarism, but of Lowry's hysterical identifications with other authors and with his dramatization of another's psyche in terms of his own—the blurring of the boundaries, as it were, between self and other—and the fictionalizing of his own inner life. This fleeting Richard Connell episode, occurring at about the same time that he was writing and publishing "Satan in a Barrel" and "The Repulsive Tragedy of an Incredulous Englishman," provides an interesting context within which to consider the stories he *did* write himself.

To read the juvenilia straight through in the order in which they were published (without manuscript evidence there is no way of determining exactly when he wrote them or whether they underwent revision)[1] is to observe several interesting features about the stories themselves and, of course, about the young Lowry as a writer. Although I find merit in each piece, I also think it is obvious that Lowry's stories become more complex and that his control of prose style, narrative form, what today I would call focalization, and intertextuality increase noticeably. "The Light That Failed Not," "Travelling Light," and "The Blue Bonnet" are clever, but basically ephemeral; in these the young writer is trying on styles and short story modes derived (a term I use advisedly) from other popular writers of the day, notably Michael Arlen. In "A Rainy Night," "Satan in a Barrel," and "The Repulsive Tragedy of an Incredulous Englishman," he has moved on, freed himself from "Arlenesque" influences, and found his models in other, better writers such as Marlowe, Goethe, and O'Neill. Moreover, the latter three stories are both more densely textured in imagery and allusion than the first three and considerably more complex in narrative structure. But perhaps what is most fascinating—a key reason for taking juvenilia seriously in the first place—is that these stories reveal many capillary links with Lowry's mature fiction.

All these stories demonstrate Lowry's early love of puns and verbal witticisms; for example, one of his best quips comes at the end of "The Light That Failed Not," when his erring schoolboy turns a familiar axiom, "There's many a slip 'twixt cup and lip,'" into a clever Leysian in-joke (see *Satan*, note 17, 7). They also demonstrate Lowry's abiding love of irony and parody, qualities that characterize his later work and his vision of life and of himself. The posing and self-mockery so evident in his letters (both those written at this time and those written later in life) and mature fiction are already present in these stories.

The main point of "The Light That Failed Not" is that the narrator has made a spectacle of himself and is only saved from further humiliation and persecution by secular intervention. But this quality of self-mockery—or what might be more properly called self-reflexive irony, when the *self* in question is the narrator or central character, not an autobiographical "I"—is also central to each of the last three stories. In "A Rainy Night," a self-righteous, middle-class man completely misreads a fellow human being, with fatal consequences; in "Satan in a Barrel," the entire plot turns on the ironic positioning of the chief character (a point I shall return to); and, in a sense, the last story, "The Repulsive Tragedy," takes the ironic exposure of the schoolboy in the first story and turns it into a much more serious exposé of a writer's pretensions. At sixteen, Lowry was well aware of the power, the limitations, the vulnerability, and the temptations to arrogance, pomposity, and vanity the creative enterprise afforded. This is an awareness that would never leave him and, some might argue, helped to destroy him.

But, on a lighter note, these juvenilia also demonstrate Lowry's developing literary awareness. Everywhere in these stories, even in as slight a one as "The Blue Bonnet," with its arch "apologies" to Michael Arlen, Lowry is both showing off his reading knowledge of writers, from those on The Leys curriculum, such as Chaucer, Shakespeare, and Wordsworth, to contemporary English writers like Kipling, Maugham, and Arlen, or a serious foreign writer like Eugene O'Neill, who would become a far more important influence than any contemporary British writer.[2] He takes great delight in both using and parodying the stylistic quirks of Michael Arlen (the dots, dashes, diction, and locutions), but this *ear* for the *voice* of another writer could be exploited in more serious ways as well, for example, in the O'Neill-inspired speech of the "old Swede" in "A Rainy Night" (*Satan*, 20–27).

Lowry was reading voraciously and far beyond the bounds of any public school curriculum during these years and, more to the point, he was already *digesting* this reading and transforming it into what I call his "caddis-worm" poetics.[3] We can recognize the beginnings of this process of borrowing and transformation for what it is: the first manifestation of a poetic. Even in these early stories, I believe, we can see Lowry gaining control over the process, tuning his ear for language and style, experimenting—through imitation—with the literary, and learning how to deploy, exploit, and transform his sources.

"Satan in a Barrel," more than any of the other stories, reveals typically Lowryan themes, or concerns, that will persist in the mature fiction (*Satan*, 28–38). Chief amongst them is the central role of self-awareness and the complexities of consciousness and perception (whether of self/writer or other, and, for Lowry, the distinction between these two would always be problematic), and, inevitably, alcohol.[4] For anyone at all familiar with Lowry's life or with *Under the Volcano*, it will come as no surprise to find drinking and drunkenness portrayed in these stories. "A Rainy Night" warns against the too-easy assumption that someone who appears dishevelled or incoherent is necessarily a drunkard, but "Satan in a Barrel" provides quite another perspective on the use of alcohol, which, of course, is but one of many resonances between this story and the *Volcano*. "Satan in a Barrel" also reveals Lowry experimenting with dreams and dreaming as both theme and narrative strategy. Where a dream mechanism facilitates and contains the story proper in "Travelling Light" and in "Satan in a Barrel," the ramifications of the dream, as theme and structure, in "Satan" are especially interesting. Lowry's use of focalization, of dream as *staging* the narrative, and of historical fact versus creative fiction sets this story apart from its companions. Moreover, its foreshadowing of characterization, themes, and narrative strategies in *Under the Volcano* only makes it more worthy of analysis.

"Satan in a Barrel" ostensibly takes place in the Tower of London, where the first-person narrator conjures up the incarcerated villain of the Bloody Assizes: George Jeffreys (1645–89), First Baron of Wem, Chief Justice of the King's Bench, and Lord High Chancellor of England. The story covers some of the last hours in the judge's life, as the wicked man struggles to repent, argues with the warden, with voices that he hears, and with God, tries to pray for forgiveness, toys with suicide, vows to stop drinking, and receives with delight (as he apparently did in life) a barrel of Colchester oysters delivered to his Tower cell. However, when he discovers that the barrel contains a halter instead of oysters—his "favorite dish" (34)—he falls to cursing: "I curse you, Jeffreys, vilest of men! I curse the sender of the barrel! I curse the halter! I curse Christianity! but above all Fate, I curse you ... Like Job, I curse the whole of my life" (34). Jeffreys cries out in vain for his voices to come back, but they are silent, and the story crashes to its close.

No doubt Lowry had studied the 1685 Rebellion and the role played by George Jeffreys, "the Judge of the Bloody Assize," in his history classes; any English schoolboy would be expected to know the events, the players, and the politics of that critical period in British history. But it is what Lowry *does* with that history that is so interesting. Yes, we will think we know what is coming, as the first-person narrator prompts his readers in the opening sentences, but, of course, we do not. What follows, after a deft segue from Ben Jonson's toe to Judge Jeffreys in the Tower of London (which at least preserves some vestige of temporal continuity in the seventeenth century), is presented as both a dream and a play.

> I feel perfectly certain that he was not there: I hunted everywhere: heaven was quite a small place. The psychology of dreams is an interesting study. Why was I, of all people, in heaven? A curtain at the back of my mind reefed up suddenly to reveal three stone walls, my mind being the fourth, a grating for a window, a hard bed, a rickety chair or two ... A cell, ostensibly, in the tower of London: most sinister; certainly an abstract creation of my fevered imagination, for I had never visited the place. Discovered—Judge Jeffreys and a warder. (*Satan*, 28–29)

The narrator's bald statement that "a curtain at the back of [his] mind reefed up" to reveal the spectacle/drama of the bloody Judge during his last hours may be heavy-handed but it is, nevertheless, the first example we have of Lowry constructing the kind of retrospective replay of events that he would handle so smoothly in *Under the Volcano* and attempt in other novels. From his position in "an ethereal stall," this narrator focuses, like a camera, on the drama unfolding in Jeffreys's cell: history is about to be pirated into story, the story of a talented but evil man's final torment and damnation. Jeffreys, as Lowry represents him through the eye of his dreamer/narrator, is Faustian. He is, moreover, an avatar of his namesake, Geoffrey Firmin in *Volcano*, who is, in turn, a complex psychological projection of aspects of his creator—Malcolm Lowry. Once we are securely into the dream mechanism in the story-within-the-story, we will stay there until the concluding phrases, when the dream will end abruptly with the crashing down of the curtain and the chiming of clocks. The dreamplay has ended but we, unfortunately, remain inside it, positioned, in fact, with Jeffreys, trapped in the hell of his cell/soul, his damnation, and the narrator's nightmare.

Within this dream structure of story-within-story (or play-within-story), Lowry explores one of his most important themes: the suffering of a soul/psyche struggling with the forces of good and evil (conveyed here in Marlovian voices, as they will also be in *Volcano*), cursing his fate and Christianity, and facing imminent demise from, among other things, "drinking too much brandy" (34). This expressionistic drama-tization of a suffering soul is heightened by the chiming of clocks which serve, through repetition, to unite the story, to enhance the "ethereal" quality of events, and to measure off time, which is running out.[5] Jeffreys, as represented in this "pirated history," is in Hell, the Hell of his story-teller's imagination, that same circle of Hell that Geoffrey Firmin (also a casualty of history) will occupy. My point is this: although Judge Jeffreys is the main focus or object of this story, the primary suffering consciousness is the dreamer/narrator's. "Satan in a Barrel" may not foreground the figure of the writer as obviously as does "The Repulsive Tragedy," but it is nonetheless, and powerfully so, *about* the creative imagination.

What, good heavens, was the sixteen-year-old Lowry going through at this time in his life? What could have provoked or elicited such a vision? Or is this grand guignol story merely the clever result of an over-dramatizing teenaged sensibility? I do not, of course, know precisely, but there is enough known about Lowry's life during these years to tempt me to suggest that in George Jeffreys Lowry recognized the potential storying of himself—of his need for attention and alcohol, his capacity for suffering and evil, and his absorption in self and self-dramatization. The devil in this barrel is the devil of self.

Malcolm Lowry left The Leys in 1927, and he would never again sign anything "CAMEL." But the boy was father to the man, and Clarence Malcolm Lowry took CAMEL with him. Shortly after leaving the school, he spent four months as a deck-hand on the SS *Pyrrhus*, discovered the poetry and fiction of Conrad Aiken, and entered Cambridge University in the fall of 1929. He would shift from being "Tilly" of Bloomsbury to being a passionate young writer actively searching for models and materials. He would discover and meet Nordahl Grieg, who, together with Aiken, was a profound and lasting influence. And he would write constantly and continuously: short stories, letters, *Ultramarine*, and *Lunar Caustic*. All of this writing was what today I would describe as a form of "autobiographics" (see Gilmore): autobiographical fiction in which the blurring of boundaries between self and other and the development of narrative and structural strategies for dramatizing that boundary shift are at least as important and interesting as any factual information the fiction might convey about Lowry's actual life (events, people, places, etc.) Only think of the structure of memory and reverie, located in Dana's perceiving consciousness, and focalized entirely through Dana in *Ultramarine*, or of the nightmare staging of consciousness in *Lunar Caustic*. While the dream-staging device in "Satan in a Barrel" may be more clumsy than the dramatization of consciousness in either *Ultramarine* or *Lunar Caustic*, I think we can trace the development of the strategy and the need to thematize such dramatization of the self right back to that juvenile story. By the time of *Under the Volcano*, Lowry was ready to write and stage his ultimate performance.

No one who has read *Under the Volcano* is unaware that the entire thrust of chapter one is to get us to the theatre, or cinema (Lowry uses both terms) in Quahnahuac. By small nudges and references—Laruelle sighting the distant lights of the town's "one cinema" (11) going on and off, his promise to meet Vigil at "the cine" (13), his memories of films he made (15), and of Yvonne as an actress (18)—we are brought to the cinema with Laruelle (29) and stand with him, out of the rain, in the darkened "shelter of the theatre entrance" (30). From this point to the end of the chapter, we are with Laruelle in the cinema/cantina, from where we can see into the darkened theatre, and we read, over his shoulder, the book of Marlowe's plays and the lost letter that the Consul wrote to Yvonne that slips from the book's pages. As the French filmmaker has already done, in conjuring up the remembered scenes of Geoffrey and Yvonne embracing in the ruins of Maximilian's garden, of Geoffrey during the war, or of Geoffrey in the Hell's Bunker when Laruelle and the "Old Bean" were young, Jacques will once more be used to stage a very dramatic scene—this time the story-cum-letter of the Consul's cry for his lost wife to return. And, as we know so well, the scenes we are about to read/witness after the burning of the letter and the tolling of the bell—"*dolente ... dolore!*" (47)—are all about Yvonne's return on the Day of the Dead one year before. Here, as in "Satan in a Barrel," Lowry uses a fictional focalizer (the "I" in the story, Jacques in *Volcano*) to see, stage, or present the performance that will unfold before us. The shift from stage play to film, while interesting for other reasons, is less important here than the strategically staged or performed quality of the scene. In a sense, *Under the Volcano* is Jacques's film; it is also his recurrent nightmare, a dream that he cannot wake up from and that we too are caught up in, an infernal machine of memory, guilt, and desire that Lowry knew would work so well.

It is Jacques who links Geoffrey Firmin with Joseph Conrad, or, more impor-tantly with a Conrad character, when Lowry has him "think of the Consul as a kind of more lachrymose pseudo 'Lord Jim' living in self-imposed exile" (39), but that comparison enables us to link Geoffrey and his story back to Lowry, who saw him-self living in a kind of self-imposed exile and who dramatized himself living that way even as a public school boy with a bizarre fascination for another exiled soul and evil genius ... George Jeffreys. While the leap from Bloody Jeffreys to Geoffrey Firmin, ex-Consul, may seem a large one, I think that both "characters" (the one no more *real* than the other) are avatars for aspects of Lowry himself. In some sense, he identified with these characters, not because they sentenced people to death or cremated captured enemy seamen, but because they had great powers, misused them, drank excessively, suffered for their sins, and lost. That Lowry does so much with this basic formula in *Volcano* should not blind us to the operation of a basic and creatively productive relationship between self-dramatization (in his life and his letters) and the projection of a dramatized self-as-other in his fiction. To move from the one mode of performance to the other, Lowry needed a narrative strategy, and that strategy is the one, tried out for the first time in "Satan in a Barrel," of a focalizing narrator who conjures up on the stage/screen of his mind the inner life and spiritual struggles of a doomed soul with whom both the focalizer and his creator are closely identified. If Jacques Laruelle sees in the Consul a "lachrymose 'Lord Jim,'" I see in the adult Malcolm Lowry the teenager, who signed himself "Camel," and the little boy, who always knew he would be a writer.

(1999)

Notes

* References to *Under the Volcano* are to the 1963 Penguin edition.

[1] In "Three Letters Home," I have discussed the fate of Lowry's papers and other possessions, which were left in the family home of Inglewood. According to Lowry's nephew, Martin Lowry, the house had to be prepared for sale in 1951, after Mrs. Lowry's death, and Martin, aged ten at the time, was responsible for carrying papers from Malcolm's former room to a great bonfire in the garden. It is possible, even likely, that many early manuscripts and school notebooks were destroyed at this time. As a result, the editing of these stories has been a simple matter of careful transcription from the *Leys Fortnightly*. Annotation has been another, more challenging matter.

[2] Although D.H. Lawrence, James Joyce, and T.S. Eliot were well-known to Lowry by the late twenties, the most significant influences upon his work are Nordahl Grieg and Conrad Aiken.

[3] In "Respecting Plagiarism," I discuss Lowry's fears about plagiarism and the poetic he developed from his practice of borrowing from other writers. The phrase "caddis-worm school of writers" is Rupert Brooke's ("Respecting Plagiarism," 113).

[4] Many other issues of importance to Lowry also emerge in these early stories, such as life at sea, the figure of the double or *Doppelgänger*, and fears about authority; the ones I emphasize are those that seem to me to have particular significance in his work.

[5] Lowry's interest in expressionism in painting, film, and theatre can be traced back to his public school days (see *Sursum Corda!* I, 38) and proved a lasting influence on his art (see Grace, *Regression and Apocalypse*, 163–84).

10

The Play's the Thing:
Reading 'Lowry' in the Dark Wood of Freud, Cocteau, and Barthes

The Author himself ... can or could some day become a text like any other .... [H]e has only to see himself as a being on paper and his life as a bio-graphy .... [T]he critical undertaking ... will then consist in returning the documentary figure of the author into a novelistic, irretrievable, irresponsible figure, caught up in the plural of its own text.

(Barthes)

JOCASTE: Oui, mon enfant, mon petit enfant .... Les choses qui paraissent abominables aux humains, si tu savais, de l'endroit où j'habite, si tu savais comme elles on peu d'importance.

(Cocteau)

To-day, just as then, many men dream of having sexual relations with their mothers, and speak of the fact with indignation and astonishment. It is clearly the key to the tragedy and the complement to the dream of the dreamer's father being dead. The story of Oedipus is the reaction of the imagination to these two typical dreams.

(Freud)

I

Many years ago I believed that I would never attempt a psychoanalytical reading of Malcolm Lowry, either of his work or of his biography. Oddly enough, however, editing his letters for *Sursum Corda!* has tempted me to do just that. The first time I gave in to this temptation was in "Respecting Plagiarism: Tradition, Guilt, and Malcolm Lowry's 'Pelagiarist Pen,'" but here I am giving in once more to the temptation to read "Lowry" through what Roland Barthes would call his *bio-graphy*.

Whether or not Lowry's letters will help me find a way through the dark wood of Lowry's imagination, they continue to beckon, to invite me to *return* once more to Lowry's texts and to some of the unfinished questions in "Respecting Plagiarism."

That study grew directly out of my work on volume one of *Sursum Corda!*, more particularly out of issues raised by two very striking letters (one to John Davenport, the other to Nordahl Grieg)[1] that threw an interesting sidelight on Lowry's early anxiety over plagiarism. In 1989 I discovered Michel Schneider's psychoanalytical analysis of plagiarism, *Voleurs de mots: Essai sur le plagiat, le psychoanalyse et la pensée* (1985), and this fascinating study supported my theory that Lowry's plagiarism phobia (Schneider considers Lowry to have had a psychosis that verged on schizophrenia) was not only deeply rooted in some early childhood trauma, but that it was fundamental to what I saw, and still see, as his poetics. The question I did not explore in "Respecting Plagiarism" (and I stress explore—this is not a matter of answers) was: if Lowry could work with this poetics, make it work for him, so powerfully, in fact, that he could write *Under the Volcano*, what happened after 1947? His poetics did not change; if anything, what I called in "Respecting Plagiarism" his "caddis-worm tendencies" intensified (119). His obsession with plagiarism continued, and to that long line of "family jewels" that he struggled to "reset" must be added his own work.

None of this, of course, is new to Lowryans, who know the post-*Volcano* story and remember Lowry's own lament:

> Success is like some horrible disastar
> Worse than your house burning, the sounds of ruination
> As the roof tree falls succeeding each other faster
> While you stand, the helpless witness of your damnation.
>
> Fame like a drunkard consumes the house of the soul
> Exposing that you have worked for only this—
> Ah, that I had never known such a treacherous kiss
> And had been left in darkness forever to work and fail. (*CP*, 214)

Many Lowryans have struggled to make sense of what went wrong. Many have wondered why, especially when he got the Random House contract with Albert Erskine in 1952, he could not produce the finished texts that Brother Albert expected. To read Lowry's letters in volume two of *Sursum Corda!* is to read a narrative of explanation, explication, and excuse—accidents, illnesses, deaths of friends and loved ones, continuing involvement with *Volcano*, cold weather, lack of money, the list goes on and on—and underlying all of these actual events is fear.

Lowry's fears were legion and he was only too aware of them, as the writing from the post-*Volcano* years shows. Working on volume two of *Sursum Corda!* brought me face to face with Lowry's fears, with the fact that he could and did write complex and exquisite letters when he could not write, or finish, what we call his fiction, and with my own recurring question: why? Perhaps it is only human to want to know why. If there is an enigma, a seeming mystery, we seem to want to solve it. Perhaps we are all, like Oedipus, challenged by the Sphinx. And Malcolm Lowry is a formidable Sphinx.

Although I am not what Douglas Day would call a "good Freudian" (466), I do think I have found a key, if not quite *the* key that Freud claimed to find; therefore, before I describe what I propose to do—and not do—here, let me say a few words about my three prefacing quotations. I begin with an epigraph from Barthes in *S/Z* for several reasons: in that exemplary text Barthes shows us how to read a text as a plurality of texts within the text; he reminds us, moreover, that an author can become a text, almost as if he had Lowry in mind. Finally, there is a warning in this passage, a warning to which I want, for the moment, to turn a blind eye, even if I will inevitably, perforce, have to return to it in the end: that the "documentary figure of the author" will escape me into his own *auto-bio-graphy*. And I will return to Barthes in other ways as well, in other citations as complex, paradoxical, and provocative as this one from *S/Z*—for example, that the pleasure of the text is its "staging of an appearance-as-disappearance ... of the (absent, hidden, or hypostatized) father" and that the "writer is someone who plays with his mother's body" (Barthes 1975, 10, 37).

The passage from Jean Cocteau's *La Machine infernale* in my second epigraph, spoken by the dead Jocasta, is my key for several reasons: it is after all the passage read and misread by the Consul in chapter seven of *Volcano*, where some crucial contextual information is withheld or even avoided and repressed (by Geoffrey or Malcolm?); it is from a play that made a great impact on Lowry, a play that he returns to in two important letters written during the last year of his life. And, finally, it is *not* the passage that Freud sees as the key to the Oedipus complex. Indeed, it could not be, because the speech Cocteau gives to Jocasta does not occur in *Oedipus Rex*, where the dead Jocasta does not return as a ghostly mother to guide her blinded son. Freud found the key he was looking for in another of the queen's speeches to Oedipus: "Many a man ere now in dreams hath lain / With her who bare him. He hath least annoy / Who with such omens troubleth not his mind."[2]

If I am not a good Freudian, it is because I have always resisted Freud's model of the human psyche, and I have always resisted Freudian readings of Lowry (or other authors for that matter).[3] However, a great deal of the recent criticism and theory that I find most useful does return to Freud, often to reread and remake him, and there can be no doubt that Lowry read Freud, read about Freud, and was influenced or inspired by Freud at second hand. If he had not already discovered Freud on his own before 1928, Conrad Aiken certainly introduced him to the subject, or at least to his interpretations of Freud, so that in later years Lowry could joke with Aiken about being an "Oedipus in his post-Jocasta period" (*SC* I, 261) and compare his works-in-progress, "Dark as the Grave," "Eridanus," and "La Mordida," to Daniel

Paul Schreber's *Denkwürdigkeiten eines Nervenkranken.*[4] Freud and the Oedipus complex were part of the literary, artistic, and intellectual discourse with which Lowry grew up, a discourse that is still very much with us and that a new generation of Lowry scholars is using to read *Lowry* (see Bock, Cross 1997, and Vice 1997).

Despite my long involvement with the Lowry letters, I am not going to discuss editing here; nevertheless, I am going to consider letters, two letters in particular—the Lowrys' relatively short 11 December 1956 letter (*SC* II, no. 698) to Elaine and David Markson, and Malcolm's long, complicated 22 February 1957 letter (*SC* II, no. 705) to "dear old Dave." What I hope to reveal is how a Lowry letter works—and believe me it does, like "a sort of machine … as I have found out" (*SC* I, 506)—and what it can tell us about Lowry and about reading Lowry. Of course, I have not chosen just any two letters. Both are from the last six months of his life, both are to Markson and are about writing fiction, and in both Lowry is deeply involved with the Oedipus story and its implications.

Lowry's ostensible reason for writing the second of these letters is to give writerly advice to Markson, "to play Goethe as well as Pushkin to [his] Eckermann-Gogol" (*SC* II, 885), and that advice begins with reiterated recommendations that he read, above all, Cocteau's *Machine infernale*. That Lowry should have stressed Cocteau's version of Oedipus above several others he mentions, including the Sophocles, Keats, Yeats's translation/transcription, Robert Graves's *Greek Myths*, and Freud should come as no surprise. We know that he saw the première of the play twice in Paris in 1934, that the performance impressed him deeply, that he owned a copy of the first French edition, and that the play operates within *Under the Volcano* as a type of *mise en abyme.*[5] What is remarkable is Lowry's vivid recollection of the play and the way in which he contextualizes it in his February 1957 letter to Markson, twenty-three years after he saw it performed.

I shall need to contextualize it as well, and to review the play itself because it has not received the close attention, in connection with Lowry, that I believe it deserves. An essential part of that context, of course, is Freud's theory of the Oedipus complex and what I see as the critical differences between the Cocteau and Freud interpretations of Sophocles, and these interpretations return us inevitably to theories of the unconscious, of trauma in childhood and family relations, and to Lowry who once said (or was it Plantagenet? or Lawhill?) that "return to the presexual revives the necessity for nutrition" (*LC*, 266). Now I am not suggesting that the play's the thing in which I'll *catch* Lowry's unconscious. However, Cocteau's play, together with the play of Lowry's memory and words that surround it in these letters, does suggest that a return to Lowry's letters will provide clues to the answers for some nagging questions: Why, for example, was he remembering Cocteau so vividly in 1957? Why was he having such difficulty completing any new fiction after the publication of *Under the Volcano* but apparently having no problem writing Markson's fiction for him? Why did he turn against Margerie with such intense hostility, notably in these latter years (see Day, 36–37), and why, in the final analysis, did his "caddis-worm" poetics fail him?[6] In what follows, I work backwards from Lowry's letters, to Cocteau and then to Freud, before returning to Lowry and these haunting questions.

II

When the Lowrys wrote to Elaine and David Markson from The White Cottage on 11 December 1956, they were only recently reunited after Margerie's collapse and month-long "snooze" in hospital. Her breakdown had come on the heels of Lowry's release from his second ordeal in Atkinson Morley's Hospital, but somehow, by December, they both seemed well and Lowry was "working like absolute sin" on *October Ferry to Gabriola*, which, so he claimed, he was "managing to eat ... a little more than it eats me" (*SC* II, 866). Markson had begun work on a novel using the Oedipus theme, and this immediately caught Lowry's attention. The letter is jointly written, and in his section, Malcolm protests that Margerie has not taken "your Oedipus book seriously enough" (865). "Have you got your Cocteau's Machine Infernale well oiled?" he asks; "sleeping with Yeats under the bed" (865).[7] And he goes on to remind Markson that, in Cocteau's play, "the Sphinx falls in love with Oedipus, & then eats him I think" (865, she does fall in love with, but does not *eat* Oedipus, which is a nice Freudian slip on Malcolm's part!).

Lowry's main contribution to this letter is a playful "blurb" for Markson's book in which he describes it as a "pulsating drama of a mother's love that triumphed even beyond the grave to give Psychoanalysis its proudest name! THE STORY *BEHIND* THE FREUD LEGEND." In a postscript he lets loose with a series of witty and outrageous declamations:

> SEE kingly pride dragged in the dust ... The Sphinx Humbled! What did Nasser's Mother really look like? You'll find out when you see Oedipus confronted by the Lion-Faced Lady! ... See the Young Oedipus & the Lion-Faced Lady! See the Sphinx feeding! ... HEAR THE FIRST AND MOST SEXUAL QUIZ ON EARTH! (*SC* II, 866)

Reading this, one could be excused for thinking Lowry was imagining a film or a play, not a novel. What Markson thought of it I can't say.

Lowry's 22 February 1957 letter to Markson is long and extremely dense, in many ways reminiscent of his 25 and 27 August 1951 letters to Markson in which he described his lost "In Ballast to the White Sea" (*SC* II, nos. 467 and 468). Douglas Day described those letters as "full of qualifications, amplifications, mystifications—so convoluted, ultimately, that one almost finds it hard to regret the loss of such an impossibly complex novel" (124). And much the same could be said about this 1957 letter to Markson, except that this time the novel Lowry was writing existed only in the letter.[8] The letter consists of five sheets of 21 x 27.5 cm letter paper, most filled on recto and verso with Lowry's tiny script, and there are several marginalia; it takes up just over seventeen pages in its published form.

Lowry expends three pages on a general description of his reading, news about a reprint of *Volcano*, and chit-chat about radio programs and plays, before coming to grips with his real subject: "I feel I have done less than justice to your idea of the Oedipus novel by simply writing you some facetious blurbs" (878), he says, and for the rest of the letter (fourteen more printed pages) he makes up for his early blurbs. Again he stresses the importance of Cocteau: "Your ideas all seem to me excellent, but you really and seriously must read Cocteau's Infernale Machine if you haven't already done so: it could not confuse your purpose and is one of the finest possible works" (878). From there he moves into a detailed analysis of "the whole Oedipus myth" (879), paying especially close attention to Robert Graves's 1955 *Greek Myths*. According to Lowry, Graves argues that the "Freudian theory that the 'Oedipus Complex' is an instinct common to all men" was suggested by a deliberate perversion of the source myths in Sophocles and other Greek playwrights, and he goes on to comment that "this does not of itself discredit the Freudian theory" so much as shift critical focus to "the curious compulsion in man ... to repeat [the story] in its perverted form" (880).[9] This perversion, so Lowry reports Graves to Markson, is that Oedipus was punished for trying "to substitute patrilineal for matrilineal laws of succession" (880), *not* for murdering his father and sleeping with his mother.[10] Lowry finds this Graves material sufficiently interesting to insist that he will copy the relevant pages for Markson if he cannot lay his hands on the book, but he warns Markson not to follow Graves by having his Jocasta throw herself from a rock like the Sphinx instead of hanging herself, as she does in Sophocles and, even more spectacularly, in Cocteau.

At this point, Lowry turns his attention to Markson's fiction, two published stories—"The Happiest Gun Alive" and "White Apache"—and the Oedipus novel in progress, and his proposal is for nothing less than a total re-scripting of Markson's published stories into a major opus on the Oedipal theme (which, as we have already seen, Lowry is attempting to modify, *pace* Cocteau and Graves). He begins with a modest demurral—a rhetorical strategy that he repeats several times in this letter: "I had and have for you one of the happiest ideas for a novel since Miss Lonelyhearts and Nathaniel [sic] West were apprentice seamen: anyway I hereby present it to you for whatever you want to make of it or not" (881).[11]

To recapitulate the details of Markson's stories would only add unnecessarily to the complexities, not to mention the length, of my argument. In any case, "The Happiest Gun Alive," which Lowry sees as something like a portrait of the artist as a young man, has not yet been located. The main points are that both stories are "westerns" ("Happiest Gun" is about the historical gunslinger Clay Allison) and that Lowry finds interesting problems for the writer in both. The hero/narrator

/writer of the stories quickly becomes, not Markson's but "*our* protagonist" (881, emphasis added), and Lowry renames him Thomas More. The artistic More, who is obliged to write "brutal if lively pieces" (881) about men of action like Clay Allison in order to make a living, then becomes a composite character split off from his active *Doppelgänger*, and the drama of the work, as Lowry proposes it, comes from More's attempts to reintegrate his personality, his psyche, and his art as Thomas Claymore. "The necessary hams," Lowry exclaims, "are by now beginning to be hung in the window": "thunder is growling as we get set for the interior & exterior drama that we now begin to see must end by the reconciliation of Clay & More; or the triumphant triumph of More; or the disastrous triumph of Clay: or catabasis into catabysses of both Clay & More or final extinction into the Ultimate Clay of everyone in the cast" (882). In this passage readers of Lowry will recognize the locutions and the theme, which has yet to be fully elaborated in structural terms, from that famous January 1946 letter to Cape. Moreover, this story (Lowry's, if not Markson's) is already sounding familiar.

Lowry makes much of the Claymore and Sir Thomas More allusions and associations of *their* protagonist's name and identity. The Sir Thomas connection takes him (via the Irish poet Thomas Moore, who did not write Thomas Wolfe's poem) to "The Burial of Sir John More after Corunna," which, in turn, reminds him of Oedipus wandering "as a blind beggar until he came to his Colonus, or Corunna."[12] But the associations are more than literary. He tells Markson that his "Clay Allison, on the cover [of the as-yet-undiscovered men's magazine], looks exactly like Juan Fernando Marquez, the original of Dr. Vigil in *Volcano*" (883) and that he, Lowry, is beginning to identify with Markson's More character: "I'm getting to identify myself a bit with your character here: but it looks to me like an excellent opportunity for abreaction,—disguised, overt, angry, understanding, bored, or all 5 at once—of your own personal experience" (883).

But Lowry is not content to leave the connections there. His own imagination, even perhaps his unconscious, is pushing him to develop the "psychoanalytic" ramifications, "secular or literary," of "More's more serious work on a novel on Oedipus" (884). Seen from this angle, says Lowry, the sheriff in "White Apache" is an aspect of More's superego, which together with the text of the successful (a point he stresses) story itself, pushes "our" hero towards his "Girl" and the "Eros-Life wish" and away from "the trigger-happy Thanatos-Bound Clay" who represents his "Dark Doppelgänger" (884).

"Are you with me?" Lowry asks, "Iss ver gut, n'est ce pas?" (884). Then he launches into a cabbalistic riff on the competing forces of creation and destruction, most notably self-destruction, the desire for death, and the temptation of suicide (885), which must be overcome and made use of, like the "Unconscious in his Art, the purely physical or sexual ... in his personal life" because, as Lowry announces, "More will fail to achieve full existence as a man (or make anyone else happy for that matter) unless equally he realises or attempts nobly to realise himself as an artist in the best sense" (885).

Just in case Markson has not followed him thus far, or is not convinced that this is all very good, Lowry blocks out the chapters of Markson's book for him. In doing so, he has "added a chapter or so" (886) and significantly altered the time scheme. The novel now has six chapters:

> I = "Happiest Gun Alive," written by More about Clay and set in Texas in 1879.
>
> II = Tom More, in New York on a night in 1957, broods on the story in I.
>
> III = "White Apache," written by More and published in the *Saturday Evening Post* for 29 September 1956.
>
> IV = More, same time and place as II, now identifying himself with Oedipus and brooding on the story in III.
>
> V = A section of the Oedipus novel that has been rejected and is set in "Thebes. Greece. BC?"
>
> VI = More broods on V. (*SC* II, 886)

This is as far as Lowry gets with the chapters because the Oedipal associations of the plot carry him off into a lengthy excursus on Freud and the "alternative endings & resolutions of his [More's] Oedipus story" (887), all of which More will brood upon while watching a film of his own "Happiest Gun Alive," while accompanied by "a girl who is really the same as the White Apache's girl in III" (887).

I will return to these endings and resolutions, but the structure of this Lowryan novel for Markson invites a few preliminary observations. Lowry has, in fact, suggested an involuted, embedded narrative structure that privileges the writer's imagination (or unconscious) as the fundamental subject of the fiction. This structure parallels very closely the kind of narrative he was struggling with himself, a narrative in which everything written was contained within everything else, connected and interconnected with everything else, in an obsessive form of *auto-bio-graphy*. It is yet another articulation of Lowry's own theme: it is the story, as he lays it out for Albert Erskine (*SC* II, no. 512), of his own protagonist of *The Voyage That Never Ends*, Sigbjørn Wilderness, who is "not, in the ordinary sense in which one encounters novelists or the author in novels, a novelist [but ...] a sort of underground man [...] making up his life as he goes along, & trying to find his vocation" (*SC* II, 538).

In short, what Lowry is doing in this letter to Markson is transferring his own themes, obsessions, anxieties, and inabilities to write, contain, or control his material to Markson and identifying Markson's protagonist with Sigbjørn whom, as we know, Lowry proudly defended as *his Doppelgänger* (*SC* II, 538). He is at once so consumed by this self-reflexive and narcissistic narrative (despite his disclaimers about who was eating whom) that he can only think in these terms. In fact, I would argue that he is asking Markson to take the story over, lock, stock, and barrel, to relieve him/Lowry/Sigbjørn of the burden of writing and, as always with Lowry, *living* it. He is, in effect, asking his literary, adopted son to carry on, to assume the creative task of integration, to, as it were, kill him off.

But let me stop there and return to Lowry's letter. After a long detour on the word "compromise," the nature of the "perfect work of art," and a speculation that Freud discovered "greater artistic integrity" (887) in the "lie" (or compromise with the truth) of Sophocles' *Oedipus Rex* than exists in the truth that Robert Graves claims to have uncovered in the Greek myth, Lowry asks Markson (or is it himself he is addressing?): "Then who, to wind up, in all this, is your Iocaste, who your Laius, who your Sphinx? [I]f the Sheriff or The White Apache or both are disguised higher selves, are they, likewise, disguised father images when we shift on to the Oedipean level to be slain?" (890).

It is at this point that the machinery of Lowry's argument shifts into high gear on the matter of Oedipus or, more precisely, "Oedipusses" (890), because Lowry sees other meanings in the Oedipus story from the one constructed by Sophocles and chosen by Freud, and he is at pains to convince Markson to depart from a rigid Freudian misreading, however artistic, at least far enough to allow other possibilities to emerge through the "contrapuntal" structure of his narrative. These possibilities include the idea that Oedipus found comfort, even happiness, being led away from Thebes by his daughter Antigone, that "Oedipus [is] an almost archetypal figure of exile & wandering" (891), and that "the most important point [is] the identity of Iocaste": "She is, of course, Art herself here, the higher Muse, the only woman with whom he can commit lawful incest, while having another wife of his own" (892).

If Markson wondered what in hell Lowry was blathering on about in this letter, the key to an explanation is not missing so much as partially hidden. Barthes would say it was veiled! Lowry has twice urged that Markson read Cocteau, and now in his "P.P.S." he returns to *La Machine infernale* for which, he tells Markson, Cocteau "presented me with a box seat for two nights in succession" (892). This time he returns to Cocteau's play to recommend that Markson borrow "the Sphinx's familiar, the Jackal God, Anubis [who] trots around dog-masked in the marital chamber on the wedding night, hissing and spilling the terrible beans into the conjugal ears while they are asleep" (892). If Markson was paying attention, he would surely have suspected that something was odd here: what's this? the conjugal couple asleep on their wedding night? and how did a dog-masked Anubis enter the room or, more to the point, why, and what does he represent? For answers to these questions I must turn, not to Sophocles or Freud, but to Cocteau and the play within the play of Lowry's fiction, of this letter to Markson, and just possibly of his *auto-bio-graphy*.

III

La Machine infernale was written in 1933, at a time when Cocteau was suffering from opium poisoning and still mourning the untimely death of his first great love, the young poet Raymond Radiquet. This was not the first time he had worked with Sophocles, and he had a profound, if idiosyncratic, interest in other Greek myths as well.[13] But it was *La Machine infernale*, in its apparently stunning Comédie des Champs Elysées production by the Théâtre Louis Jouvet in April 1934 that established Cocteau's reputation as an important, innovative French playwright. The play ran for sixty-four performances, with Cocteau playing the role of the narrator, and by the end he was a celebrity (Brown, 311).

Later responses to the play by biographers and critics have, however, been oddly mixed. For example, Frederick Brown describes it as "a dark tribute to Mme Cocteau [the playwright's mother]" (308), and he notes the degree to which Cocteau has mixed Sophocles with an "intaglio of further borrowings" (310). "*La Machine infernale*," he concludes, "has the personality of a master tinker's vehicle, composed of old spare parts ingeniously riveted together with gimmicks" (310).[14] Francis Steegmuller is dismissive; in his view the spectacular production concealed the fact that Cocteau had reduced "a high old legend ... fairly close to the level of modern situation-comedy" (431). Lowry, who was clearly impressed with the sheer spectacle of the piece (see also Landers, Wildman, and "Jean Marais, Jean Cocteau et *La Machine infernale*"), did not miss its allusions to Freud and Hamlet, its modernity, and its comedic power (Cocteau's Oedipus, remember, strikes Lowry as comforted, even happy).

Cocteau himself has described the story of Oedipus as a "frightful comedy" that he complicates in his own treatment of the subject. He makes this comment in "On Being Invisible" from *Journal d'un Inconnu* and in the context of some very interesting observations about the Sphinx. About Freud he writes: "Freud burgled poverty-stricken dwellings. Out of them he got a few pieces of wretched furniture and a few erotic pictures. He never sanctified the transcendental in the abnormal. He did not offer a welcome to the great disorders. He offered the pestiferous a private confessional ... Freud's error is to have turned our tenebrosity into a protection for bits of furniture, and this discredits it" (Cocteau 1959, 23, 25). And the reason—or a reason—for this attack on Freud can be found in the same passages when he insists upon the importance of the Sphinx, whom, so Cocteau argues, the gods trick Oedipus into betraying (25). It is this betrayal, insists Cocteau, that makes Oedipus like Orpheus, in that both figures are punished by being robbed of their muse. Who plays the muse in Cocteau's revisioning of the Oedipal drama remains to be seen, though Lowry has already given Markson his opinion.

In *La Machine infernale*, it seems to me, Cocteau creates a parody of Sophocles and a radical rereading of Freud. The play has four acts: act one takes place during a stormy summer night on the ramparts outside Thebes; act two takes place simultaneously on a deserted hillside over-looking Thebes (the narrator tells us to "imagine that we can wind back the last few minutes [of act one] and relive them elsewhere" [33]); act three is the famous bedroom scene that so impressed Lowry; and act four, which takes place seventeen years later, is the revelation and resolution.[15] Each act is introduced by the narrator (there is no chorus), whose remarks are prophetic, ironic, and slightly cheeky. To introduce the third act, for example, he tells us that Oedipus and Jocasta are "asleep on their feet" ("Ils dormant debout") and, despite "a few polite hints," are "too tired to see the trap that is closing on them forever" (60).

Act one is, in many ways, a parody of *Hamlet*. The ghost of Laius appears to a couple of soldiers, but he is a very pale imitation of King Hamlet. When Jocasta shows up with Tiresias to confirm the rumour that someone is trying to warn her of something, the Ghost is incapable of being seen or heard. He babbles fretfully from the sidelines and is finally hauled away by "invisible guards" (31) before he can utter the word "son," let alone allow his full, frightful tale to unfold. In any case, no one is listening. Jocasta is preoccupied with her scarf, which keeps trying to strangle her, her dreams about a baby that becomes "a sticky pulp" and fastens itself to her mouth and belly (18), and the handsome young soldier who has clearly caught her fancy. As she reminds the querulous Tiresias, "All little boys say, 'I want to be grown up so I can marry my mother.' It isn't foolish, Tiresias. Is there a liaison sweeter, more cruel, and yet more proud, than that of a son and a young mother?" (28). Incest is not a problem for this Jocasta, at least not yet.

Half of act two is over before Oedipus comes on stage, and when he does appear he is a decidedly adolescent character—vain, rather stupid, intemperate, and childish, rather like a teenager in search of adventure. The Sphinx, dressed as a seventeen-year-old girl in white, dominates the act, first with Anubis, whose head she cradles in her lap, then with a passing mother and son, and finally with Oedipus. Cocteau's Sphinx is tired of killing young men, and she vows to fall in love with the next one who comes along, give him the answer to the riddle, and then die. Anubis warns her that it will not be quite so easy, but when Oedipus shows up, things unfold according to plan. Oedipus boasts to her that he is off to "kill the monster" whom he will recognize from her "breast and claws" (46), and when she asks him if he has ever killed anyone, he tells her about accidentally killing an old man at the crossroads to Delphi and Daulia. The Sphinx, realizing that this is her man, goes through a splendid staging of her powers, reduces Oedipus to a grovelling boy calling his mother, and tells him the riddle and its simple answer. When she then asks him the riddle—for real, as it were—he repeats what he has just been told, shouts that he has won, and runs off towards Thebes. Moments later he reappears because it has dawned on him that he had best have some visible proof of his victory. Again the Sphinx helps him. She borrows Anubis's head so that when Oedipus carts her body off to Thebes, she will be recognizable as the monster. Oedipus, impressed, exclaims: "Amazing … women think of everything" (57).

Act three is, for my purposes, the most important. It opens on the wedding night in "Jocasta's bedroom [which is] red as a butcher's shop set down among Municipal buildings." At the centre of the platform is the bed, "covered with white furs"; "at the foot of the bed [there is] an animal's skin and a cradle to the left" (61). Jocasta and Oedipus enter, and his first pronouncement—meant to reassure Jocasta—is that "you are me, and I am you" (61, "C'est pareil"). There is a major confrontation with Tiresias, in which the seer warns him and is nearly strangled for his pains, but the key exchange between the two men goes as follows:

TIRESIAS: Do you really love her [Jocasta], Oedipus?

OEDIPUS: With all my soul.

TIRESIAS: Do you love to take her in your arms?

OEDIPUS: Most of all I love to be taken in her arms.

TIRESIAS: Thank you for making the distinction. You're young … very young. Jocasta is old enough to be your mother. Yes, I know what you are going to say …

OEDIPUS: I am going to say that I have always dreamed of that kind of love … a love—almost maternal. (66–67)

And so the stage is set for the rest of the act, an act in which the newly married couple talk, dream, and sleep, but certainly do not make love.

Clues as to what is really going on here are scattered liberally about the dialogue and stage. Oedipus tells Jocasta a fabricated version of his meeting with the Sphinx, but Jocasta has fallen asleep; then, they both fall asleep only to have Anubis pop out from under the animal skin parroting Oedipus's boasts and threats from act two (see SC II, Figure 24); Oedipus wakes screaming from his nightmare and Jocasta soothes him. "What a big child!" she sighs, as she tries to change his clothes. "Yes, mother," he replies (78). When she sees the holes in his feet, she is horrified, and this leads her to describe how she abandoned her own baby nineteen years ago.

Oedipus, however, just cannot stay awake. He lies across the bed with his head on the cradle and falls asleep while Jocasta listens to a drunk singing about her age and stares into a mirror. Act three closes with Jocasta carrying the mirror frame to centre stage and staring through the frame at the audience. The effect of this tableau must have been stunning: the audience is face to face with what I will call its Symbolic Mother, who stares at it, unseeing and all-seeing, just like the Sphinx, the perfect image of its deepest fears and needs. Oedipus, meanwhile, "is snoring gently" (83).

Affairs move swiftly in act four, and this is the only act that follows Sophocles at all closely. Oedipus learns the truth from the Shepherd; Jocasta hangs herself, off-stage, with that troublesome scarf from act one (Cocteau was apparently recalling Isadora Duncan's death); and Oedipus blinds himself with her brooch. However, the ending of the play is pure Cocteau and very important to my reading of "Lowry." As Oedipus is stumbling about blind and bloody, the stage instructions inform us that "*Jocasta's ghost appears in the doorway, white and beautiful, with the long red scarf wound around her neck and her eyes closed*" (93). Oedipus thinks she is alive, but it is only because he is blind that he can see her. She explains that his wife is dead and that she is his mother come to help him. She leads him away, as he clutches her dress and sobs, "Mother!" (95), and Antigone follows, holding his hand. Together, Antigone and Jocasta (who, in her white dress, closely resembles the Sphinx in act one), "speaking in perfect unison" (96), count the steps Oedipus must take as they leave the stage. Mother leads son and daughter on their collective dark journey into … what? The unconscious? Death? A return to the womb? Or a truly innovative rereading and restaging of the Oedipus story? Whatever else it may be, Cocteau's Oedipus has found what he was looking for all along—a mother's guiding, supporting, unconditional love. Laius is out of the picture, irrelevant, an accident.

But for Freud, in *The Interpretation of Dreams*, one text we can be reasonably certain that Lowry knew at first- and second-hand, the mother has a less prominent and positive role. Freud saw in the Oedipus story a narrative of the Oedipal stage of heterosexual male development (females behaved analogously, as far as Freud was concerned). In order to reach "normal" adulthood, the boy had to reject his attachment to his mother, transfer his identification to his father, while repressing the desire to replace the father with the mother, and sexually objectify his mother in a mother substitute. It is "Nature" (365), says Freud, that forces these Oedipal wishes and ordeals upon us, and the role of the father is crucial to the healthy development of the son. When something goes wrong, as it often does, various problems arise. The one that seems to fascinate Freud in this section of *The Interpretation of Dreams* is an incestuous desire of the son for the mother, and Freud goes on at some length to explain *Hamlet* in these terms. (This is yet another point at which Cocteau parodies Freud by making his *Hamlet* parallel—the Ghost figure—such an obvious failure). Other psychological problems that can arise from a failure to pass through the Oedipal stage successfully include, according to Freud, latent homosexuality, regression to orality, hallucinations, and failure to establish a stable patriarchal family unit.

Freud takes up the question of homosexuality in another essay that Lowry may have read—"Leonardo da Vinci and a Memory of His Childhood"—and it is here that Freud develops his theory of how a castration complex associated with the phallic mother can lead to types of homosexuality.[16] In Leonardo's case, Freud argues that the great artist's strong love for his mother, from whom he was separated by his father and stepmother (a second mother), led him to identify with his mother in a form of auto-eroticism. And, of course, Freud also explores homosexuality and male hysteria in his study of Schreber.

Now I am not for a moment suggesting that Freud has satisfactorily explained Sophocles' *Oedipus Rex*, or Shakespeare's *Hamlet*, let alone the creativity of Leonardo da Vinci. However, he has given us an interpretation, a reading as it were, that had a tremendous impact upon the twentieth century. So, beginning with Freud and his starting point of the Oedipus complex, I would like to explore two responses to Freud that expand and elaborate upon his theories and bring me closer to my reading of *Lowry*—these are Ruth Brunswick's essay "The Preoedipal Phase of the Libido Development" and Michel Schneider's psychoanalytical study of plagiarism, *Voleurs de mots*.

If the successful negotiation of the Oedipal phase prepares a boy for adult heterosexuality in a stable patriarchal family, then failure to negotiate this stage can lead to a neurotic man who, in Brunswick's terms, has a "negative" or "passive" Oedipus complex (235). Such a man has been unable to give up or repress his attachment to the mother and this results in a form of identification with the mother and a passive relation of fear of and/or submissiveness to the father. Although Brunswick allows that this can lead to homosexuality, latent or not, she is much more interested in what the negative Oedipus complex reveals about the preoedipal stage. "The clinical picture [of the little boy]" she suggests, "is that of a profound mother fixation ... but closer study reveals that much of the fixation is passive instead of active, and preoedipal instead of oedipal" (248). In other words, a negative Oedipal complex in a man is, more accurately, designated as passive, preoedipal, and non-sexual, in short, as a need for nourishment. A man with a negative Oedipus complex who develops a mother fixation (which is not the only path he may take; see 251–52) is unable to give up, not the Oedipal or good mother, but the punishing phallic mother. As Brunswick explains it, "because of the primitive nature of this passive, tenacious attachment to the mother, an intensely ambivalent relationship between the man and his mother-substitute[s] results. His passivity and his dependence upon the phallic mother are resented and rebelled against by his entire masculinity" (252–53). If this man is an artist, more particularly a writer, a mother fixation could be crucial to an understanding of much more than his aetiology or his social and sexual adaptation in marriage. But for insights into the question of creativity I must turn to Schneider.

To be a successful, productive writer, Schneider tells us, one must separate oneself from language in order to be able to use it, to control and deploy it, to master it ("Pour écrire, il faut se séparer du langage, et c'est le plus lent des deuils," [227]). Moreover, one must, says Schneider, accept the Oedipal fact that one is never *first* with the Muse, the Mother tongue (286), or what I am calling the Symbolic Mother. The plagiarist, or the writer who fears he is a plagiarist, is unable to take up this active, even aggressive position; he is unable to move through the Oedipal stage and regresses to the preoedipal: "dans le plagiat, on demeure dans une sorte de violence pré-oedipienne, á l'intérieur d'une fusion ou d'une relation duelle" (282).

However, Schneider argues that many great writers are plagiarists in the sense that they borrow words, that all writers are under the influence of the (m)Other, and that male creativity in language cannot be adequately explained as Oedipal desire. Instead it must be seen, or so Schneider thinks, as the cathexis of the son with his mother, and it involves a very complex set of needs and anxieties.[17] The writer needs nourishment from the mother, who is the source of language and ideas (insofar as these exist in language); this access to the mother (tongue) must not be prohibited by the father or blocked by the mother herself; and the precariousness of this cathexis results in potentially crippling guilts, insecurities, and profound doubts about one's sexual identity, one's authorship and originality (a problem exacerbated in an age obsessed with the legal ownership of words), and one's ability to write *instead of being written*. This last anxiety is the most psychologically crippling because it can lead to a plagiarism psychosis, such as the one suffered by Lowry (according to Schneider [see 21–22, 93]), which consists in the inability of the writer to separate himself from his own work, or to separate his words from those of others whose work he has read. Such a writer both fears and desires cannibalization of and complete absorption in the mother. Thus, in a patriarchal, masculinist culture like our own, this writer has come to identify himself completely with the despised and castrated female. Not surprisingly, Schneider includes in his list of symptoms for the neurotic or psychotic plagiarist—orality, paranoia, latent homosexuality, a fascination with doubling (or narcissism), hysterical identifications with the Other, and suicide.[18]

IV

But what, if anything, does all this tell us about Malcolm Lowry? Can we speculate about what happened to him after 1947, about his state of mind and his creative powers in 1957, on the basis of this psychoanalytic narrative? Is there anything here that strikes a resonant chord with the long letter to Markson with which I began? Indeed, I think that there are at least three categories of useful insight here, and within each there are many separate and worthwhile trails to follow. Let me describe these categories, as I see them, and point to a few of these trails.

Beginning from my initial working assumption that, as Barthes points out, the documentary author can (if not *should*) be read as a text—a point with which, after all, good Freudians and other psychoanalysts would agree—I see three categories of *Lowry* text represented here: the text of his life, or biography; the text of his literary works, or Barthesian *bio-graphy*; and, the life as written and endlessly rewritten in and by the work, which is acutely the case with Lowry and which I am calling the auto-bio-graphy. I will begin with the biography because editing letters always tells us a great deal about the facts and concerns of the writer's life. Very few of Lowry's letters to his family have survived.[19] Those that have, however, tell us much of what we know from the biographies about his extremely difficult relations with his parents, and this state of affairs appears to be confirmed by scattered comments that Lowry made in letters to other people. We know that he feared and resented his "Old Man," upon whom he nonetheless depended for money, and that he blamed his parents for not understanding and appreciating him, for ignoring him (even when he had a severe eye infection), and, in the case of his father, for attempting to control him. Father-figures do not fare well in Lowry's fiction, either, and mothers rarely appear.

Day argues that Lowry suffered from an "aggravated Oedipal situation" (64), while also noting what he calls Lowry's "orality " and "markedly regressive, infantile" state in the latter years of his life (69–70). He takes Lowry's stories about sadistic nannies seriously as "screen memories" (67), notes Lowry's inability to distinguish self from other (69), and describes Lowry as a classic manic-depressive (30). In attempting to understand Lowry through this Freudian approach (which I must say I have come to respect because Day does not, finally, claim that it *explains* his subject), however, Day stresses the role of the father to the exclusion of the mother. He does this despite some important hints provided by Lowry himself, hints that he records. The sadistic nannies are one of the most important of these hints, but also important are these facts: that Lowry claimed he rarely spoke of his mother or did anything nice for her because Stuart resented it (26), that Lowry apparently looked a lot like his mother, and that he wrote to her regularly and affectionately (62). Stuart, Lowry's eldest brother, appears to have been much admired by the young Malcolm, and in many respects he stood in for Arthur Lowry after his death by representing the family in dealings with Malcolm. Within the family structure, I am suggesting, Stuart replaced the father and so his prohibition on the mother is significant.

Indeed, there appears to have been a marked prohibition among the Lowry sons regarding Evelyn Lowry. It has proved almost impossible to glean much information about her, and Russell Lowry, Malcolm's surviving, elder brother even refused to discuss her.[20] Gordon Bowker, however, has provided some facts: we now know for certain that she was from a respectable but poor working-class background and, thus, out of her element in her husband's rising middle- and upper middle-class world; we know that she often accompanied her husband on business trips, that she had difficulty managing servants and her home, that she often left the boys, notably the youngest, in the care of nannies, and that she had hoped her last child, born in her middle age, would be a girl.[21] It is time, I believe, to put Evelyn Lowry back into Malcolm's life, not to the exclusion of Arthur, but nonetheless in a central position. To do so not only helps us better understand Lowry's biography, but it also illuminates both his *bio-graphy*, as Richard Cross has already shown in his important study "*Ulysses* and *Under the Volcano*: The Difficulty of Loving," and the crippling problems he suffered with his *auto-bio-graphy*.[22]

Whatever actually happened to traumatize Lowry when he was an infant or very young child we will never know. We can, however, learn something by contextualizing these early years in the light of post-Freudian theories of preoedipality and plagiarism, and by situating Lowry in his socio-historical context.[23] In chapter two of *Imperial Leather*, "'Massa' and Maids: Power and Desire in the Imperial Metropolis," Anne McClintock dismantles what she sees as an intricate complex of repressed associations of class, sexuality, gender, and power in Freud's Oedipal family romance. The central character, says McClintock, in this childhood real-life drama is not the father but the nurse or nanny, a figure whose agency and presence Freud erased in order to "safeguard the male's historical role as sexual agent" (88). For Freud, McClintock argues, the nurse "is the repudiated, working-class other: the expelled abject from which he could not part" (89). By historicizing the Freudian bourgeois family in this way, McClintock alerts us to several things: the ambivalent (vulnerable yet powerful) and potentially resentful position of the nurse/nanny; the class structure of the upper middle-class home signalled most forcefully by the accent of speech in the mother tongue; and the doubling, or splitting, of the maternal role, which whether as nanny or biological mother, is abstracted, abjected, and excluded from the action of the drama.

When we remember that Lowry was born into a similar family, we can then re-evaluate the position of his mother and her surrogates, the nannies.[24] Lowry's family was an aggressively masculinist and patriarchal one ruled by an ambitious, autocratic Victorian *pater familias*; Arthur and his three oldest boys were successful at sports, at business, and at war. Arthur built the family fortunes with the family business and removed his family to a large, impressive, prestigious house, where his wife and servants were expected to manage domestic life on a suitable scale. Evelyn, however, was a working-class girl, who, despite her pretentions to upper-class identity and her efforts to alter her speech through elocution lessons, could never entirely mask her origins. She was, quite simply, *déclassé* in her own home; she could not keep up and would remain a constant reminder to husband and sons of the lower-class origins of the family. In the light of this situation, is it not possible that her growing sons found her embarrassing and that her life might have been crippled by a sense of her own inadequacy, in the face of which it was better to refuse visitors, to keep her mouth shut, or even to affect disinterest in her boys lest she pull them down to her level? Is it not possible that the sons developed a hatred of this mother that was both Oedipal (as a sexual desire repressed, if not successfully transferred to an alternative object under threat of castration from the father) and class-based? And that the youngest, last-born son, who was supposed to have been over-protected and much fondled by his mother, never successfully negotiated his Oedipal stage, displaced a set of very early fears and resentments connected with fondling, separation, and loss onto the nannies, and harboured an identification with and affection for this doubly prohibited mother that led to an exacerbated preoedipal regression? If I add to these speculations the scattering of other biographical details—Lowry looked like his mother, Lowry inherited her talent for storytelling (if Russell is to be believed) and, thus, her attraction to language, Lowry expected his wives to mother him (something Margerie carried to an extreme)—is the possibility of preoedipal regression, with all its consequences, not enhanced? I think it is. Moreover, I also think that Lowry's work, his plagiarist's pen or poetics, and his final collapse under the weight of his *auto-bio-graphy* support this possibility.

Now it is quite impossible for me to explore all of Lowry's work here in search of evidence to support this possibility—that is a subject for a book. But I can return to Cocteau and *La Machine infernale* for what I believe is strong evidence of Lowry's preoedipal identification with the mother on the level of *bio-graphy*. As we have seen, this play and Cocteau's reading of the Oedipus story, one that privileges the Symbolic Mother (as Muse), held great significance for Lowry: it influenced him in 1934; he used it in *Volcano*; and he returned to it at the end of his life.

To judge from Ackerley's *Companion to "Under the Volcano,"* there are no mothers in that novel, and, indeed, mothers are rarely mentioned by any of the characters. However, we know from Laruelle that Geoffrey lost both his parents (his mother died and his father disappeared), that his stepmother, Hugh's mother, also died, and that the mere mention of the words "father" or "mother" would cause the young Geoffrey to "burst out crying" (16). On one occasion, and *en passant*, Geoffrey recalls the death of Hugh's mother (78). However, there are two extremely interesting allusions to the mother in *Volcano*, one overt, the other suppressed or veiled. Both occur in chapter seven, Geoffrey's chapter, the symbolic chapter seven, and the chapter in which he enters his own infernal machine.

In the first, with the "clubs of the flying machines seen out of the corner of his eye" (197), Geoffrey faces Yvonne who merges with his mother and stepmother:

> And yet, he was thinking all over again, and all over again as for the first time, how he had suffered, suffered, suffered without her; indeed such desolation, such a desperate sense of abandonment, bereavement, as during this last year without Yvonne, he had never known in his life, unless it was when his mother died. But this present emotion he had never experienced with his mother: this urgent desire to hurt, to provoke, at a time when forgiveness alone could save the day, this, rather, had commenced with his stepmother, so that she would have to cry: "I can't eat, Geoffrey, the food sticks in my throat!" (197–98)

What Geoffrey has unconsciously revealed here is that he is redirecting (as he did in the past) his anger and hostility against his mother for leaving him, thereby depriving him of her Self, to his stepmother and wife, both of whom he classifies as stand-ins for the lost mother.

The second occasion is even clearer, if only we know how to read it. This time Geoffrey, in a vertiginous, hallucinating state of drunkenness, consumes the contents of the cocktail shaker, which enables him to descend the stairs in Jacques's tower to the living room where he finds and (mis)reads a passage from Cocteau's *La Machine infernale*: "'Oui, mon enfant, mon petit enfant,' he reads, 'les choses qui paraissent abominables aux humains, si tu savais, de l'endroit où j'habite, elles ont peu d'importance.'"[25] Clearly this is a speech from a play and, therefore, it must be part of the dialogue; it is addressed, after all, to "mon enfant, mon petit enfant." As I noted above, this speech belongs to Jocasta in act four of the play just after she has returned from the dead as Oedipus's mother. Here is the complete exchange between mother and son:

> OEDIPE: Femme! Ne me touche pas ...
>
> JOCASTA: Ta femme est morte pendue, Oedipe. Je suis ta mère. C'est ta mère qui vient à ton aide ... Comment ferais-tu rien que pour descendre seul cet escalier, mon pauvre petit?
>
> OEDIPE: Ma mère!
>
> JOCASTA: Oui, mon enfant, mon petit enfant ... Les choses qui paraissent abominables aux humains, si tu savais, de l'endroit où j'habite, si tu savais comme elles on peu d'importance. (214)

Jocasta has returned from the dead and from Oedipus's unconscious (states closely related in Cocteau's personal mythology) to guide him down the stairs from the platform of the play's staging and into the unknown. Geoffrey has needed many drinks, topped off with the contents of the cocktail shaker, to enable him to descend the stairs in Jacques's tower so he can find and read this message from his absent—yet present if only he could see her!—mother. But he does not see her and consequently will be left with her surrogates—Yvonne and the now empty cocktail shaker. Tragically, for Geoffrey, and for Lowry, the help he needs is before his eyes in the sound of a voice from the past, from a Paris stage in the spring of 1934, and in the shape of advice from an older, wiser writer who knew that Freud's Oedipal complex was not the only answer, especially for the writer. This writer (Cocteau) who knew what Lowry should have known but would not articulate clearly until 1957 in his letter to David Markson—that Jocasta is *more* than the mother; she is "Art herself ... the higher Muse," and, I would add, the mother tongue.

By 1956–57 and by the time of the two letters analysed above, Evelyn Lowry had died, Malcolm had returned to his mother('s) country, and he had undergone psychiatric investigation and brutal treatments for alcoholism. He had been told *not* to attempt writing again and had only gradually and partially returned to the manuscript of *October Ferry to Gabriola* and his plans for his masterwork of interrelated novels, *The Voyage That Never Ends*. His letters show that he was still preoccupied with *Volcano*, the separation from Dollarton, the loss of his beloved pier, and the dilemma—or is it terror?—of the writer who is always already written. If I have read Lowry's February 1957 letter to Markson correctly, Lowry's repressed need for his lost, rejected, prohibited mother had returned with a vengeance. His extreme hostility towards Margerie, who had mothered him and taken over a very large role in his authoring, is not surprising. As Brunswick reminds us, the preoedipal man is characteristically aggressive and hostile towards mother substitutes (251–53). But, on the level of *auto-bio-graphy*, it is Lowry's plagiarism with its associated terrors and obsessions that is of primary interest.

Lowry's plagiarism, I believe, his hysterical identifications with the words and works of other male writers, had caught up with him in the form of auto- or self-plagiarism. His unsatisfied and insatiable desire for the mother was not phallic but oral, pre-sexual; it was a desire for language, words, the mother tongue, which he longed to absorb into himself but to which he found access blocked or denied. He had turned narcissistically in on himself and was attempting to write his life when he could no longer, or at least only with extraordinary effort and difficulty, live it. His complete identification with the Symbolic Mother had rendered him speechless except through stolen words, even when those words were stolen from himself. What the letter to Markson shows us is Lowry writing his own death in a text that is not one, a text that *cannot, should not* be one.[26] This letter bears witness to his artistic absorption in and cannibalization by the (M)Other (the words, the narrative, the structure, in short the story) that is himself in a narrative where it becomes impossible for him to distinguish self and other. His claim that he was eating *October Ferry* more than it was eating him notwithstanding, Lowry was, in fact, eating himself. As Schneider tells us, the ultimate desire of the plagiarist is his own death: "la mort est ... au fond du plagiat. La mort pour celui qui est plagié ... mais aussi, plus secrètement, la mort pour la plagiaire, détruit dans son espace psychique propre" (302).

When Barthes traces the pleasure of the text to its "*staging* of an appearance-as-disappearance" of the *father*, he describes an Oedipal formula for pleasure that erases the mother and the preoedipal desires of the writer (and reader)—or of a writer like Lowry for whom the *mother's* "appearance-as-disappearance" is more important. But he is closer to the truth (of the larger, more complex picture) when he says that "the writer is someone who plays with this mother's body" (Barthes 1975, 37), whether to "glorify" and "embellish" it or to "dismember" and disfigure it. What reading "Lowry" in the dark wood of Freud and Cocteau shows us is that, by 1957, Lowry had passed beyond his capacity to distance himself (as Schneider would put it) from the mother's body enough to glorify it in independent, finished, great works of art. Instead, the necessary gap between self and other had irrevocably closed until he had no choice but to lose and disfigure himself in the text of his own life. What that letter to Markson stages is Lowry returning "the documentary figure" of himself "into the novelistic, irretrievable, irresponsible figure, caught up in the plural of its own text" (Barthes 1974, 211).

(2000)

NOTES

* All references to *Under the Volcano* are to the 1947 first edition.

[1] These letters are numbers 25 and 35 respectively in *SC* I. For a discussion of the letter to Davenport see Grace, "Thoughts towards the Archeology of Editing: 'Caravan of Silence.'"

[2] Freud is quoting from Lewis Campbell's translation of Sophocles; see *The Interpretation of Dreams*, 366. Among the many changes that Cocteau makes to the story he inherited from Sophocles is the excision of this speech. Lowry's copy of the 1934 first publication of *La Machine infernale* would not have reinforced so much as contradicted Freud.

[3] It is a pleasure to thank my colleague Michael Zeitlin for his advice and help on Freud; any errors and misinterpretations in my application of Freudian or other psychoanalytic theories are my own. I have been influenced in my approach to Freud by recent feminist and cultural theory, much of which is critical of Freud and Freudian or Lacanian thinking. I would also like to thank my research assistant Lisa Chalykoff for her help and the Social Sciences and Humanities Research Council of Canada for their funding in support of this work.

[4] At the time of this remark, in 1947, Lowry could only have known Schreber's memoir at second hand, probably through Freud, because Schreber's text, which has been called "the most-quoted unread book of the twentieth century" (Kendrick, 33), was not fully translated into English until 1955. See my discussion of Schreber in *SC* II, 100–101.

[5] See Lowry's 1 March 1950 letter (*SC* II, 389) to Clarisse Francillon for his praise of Cocteau. Lowry's copy of the play has not survived with his library, but according to Bowker (229), he had it with him in Mexico in 1937. Lowry met Cocteau through Maurice Sachs in 1934 (Bowker 178–79) shortly after his marriage to Jan Gabrial and during their initial months in Paris.

[6] An enquiry into questions of theatre, performance, and spectatorship would take me far beyond the parameters of this paper; however, I think it should be done. One of the passions of Lowry's life was the cinema, with theatre not far behind, and he and Margerie devoted most of 1949 and early 1950 to the writing of their screenplay of *Tender Is the Night*. Comments made about incest, suicide, Oedipal problems, dreams, and psychoanalysis in his letters about the novel and in the screenplay itself suggest that he was fascinated by the challenge of staging Nicole's disturbed psyche and its aetiology filmically; see *SC* II, nos. 374 and 397.

[7] Lowry is referring to W.B. Yeats's 1928 translation/transcription of *Oedipus Rex* for the Abbey Theatre.

[8] Markson did not complete or publish his Oedipus book, but that is surely another story, and I do not know what effect Lowry's appropriation of the book—*if* Markson even viewed Lowry's letter in that light—may have had on its fate. The influence of Lowry and his prose

on the younger writer has been, I would suggest, enormous. Markson's *Wittgenstein's Mistress* (1988), to my mind his masterpiece, is at once the opposite, in its honed brevity, of anything Lowry could have written and profoundly Lowryan in its representation of consciousness through a "caddis-worm" style and language.

[9] Lowry's wording here could be a quotation from Freud's *Beyond the Pleasure Principle*; see, for example, pages 13–17. Whether he is quoting or not is of less significance than the fact that, at many points in this letter, he is repeating central ideas about repetition and the forces of self-preservation and self-destruction explored in that text.

[10] Graves argues that Oedipus was an invader of Thebes who tried to suppress the Minoan cult of the Moon-goddess by misrepresenting the death of the old king and the remarriage of the queen, the priestess of the Moon-goddess, as parricide and incest, and then by transforming the goddess into the evil Sphinx (374–75). Given what we know about modern conquest and imperialism, this propoganda sounds like a most plausible theory.

[11] A few pages later he interrupts his narrative with another demurral—"I hope you'll excuse my intolerable arrogance in making these suggestions at all but your Demon has only to reject them if he doesn't like them" (*SC* II, 884)—and later still he writes: "Well, I can scarcely [go] on without spoiling your story for you" (888). But go on he does, for four more pages, his purpose being "to set the fires of your imagination burning with the very tinder that it is only natural for it to despise or reject" (890).

[12] My annotation to this reference in the letter (*SC* II, 893) is incomplete. Lowry must be thinking of Thomas Moore (1779–1852), the well-known Irish poet, and conflating him with Sir Thomas More.

[13] Cocteau's book of poems called *La Danse de Sophocle* appeared in 1912, he wrote *Orphée* in 1926 and the script for Igor Stravinsky's oratorio *Oedipus Rex* in 1927, and after *La Machine infernale*, he returned to the Oedipus story in two more plays: *Les Parents terribles* (1938) and *Antigone* (1943). After Radiguet's sudden death in 1923, Cocteau began taking opium regularly and he was not cured of the effects of opium poisoning until the mid-thirties. Cocteau's homosexuality is essential to an understanding of his life and art, and Lowry, who met Cocteau through Maurice Sachs, could not help knowing this, whether or not he appreciated the degree to which the poet and playwright's sexual orientation affected his interpretation of the Oedipus story. We should not forget the later impact on Lowry made by Cocteau's films *Le Sang d'un Poète* (1932) and *Orphée* (1950); see Bowker, 468.

[14] Although both Brown and Steegmuller document the importance of Mme Cocteau in her son's life, Brown is the only one, to my knowledge, to have explicitly linked her with *La Machine infernale*. In a 1930 meeting with Cocteau, whom he saw in a dressing gown with a ribbon around his neck, Brown says he looked like his mother (287), and Steegmuller provides important information about Cocteau's childhood (including a crucial dream about his father appearing as a parrot at the table where he and his mother are eating), his father's suicide, and his close and complex relations with his mother, with whom he lived until her death (9–22). Steegmuller disputes Cocteau's claims to heterosexual affairs and argues that he was, sexually, always and only homosexual.

[15] All my quotations from the play are either from the English translation by Albert Bermel or from the original 1934 publication.

[16] I have found no concrete evidence that Lowry knew this essay, which was first published, in German, in 1910. However, the essay was well-known and would have been of interest to

artists. Certainly, Cocteau knew it and was scathing; see his comments in *The Hand of a Stranger* (24–25).

[17] The following summary of Schneider's long and complex argument is drawn from pages 160–67. All translations from the French are my own.

[18] Questions have been raised about Lowry's sexual orientation, both in connection with Paul Fitte's suicide and with an episode in New York in 1936 (see Levy, and also Bowker, Bradbrook, and Day), which Jan Gabrial describes as a homosexual encounter in her memoir. A discussion of homosexuality, or even of what Eve Kosofsky Sedgwick calls homosocial triangulation (with its debt to Freud's Oedipal theory) is beyond the scope of this discussion and is a different, if connected, issue.

[19] Volume I of *Sursum Corda!* contains four letters to Arthur Lowry and one to Evelyn; volume II contains one letter to each. Since the publication of the collected letters, three new letters have come to my attention; see Grace, "Three Letters Home" in *A Darkness That Murmured* (14–28).

[20] In *Malcolm Lowry Remembered*, Russell insisted that he would "rather not talk about Mother" (18), and in conversation with me in 1989 he was extremely derogative about her, parodying her false upper-class accent and locutions, criticizing her antisocial behaviour— she would not welcome her sons' friends in the family home—and expressing a lasting resentment over her attempt to block his marriage. He did describe, however, her ability to tell stories, and he suggested that she enjoyed doing this.

[21] Bowker describes the family in some detail, noting Arthur's ambition, Evelyn's inadequacies, and the harsh treatment of Malcolm by one of the nannies (2–11).

[22] Cross explains that it is his mother's love, "of which he has been so early and cruelly deprived" that the Consul is seeking in his wife, Señora Gregorio, and the Virgin "for those who have nobody with" ("*Ulysses* and *Under the Volcano*," 68). Both Sue Vice and Martin Bock also challenge received opinions and Freudian readings of *Volcano* and suggest new ways of thinking about the novel.

[23] As Laplanche and Pontalis remind us, the preoedipal stage, while eventually recognized by Freud, was never granted the status of the Oedipal by him, and it has been up to other theorists to articulate the function and structure of the preoedipal. See also Swan.

[24] As an adult, Lowry sought out a succession of mother substitutes, from Anna Wickham to his wives and his mothers-in-law. In a 1953 letter to Albert Erskine (*SC* II, 640), Lowry tries to blame Margerie's illness on the "mother-imago" at a time when Mrs. Bonner was neither ill nor dying, but when he himself had suffered a serious collapse and was unable to write.

[25] Geoffrey is misreading—see my prefacing quotation for the correct Cocteau text— which, given his alcohol consumption and his misinterpretation and misattribution of the following line "Les dieux existent: c'est le diable" by Cocteau, not Baudelaire, which prefaces the play and translates as "The gods exist—that's the devil of it," is scarcely surprising (see McCarthy 1994, 80).

[26] I invoke Irigaray here to underline Lowry's dilemma. In a masculinist, Freudian psychological and social order, Lowry could not valorize himself in any other way than as a unitary masculine Subject that erases the feminine other. He could find no legitimation of his dialogic self as a sex/text that is not one, on one hand, and yet, could not function as a unitary subject on the other. The result for him was abjection and a crippling sense of failure.

My use of the term Symbolic Mother also invokes Irigaray, for whom (unlike Jacques Lacan) the symbolic is absolutely distinct from the imaginary, which includes language and, thus, writing.

11

Lowry, Debussy, and Under the Volcano

One serious intention was to write a work of art—after a while it began to make a noise like music, when it made the wrong noise I altered it—when it seemed to make the right one, finally, I kept it.

(Lowry)

Malcolm Lowry made this remark in his 6 March 1950 letter to Derek Pethick, who was preparing a CBC radio program on *Volcano*, and it underscores a view of the novel (and of all his writing) that Lowry had held for many years: *Under the Volcano* functions like music. In his famous January 1946 letter to Jonathan Cape, Lowry repeatedly defends his novel in musical terms—as chords, rhythms, tempi, jazz breaks, and counterpoint—but these are not the only ways in which Lowry talks about *Under the Volcano* in this letter to Cape. Elsewhere he tells Cape that his novel

> can be regarded as a kind of symphony, or in another way as a kind of opera—
> or even a horse opera. [...] It is a prophecy, a political warning, a cryptogram,
> a preposterous movie, and a writing on the wall. It can even be regarded as a
> sort of machine. (*SC* I, 506)

Over the years, I have often pondered the synergy between Lowry and the other arts, and I have tried to trace his awareness of the sister arts and to locate other artists' responses to him.[1] But I continue to find new examples of both types of Lowry's cross-artistic activity in popular and high-brow culture, and I continue to be somewhat dissatisfied with the explanations I have come up with to date. Therefore, when I was asked to participate in a panel on literature and opera in 2002, I decided to explore further some of my thoughts and speculations about Lowry and one particular *confrère*—Claude Debussy.[2]

As my opening quotation makes clear, Lowry was deeply attuned to music and to the musical possibilities of language and narrative form. He played music, loved jazz, and followed classical music closely, listening regularly (when he could) to CBC Radio's *Saturday Afternoon at the Opera* and attending concerts and opera. He was, so the story goes, listening to Stravinsky's *The Rite of Spring* on the night he died. Contemporary "white" jazz was important to him, as the many references to Bix Beiderbeck, Ed Lang, and Joe Venuti in *Volcano* and *Lunar Caustic* demonstrate, and Lowry scholars have examined his use of jazz, arguing for music/text analogies as well as tracing references (see Epstein). Moreover, Lowry puts popular songs, hymns, and the canon "Frère Jacques" to structural uses in all his work. For example, the children's round is a key intertext in *Volcano*, and, in "Through the Panama" from *Hear us O Lord from heaven Thy dwelling place*—the very title comes from the Manx fisherman's hymn that is reproduced at the beginning of the volume—"Frère Jacques" functions as a *leitmotif,* a verbal/visual cue, and a thematic reference point.

In "The Operatic Paradigm: Voice, Sound, and Meaning in Lowry's Fiction," Mathieu Duplay has pushed the musical mapping still further by examining Lowry's references to opera, notably to Gluck, and by arguing for the importance of the "operatic paradigm" to our understanding of his prose (165). As Duplay explains,

> The operatic paradigm [in *Volcano*] illustrates the novel's preoccupation with the limits of language; but its main purpose is to define a modernist theory of writing based on the affinity between voice and the Word, between the self-sufficiency of music and the wealth of latent meanings that it eventually conjures up. (163)

References to classical music and to composers are omnipresent in Lowry's work, from Gluck, Mozart, and Bach, to Alban Berg (notably *Wozzeck* in "Forest Path to the Spring"), Wagner, and Debussy. More often than not, Lowry's references to operas are to works with themes that resonate for him; thus, *Wozzeck* is about marital infidelity and a husband's murder of the thing he loves; *Parsifal,* with its dangerous, seductive Kundry and its search for the Grail, provides Lowry with a rich source of symbols and allusions in *October Ferry to Gabriola;* and references to Mozart, especially to *The Magic Flute,* serve to underscore the magical or even Cabbalistic aspects of life in *Under the Volcano.*

But a study of Lowry and music could well be a book, and I want to single out just one example of Lowryan musicality, an example that is not primarily a thematic influence or the source of some particular symbol or intertext. The comparison I want to make is between Debussy's *Pelléas et Mélisande* and Lowryan narrative in *Under the Volcano.* I believe it is possible to argue that this particular opera demonstrates a special interrelationship of orchestration with dialogue/voice that is analogous with Lowry's narrative form in all his fiction, but I will limit my comparisons to *Volcano.* First the opera.

Pelléas et Mélisande premièred in Paris in 1902. It took Debussy nine years to complete and it is based on Maeterlinck's symbolist play. We know that Lowry was not only familiar with this work but that in September 1944, while staying in Ontario, he and Margerie attended the Toronto première of *Pelléas et Mélisande.*[3] In a letter to friends (*SC* I, no. 198), Lowry writes that "in order to reestablish our awareness of reality, we ... made an enormous pilgrimage [to Toronto] to see— what but Pelléas and Mélisande [sic]?" In one sense this reference to "reality" is an in-joke; Lowry knows full well that this opera is anything but *verismo*. But there is another sense in which Lowry is not joking. He and Margerie were in Ontario in the fall of 1944 because their little home on the foreshore at Dollarton had burned down, taking with it all their possessions and many of his manuscripts. To attend an opera was, for Lowry, a way of restoring some sense of order and reality to his otherwise shattered life. Predictably, Lowry was impressed with the opera's themes of jealousy, betrayal, lost love, death, and darkness, and in an allusion to *Volcano* he tells his friends that he and Margerie listened to the opera "in the middle of a dark wood, in the Massey Hall" (*SC* I, 464). I am certain that the many other parallels between the two works could not have escaped him: the love triangle (two half-brothers and a woman they both love); the ambiguous, troubled background of the woman; the strategic importance of the number twelve; the rearing horse, the storms and forest; the view down into an abyss; flight through a dark wood ending in death; the crucial importance of silences; the cyclic imperative of the plot; the symbolic values of the characters; and the shifting scenic structure of scene and counter-scene that focuses on a single or a shared perspective.

Lowry goes on in this letter to comment on what I see as the deeper significance of this opera for him: he quotes two passages from the libretto as examples of "Debussey's [sic] whole tone harmonies expressing such words" as Mélisande's question—"Where are you going?"—and Golaud's response—"I do not know ... I am lost also" (*SC* I, 464). Whether he had simply read the program notes or had immediately grasped something unique about this opera, Lowry's attention was drawn by its form and by the relationship between music and words that has made this work so unique and influential in the twentieth century (see Nichols and Smith). Central to that form (what Osborne has called the intimate "music-drama," 10) is Debussy's subordination of the words to "continuous symphony"; he argued that "People sing too much" in operas, and he wanted "short librettos, shifting scenes ... diverse in setting and mood; characters not arguing, submissive to life, fate" (Porter, 11). Silences are crucial to the opera, and the characters are elusive, symbolic, rarely connecting with each other in realistic, or even dramatically motivated ways. The mood, the mystery, and the sense of fate overhanging the somewhat abstract, minimal plot, are primarily conveyed through the music. It is Debussy's music that talks to us, that tells us a story we can feel but never quite pin down.

Much the same can be said of *Volcano* (and of *Hear us O Lord*), where characters and plot are fully subordinated to the continuous musical textures of Lowry's metaleptic prose narration (exposition, description, imagery, symbolic tonalities, rhythmic phrasing, character motifs, onomatopoetic word choices, etc.) Indeed, Lowry defended himself against charges that his character drawing was weak by insisting that he had "not exactly attempted to draw characters ... there just isn't *room* ... the character drawing is not only weak but virtually nonexistent ... the four main characters being intended, in one of the book's meanings, to be aspects of the same man, or of the human spirit" (*SC* I, 500–501). Thus, in chapter two, when Geoffrey and Yvonne are reunited and as they return to their home, we do not learn more about who they are and why they are seemingly estranged because they do not talk to or with but past each other in brief phrases, incomplete sentences, and silent gestures (which Lowry indicates with gaps and dashes):

> "It's a pity because—but look here, dash it all, aren't you terribly tired, Yvonne?"
>
> "Not in the least! I should think you're the one to be—"
>
> —Box! *Preliminar a 4 Rounds.* EL TURCO (*Gonazalo Calderón de Par. de 52 kilos*) *vs.* EL OSO (*de Par. de 53 kilos*).
>
> "I had a million hours of sleep on the boat! And I'd far rather walk, only—"
>
> "Nothing. Just a touch of rheumatiz.—Or is it the sprue? I'm glad to get the circulation going in the old legs."
>
> —Box! *Evento Especial a 5 Rounds, en los que el vencedor pasará al grupo de Semi-Finales.* TOMAS ÁGUERO (*el Invencible Indio de Quauhnahuac de 57 kilos, que acaba de llegar de la Capital de la República*). ARENA TOMALÍN. *Frente al jardin Xicotancatl.*
>
> "It's a pity about the car because we might have gone to the boxing," said the Consul, who was walking almost exaggeratedly erect.
>
> "I hate boxing."
>
> "—But that's not till next Sunday anyhow ... I heard they had some kind of bull-throwing on to-day over at Tomalín.—Do you remember—"
>
> "No!" (*UV*, 54)

Their fragments of speech are surrounded, carried away, *lost* amidst the portentous signs of aggression pressing in on all sides from an external world over which they have no control. As with the opera, dialogue in *Under the Volcano* is basic, stripped down, and overpowered by the surrounding textuality.

This subsuming of speech (represented speech in the novel; sung, embodied speech in the opera) occurs in other ways too—for example, through what I will call interludes. Consider this scene from chapter three of *Volcano*: when Geoffrey tries to make love with Yvonne as a gesture towards reconciliation, we are not given a description of the action or any dialogue between the husband and wife. Instead we have a very long prose interlude that conveys the emotion and thought of the Consul in hesitant phrases, long, right-branching, metaleptic sentences, and clauses that halt and then move forward only to stop abruptly against the punctuation (colons, long dashes, and ellipses):

> But he could feel now, too, trying the prelude, the preparatory nostalgic phrases on his wife's senses, the image of his possession, like the jewelled gate the desperate neophyte, Yesod-bound, projects for the thousandth time on the heavens to permit passage of his astral body, fading, and slowly, inexorably, that of a cantina, when in dead silence and peace it first opens in the morning, taking its place. It was one of those cantinas that would be opening now, at nine o'clock: and he was queerly conscious of his own presence there with the angry tragic words, the very words which might soon be spoken, glaring behind him. This image faded also: he was where he was, sweating now, glancing once—but never ceasing to play the prelude, the little one-fingered introduction to the unclassifiable composition that might still follow—out of the window at the drive, fearful himself lest Hugh appear there ... (*UV*, 92)

It is no accident that Lowry's governing trope for his prose style at this point is, in fact, music. However, his medium is words and what follows is an evocation of the cantinas, with their sights and coarse sounds, that culminates in a stunning visual image—not of physical tenderness or sexual ecstasy but of the sunlight "falling like a lance straight into a block of ice" (93)—from which we must infer what is never presented, never stated, never embodied in the common modalities of fiction.

Debussy achieves a strikingly similar effect with his orchestral interludes which interrupt the dialogue but also continue the story in music and create a musical bridge between one scene and the next. For an example of what I mean, consider the closing speeches of Pelléas and Golaud from act three, scene one, followed by the Interlude, and then the opening of the next scene with Pelléas and Golaud. In this so-called Rapunzel scene, Pelléas and Mélisande have been flirting at night; she has leaned from her tower window as he waits below; her long hair has fallen down and he catches it, refusing to release her. Suddenly Golaud enters; he is angry and calls them careless children. Speech stops abruptly, and the scene gives way to a gradually darkening orchestral interlude in which Debussy repeats motifs and phrases from earlier in the score. When the interlude ends we hear Golaud and Pelléas in a brief but frightening, ominous scene. Golaud leads Pelléas underground to the castle vaults and forces him to lean over and look down into a stagnant pool. "Do you smell the scent of death which comes from it?" Golaud asks. Pelléas can smell death and exclaims: "I can't breathe here. Let's go out." (act three, scene two, libretto, 113). The two brothers leave in silence.

In both the novel and the opera, two characters confront each other before and after the interlude; there is great tension between them and a wealth of unspoken/sung explication and exposition, which the reader/listener must *get*, as it were, from the cadences, motifs, verbal, and musical themes. Narrative meaning is evoked, suggested, implied, but not spelled out in extra chatter. Personally, I find this indirection, if that's what it is, to be profoundly moving, haunting, and dramatic, as if larger forces—the fates, the gods—were controlling the story quite apart from what the characters think, say, or do.

For my third and final comparative example, I want to return to dialogue. In chapter nine of *Volcano*, when Geoffrey and Yvonne have their one brief moment of *rapprochement*, it is conveyed in snatches of dialogue, strangely reminiscent, to my ears, of those passages from the libretto of *Pelléas et Mélisande* that Lowry quoted in his 1944 letter, or of the love scene between Mélisande and Pelléas in act four. Their comments are pitched against the descriptions of tedium, silences, sudden bursts of noise, and the violence of the bull ring, which overwhelm and nullify the dialogue and any action that might—in other novels—follow from such a moment. Here is Lowry's text:

> "Yvonne?"
>
> "Yes, darling?"
>
> "I've fallen down, you know … Somewhat."
>
> "Never mind, darling."
>
> " … Yvonne?
>
> "Yes?"
>
> "I love you … Yvonne?"
>
> "Oh, I love you too!" (*UV*, 279)

And here is Debussy's text (the music must be imagined):

> MÉLISANDE: Why do you always say you're going away?
>
> PELLÉAS: Must I tell you what you know already! Don't you know what I am going to say?
>
> MÉLISANDE: No, no. I know nothing.
>
> PELLÉAS: You don't know why I must leave? You don't realize that it's because … I love you.
>
> MÉLISANDE: I love you too. (*Pelléas et Mélisande*, 155)

My colleague, musicologist Vera Mizcnik, describes this moment as "the emptiest, lowest point in the drama."[4] The very same could be said of the hurried snatch of conversation between Yvonne and Geoffrey. And yet, it is a crucial moment in both texts; time is running out for both couples; the forces of death and darkness are rushing forward (Golaud approaching through the forest and the glasses of mescal lurking in the opening words of chapter ten); if this turning point is not seized, then all will be lost—as indeed it is. Pelléas will be killed/Geoffrey will drink those mescals; Mélisande will flee through a dark wood towards her death/Yvonne will stagger through a dark wood and be trampled to death just as Geoffrey is being shot. Love, in both texts, is doomed. Death and darkness prevail.

What I am trying to isolate through my three comparative examples—characterization through fragmented, silenced dialogue; prose or orchestral interludes; and the anti-dramatic crises—is not so much *what* is happening in the novel or the opera, but *how* it is being made to happen in words and music. The opera helps me to appreciate what Lowry was doing and why, for example, readers who expect *characters* in a novel might be critical or readers who want clear narrative action and motivation might be frustrated. The opera helps me to hear what the prose is and is not doing. And the opera helps me *hear* Lowry's words and silences, the way, as Duplay phrases it, in which "sounds turn into signifiers, and meaning emerges out of silence" (165). By the same token, *Under the Volcano* has helped me appreciate *Pelléas et Mélisande*, an opera I initially found difficult, remote, intellectual, and abstract. I came to it attuned to *bel canto* and *verismo*, but seeing it through Lowryan lenses helped me to stop missing arias, duets, and sung story.

I wish I could end this brief analysis with a discussion of an opera based on Lowry and his work. But I cannot. If such a work exists, I am unaware of it.⁵ The closest thing I know of to date is Graham Collier's jazz cantata *The Day of the Dead*. I can imagine such an opera, however, and it might be a bit like Gounod's *Faust*, with its myth, magic, and temptations, and a bit like Bartok's *Bluebeard's Castle*, with its dark world of death and entrapment that images contemporary existence, and certainly a lot like *Pelléas et Mélisande*, where symbolism and orchestration carry an otherwise minimal plot, heightened but stripped down dialogue, and two-dimensional, fated characters. It would be set—*absolutemente necessario*—in Mexico and staged against a stylized set of the volcanoes. The mezzo-soprano (Yvonne) would end up dead—which must happen in grand opera—the tenor (Hugh, or could this be Laruelle?) would die broken-hearted, and the baritone (Geoffrey), not an outright villain—for neither Debussy nor Lowry created such villains—would suffer in darkness and fail. And the opera would end—as does *Pelléas et Mélisande*, as does *Under the Volcano*—with a reminder that the entire cycle will begin again: "Il faut qu'il vive, maintenant, à sa place. C'est au tour de la pauvre petite," says Arkel (*Pelléas et Mélisande*, 191); "Over the town, in the dark tempestuous night, backwards revolved the luminous wheel._____" (*UV*, 43).

(2001)

NOTES

* All references to *Under the Volcano* are to the 2000 Perennial Classics edition.

¹ My study of Lowry's interest in the arts began first in the late 1970s with an exploration of his debt to expressionist film (see Grace 1978, and *Regression and Apocalypse*). From this I moved to painting (see Grace 1990) and then theatre (Grace 2000). Others have paid considerable attention to Lowry's love of music, especially jazz (see Epstein, and Collier) and,

most recently, opera (see Duplay). My initial thoughts about Lowry and Debussy began when I was the Malcolm Lowry Professor, in Mexico, for 2000, and presented a lecture on "Lowry and the Sister Arts."

[2] My great thanks to friend and colleague Linda Hutcheon for asking me to appear with her on this panel for the Rocky Mountain Language Association meetings of October 2001. I have revised the essay to include some recent news about a possible opera of *Under the Volcano* and the insights of Mathieu Duplay; see note 5.

[3] It is a special pleasure to thank my colleagues Bryan Gooch, Vera Micznik, and Paul Stanwood for their assistance with Debussy's opera. My thanks as well to Florence Hayes, Music Division, the National Archives of Canada, for locating production details for the Toronto première of *Pelléas and Mélisande* in Massey Hall on 21 September 1944: Wilfrid Pelletier directed the Metropolitan chorus, with Bidu Sayao as Mélisande, Martial Singher as Pelléas, and Lawrence Tibbett as Golaud.

[4] She made this observation in a conversation about the opera, and I am grateful to her for her insights.

[5] As I prepare this essay for publication at the end of the 2009 Lowry Centenary Conference, plans are underway to create an opera of *Under the Volcano* and, as Mathieu –Duplay insists, Yvonne must be a mezzo soprano opposite Geoffrey's baritone. If this does come to fruition and if Hugh is a tenor, then this would be one of those rare grand operas in which the female and male leads die and the tenor lives.

12

Remembering Tomorrow:
Malcolm Lowry, War, and Under the Volcano

> *The thing is not to make excuses for the way you behaved—not*
> *to take refuge in tragedy—but to clarify who you are through*
> *your response to when you lived. If you can't do that, then you*
> *haven't made your contribution to the future.*
> (Findley, *The Wars*)

> *"Do you remember—" "No!"*
> (*UV*, 55)

> *"Do you remember the Armadillo?"*
> *"I haven't forgotten, anything!"*
> (*UV*, 334)

> *"Do you remember tomorrow?"*
> (*UV*, 358–59)

I: Remembering Lowry

Under the Volcano is a novel drenched in memories, in remembering *and* forgetting, because, like war and peace, remembering and forgetting cannot be "cleaved into two convenient halves" (Dennis Bock, 206). Readers of the novel have always recognized this characteristic of the text, just as they have always acknowledged the importance of war, notably the Spanish Civil War and World War Two, for its setting and themes: Hugh is identified by the refrain, "They are losing the battle of the Ebro" (101); Yvonne is haunted by memories of her father, Captain Constable, whose picture, in uniform, she still carries with her (268–70);[1] Hugh and Geoffrey, flinging references to *War and Peace* at each other, argue savagely over the looming threat of World War Two, the wars in Spain and China, and the pros and cons of interference (322–25); and the closing passage describing Geoffrey's murder unequivocally connects his dying with the horrors of war (390–91).

In the light of readers' familiarity with *Volcano* and with the role World War Two plays in its multiple stories, I have asked myself why I wish to focus on the subject of war now, why I understand this subject as a key to the complex functioning of memory across the text, and why I am prepared to argue that *remembering*, specifically remembering war, constitutes one of the most important aspects of the narrative system of the novel. This new awareness results, in part, from a close study of the novel with students during 2008–09 and the opportunity to see the novel through the eyes of a young generation of Lowry readers for whom war and terror have once again become oppressive realities in daily life. But another reason for my interest and approach to the novel arises from my current research on the representation of war in literature and the arts and my attention to debates about memory, trauma, and commemoration, issues that have acquired prominence in literary and cultural studies and have provided me with fresh tools, new lenses, as it were, for re-reading a much-loved work I thought I knew by heart.

I began my investigation of Lowry's thoughts on war in general and on specific wars by re-reading his letters, early fiction and biography, and the results were surprising. On the one hand, I found more references to war than I had anticipated—or remembered—but on the other hand, I found some puzzling silences. After I have described the results of my preparatory research, I will turn to the *Volcano* to explore the constitutive function of memory and the central position of war within the narrativization of remembering in the novel. Some of the current discussions of memory, mourning, and trauma have been very useful—notably those by Dominick LaCapra, Pierre Nora, and Lawrence Kirmayer, and some relevant concepts articulated by Giorgio Agamben help me to see the *Volcano* from a fresh and important perspective. However, I can offer one observation from the start, an observation that informs the basis of my argument: I believe that *Under the Volcano* mobilizes memory ethically in an effort to overcome willed forgetting, that the text (in Freud's terms) works through a state of melancholia to a state of mourning from which it is possible to move forwards into a future.[2] I believe that Lowry *wants* us to remember the past, the world around us, and our responsibilities to that world, to our common humanity, our future, and future generations. Now more than ever, since the end of World War Two, this duty to remember and mourn the past is urgent, and Lowry's treatment of war in *Under the Volcano* speaks directly to contemporary twenty-first century experience.

In light of the biographical facts that he was just five at the beginning of the Great War, that he was an adult in Europe during the early thirties when the warning signs of Hitler's rise to power and the looming threat of imminent war in Spain were clear, and that he lived through World War Two, it might seem surprising that relatively few *direct* comments about these wars crop up in his letters. For example, I have located nothing of particular note about World War One in his letters. In a 1931 letter to Nordahl Grieg (*SC* I, 103), he makes a passing reference to that war in the context of discussing Rupert Brooke, and he admired both Brooke and Grieg as men of action who were also artists. The next war prompted a few comments in his letters without, however, producing any close analysis. Grieg, who had become one of Lowry's symbolic heroes (notably for *In Ballast to the White Sea*), continued to be important to him; he kept track of Grieg's activities during the war (as his 1940 letter to Aiken makes clear, *SC* I, 295), and included Grieg's death in his list of personal losses in a December 1944 letter to Aiken in which he thanks Aiken for sending him a copy of *The Soldier*.[3] The background for this letter is his plan to return to Dollarton after the fire, and the losses and worries he lists are "The old man dying, Nordahl dead. In Ballast is no more. Brother Wilfrid in the Royal Artillery, Russell in the police" (*SC* I, 469).[4]

His early letters to Margerie also demonstrate his concern about World War Two and his attention to news reports. Writing to her from Vancouver in early September 1939, he describes the war-mongering in the streets—"the Irish Fusiliers ... playing recruiting songs," "a child of six ... waving a baton at a bunch of bulgy plug-uglies"—and comments that "The face of the war is an ugly one" (*SC* I, 224). He is anxious about the prospect of enlisting in Vancouver, but apparently even more concerned about his separation from her. A few days later, on 9 September 1939, he writes to her again and this time, with Canada's entry into the war just hours away (on 10 September) and his duty to enlist ever more pressing, his comments are more extensive and, I think, very telling:

> There is no question of sheep or being *drawn* in to this war, but I am sick of the subject & if we must talk about it, we must do so as dispassionately as we can. [...] War is being declared to-morrow here so perhaps you can understand that I have been working under difficulties, but difficulties negligible compared with what others have to go through. If you feel like breaking, think of all the other dreams unfulfilled, the children unseen, the books unwritten, the work never to be done, the last nights together, the countless acres of anguish and the darkened haunted cities: consider the pity war distils & ourselves as creatures of luck, compared with the others who can gain no last moments more. (*SC* I, 228)

As we know, Lowry did not enlist or, at least, he was not accepted when he tried.[5] But his sentiments in this letter are measured and generous (albeit lifted from an unacknowledged source)[6] so that I am tempted to say that for once he is fully aware of his *relative* good fortune.

What the Lowry family in England was enduring and what they thought or felt about his position regarding this war (or war more generally) must now be pieced together from fragments of surviving correspondence, Russell's commentaries, and from Lowry's biographers. Douglas Day has almost nothing to say about the two

World Wars or their impact on Lowry, and Jan Gabrial claims that, when the Spanish Civil War erupted, "we remained uninvolved" (95). Although Sheryl Salloum says little about the Vancouver wartime scene, she reprints an interesting piece Lowry wrote for the *Vancouver Sun* called "Hollywood and the War" (Salloum, 142–44), but Gordon Bowker draws on a wealth of British war memories (his own and Russell Lowry's) and context to relate Lowry's growing up, his family's experiences, and Lowry's work, to the wars. Malcolm was simply too young—a school boy aged five to nine years—during the Great War to be very aware of events, but his eldest brother Stuart (born in 1895) fought in the war, saw action in France from 1916 on, and was idealized by his kid brother as a heroic soldier. Some of Stuart's letters home have survived (they are with the Lowry Family Fonds), but his remarks about the war are brief. When he returned home he had been promoted to the rank of Captain, but any career in the army he might have wanted was curtailed by arthritis. Possibly the progress of the war was discussed at home, but the boys were often away at school and it is unlikely that Evelyn or Arthur Lowry would have dwelt on their fears for Stuart or their views about war in front of the younger boys. In short, Malcolm's knowledge of events had to be second-hand. Nevertheless, it is not idle speculation to suggest that the family was proud of their soldier son Stuart, relieved when he returned to them in one piece, and that the younger brothers admired him and felt they had missed out on an exciting adventure.

By 1939, Malcolm's relationship with his family was radically different. If he felt guilty about not fighting—and I believe he must have felt considerable social, political, and familial pressure—or defensive about his anti-military views, he does not declare these feelings clearly in his letters. The one brief exception was his insistence to his father that he has been "very anti-Hitler for years," is "no pacifist," has "no intention of ducking out of the war" and detests the Oxford Group (see *SC* I, 300). But the inescapable facts were that throughout World War Two, Lowry was living safely on the west coast of Canada completely removed from any first-hand witnessing of the appalling realities of the war. And yet, despite living in comparative isolation on the beach, he could not ignore the black-out curtains, the siren warnings, the constant headlines, reports of casualties, and propaganda in the papers, and the militant, aggressive attitudes of most Canadians, and he may very well have seen the CPR memorial to the Great War on Cordova Street on his trips into Vancouver (see Figure 1). Nevertheless, he could not, in all conscience, speak as a witness (never mind as a combatant) or even as a survivor. Of course, his distance from wartime realities did not preclude his need to address the challenges and obscenities of war in general and of this war in particular, as is clear from "Hollywood and the War." To learn more about his attitudes towards war in general, however, we must look to his fiction where he has much of value to say and where his deepest feelings and convictions are made clear. Indeed, I would go so far as to say that the subject of war, which dominated the past century and framed Lowry's

Figure 1: CPR War
Memorial, Vancouver.

life, is a fundamental one for him and that it haunts almost every page of *Under the Volcano.*

By the time Malcolm went to The Leys in 1923, the school had a well-established and honoured tradition of military training pre-dating the first war. But during that war, according to James Hilton, "it was a frantic world; and we knew even if we did not talk about it. Slowly, inch by inch, the tide of war lapped to the gates of our seclusion ... " (quoted in Houghton, 180). Of the one thousand boys attending when war broke out in 1914, nine hundred and twenty-two served and by the end one hundred and forty-six had not survived. After the war, the Leys Chapel walls were "lined with memorial tablets" bearing the names of The Leys war dead, and in 1922 a special Memorial was unveiled outside the Chapel by the Duke of York, later King George VI (see Houghton, 181, 200). The base of this Memorial bears this quotation from *Pilgrim's Progress*: "My marks and scars I carry with me to be a witness for me that I have fought His battles Who will be my Rewarder." During his years at The Leys Malcolm would have seen the Memorial and the Chapel tablets on a daily basis.

The Leys had established an Officers' Training Corps (OTC) at least as early as 1905, and this made military activities a regular part of school routine. Malcolm joined the OTC upon his arrival, but he was a reluctant participant and went so far as to mock the entire business in a 1925 story published in the *Leys Fortnightly*. This story, called "Travelling Light," is an interesting piece of juvenilia for the light it sheds on a sixteen-year-old Lowry's antipathy for the trappings of military dress, protocol, and behaviour, as well as for its use of what would become familiar Lowryan devices and images (of trains, black dogs, symbolic landscapes, literary intertexts, and above all dream-narratives). The first-person narrator is returning by train to his school after a family wedding (as Lowry did from Wilfrid's wedding, in fact). He is supposed to arrive in time "to attend a full dress Corps parade" (8), but he loathes the prospect—the "black dog of this parade had sat on [his] back" throughout the wedding festivities and spoiled his fun by reminding him that his uniform was dirty, his "cap badge was missing" and worst of all, his "puttees still retained the mud of the last field-day but one" (9). In a flourish of literary panache, the narrator sums up his feelings in "the words of the poet": "A curse it is these nights to be alive: / To be arrayed in panoply of war / Doth aggravate the evil" (8).

However, lulled by the motion of the train, he falls asleep only to have "a dreadful dream":

> I dreamt that on arriving at the School I found it burnt to the ground. A few charred puttees, a smouldering tunic, a pair of bags too wide to be wholly consumed were all that was left of the Leys .... As I walked over the ashes that once had been the King's Building I tripped over .... a human foot in a Corps boot. (11)

The parallel between this grisly scene and any number of reports Lowry could have heard or read about No Man's Land is obvious, but the point of the story is that by falling asleep he has missed his connection and has ended up in Edinburgh. This discovery fills him with "rapture" because now "I need not stick my bayonet into the back of my trousers, and [because] I was, in a word, saved!" (12). Except that he is not really saved at all, as he quickly admits; he must make up for the missed parade. Therefore, he has told his little "account of the tragedy" to soothe his "troubled feelings," although precisely which feelings—of regret, of guilt, or of annoyance at not being saved after all—he never says. The tone of this little piece is cheeky but also ambivalent, with touches of the ludicrous and of self-mockery (that bayonet in the backside, for example). Nevertheless, it is clear enough where Lowry's sentiments lay when it came to the OTC, what it represented, and his awkward inability to belong.

That said, "Travelling Light" is insignificant when compared with a mature story written in France in the early thirties. "June 30th, 1934" has a simple plot: two Englishmen are travelling by train through northwestern France to catch the boat train from Calais to Folkstone on the way to London. During their journey, they comment on the past war, about which the older man, a World War One veteran called Firmin, is constantly reminded as they pass through the landscapes, former battlefields, and the towns of the Somme. Firmin's constant refrain is, "There was a lot of fighting here" (58), as he remembers his injuries, the severe cold of the trenches, the battles, the places (Amiens, Boulogne), and the "terrible" Café Cristol (39). We see the passing scenes and hear the conversation through the focalization of his travelling companion, the Reverend Bill Goodyear from "West Kirby, Cheshire, England" (56), who is younger than Firmin, in fact, "too young for the war" (38), as Firmin assumes. Through Goodyear we see the billboard signs and advertisements for Cocteau's *La Machine infernale* or for Charles Boyer in *La Bataille* (36) as the train makes its way to the coast, and Goodyear also reads the French newspaper account of the riots caused by the Stavisky case and for some unstated reason begins to feel "a bit like Stavisky himself" (36). Why he should feel this identification with the famous swindler (who was also Jewish and whose case fuelled increasing anti-Semitism in early 1930s France) is left for the reader to ponder. However, Goodyear is especially perplexed (his French is poor) and troubled by the newspaper's apparent linking of the need "to promote peace" with closer relations between the French market and German steel cartels (36). Here Lowry is deploying a narrative strategy that has become familiar from *Under the Volcano*; he is hinting at the political and economic machinations behind war, scattering clues about covert operations, and establishing fragments of the context for looming threats of war and a dubious, fragile peace. War and peace are, indeed, the subject of this story, as they would be once more for *Volcano*.

"June 30th, 1934" deserves closer attention than I can give it here, but there are a few more details that I want to note before moving on because they situate this story as an important precursor to the *Volcano*. The full title of the piece refers first and foremost to 30 June 1934, when Hitler began the "Night of the Long Knives," the execution of members of his SA Brownshirts (the *Sturmabteilung*), to suppress a revolt, but the date inevitably recalls the horrors of the Somme during June and July 1916. By the time Goodyear and Firmin reach England and board the train to London, they have purchased British newspapers with headlines screaming: "*Hitler*

Atrocities. Germany Under Arms" (46, 47). The two men fall into conversation again when Firmin remarks that "They're at it again .... They're forcing another war on us now" (46). Goodyear is not so sure and replies: "I don't really think this [Hitler's purge] means war" (46), but then he wonders if he is perhaps deceiving himself.

If he is indulging in self-deception by dismissing Firmin's gloomy fears about the potential for interests behind the scenes to make money from another war, then this is not his only deception. While still in France, Goodyear told Firmin two deliberate and astounding lies—he said that he too had fought in the war and that his only brother was killed in the fighting: "We used to like to think that he's buried in France," Goodyear claimed. "His body was never identified and we don't care to speak of it" (40). Goodyear's unspoken reflections and rationalization for this fabrication are interesting—

> Goodyear didn't understand why he had told his untruth. Had he wanted to be this man's comrade; to make up to him somehow, for his wounds, and had thought by this falsehood about the war, to bring himself nearer to him, and so to humanity, towards which was his responsibility, and in whose eyes—and were not these Firmin's eyes?—his failure would seem the more excusable? (40–41)

It seems clear from this passage that Goodyear's embarrassment at not having fought and at not having suffered any direct loss from the war motivates, at least in part, his "curious falsehood." He sees himself as having failed—failed Firmin, failed humanity, failed his responsibility to society, maybe even to history—and he feels himself excluded, not this man's "comrade," because he did not fight. In short, Goodyear feels guilty, even though he was only a boy (the same age as his son, Dick, is now in 1934) during the war. As is always the case with Lowry, there is a decidedly thin line separating autobiography from fiction, and I suspect that in many ways Goodyear speaks for and represents aspects of Lowry himself, such as his acknowledgement that he did not fight, that he may be dangerously naïve about current events in Europe, that he feels like a failure who is excluded from the brotherhood of valiant men (like Stuart, like Rupert Brooke, and like those boys whose names line the walls of the Leys Chapel), and that he longs for acceptance.

Insofar as the Firmin of "June 30th, 1934" points forward to the Consul and is a spokesman for *some* of Lowry's anxieties about military aggression, self-interested economic schemes, and the threat of another war, he is also an example of what Goodyear calls an "ominous" and "sinister contradiction" because, despite being "badly wounded in the war," he is now employed by "a German company" prospecting for metals (42). Firmin seems positioned to benefit as much as possible from the materials needed in Europe's race to re-arm, and the fears aroused by his post/pre-war prospecting will be transformed into Goodyear's terrifying closing vision of fire and violence as the train screams "like a shell, through a metal world" (48). But it is Goodyear (a Lowry focalizer after all) who is left with the responsibility, in this story, of posing the most searching questions, questions that plagued Lowry and to which he would return in *Volcano*:

> Was there really a sort of determinism about the fate of nations? Could it be true that, in the end, they too got what they deserved? What had a given people done or not done that they should be obliterated? ... [And] What about England? ... What is wrong with *us*? ... And what is wrong with me? (43)

II: *Volcano* and the Landscape of Memory

After Margerie joined him in Vancouver, Lowry began planning the revisions to his "Volcano" manuscript that he would undertake as soon as it reached him from Los Angeles in January 1940. With the possibility of enlisting pressing in on him, he worked frantically over the next six months to complete what we know as *The 1940 Under the Volcano*. Thanks to Paul Tiessen and Miguel Mota, this early draft of the novel (the one rejected by twelve publishers) was published in 1994, and Frederick Asals wrote an excellent introduction for the volume. As Asals reminds us, Lowry "was an ocean away" from the Spanish Civil War "during its entire course" and while

> Lowry like others of his generation was moved by its issues and implications ... it touched him less directly than the war now directly menacing England, one in which his own participation threatened not to be a matter of choice. The European conflict is a palpable presence in the 1940 *Volcano*; the particularities of the Spanish war he would have to work up later. (xvi)

And World War Two *is* palpably present on every second page, or so it seems. However, World War One retains its ghostly grip on the 1940 text and the Spanish Civil War, albeit little more than a few noises off, remains lurking in the wings waiting for the revisions required to bring the final novel to fruition seven years later.

It is important to remember that during the six months of work in 1940, and again over the following years of extensive re-structuring and re-conceptualization, Lowry was surrounded by constant reminders of the war in Europe and then the war in the Pacific. Although his anxiety over enlisting, or even being conscripted, was eventually allayed, daily newspapers, radio broadcasts, and local events kept the war before him.[7] Vancouver was always comparatively safe; nevertheless, its citizens were subjected to a barrage of propaganda, war-mongering, and racial profiling, and they suffered a share in the inevitable tragic losses of local men killed overseas. After Pearl Harbor, the west coasts of Canada and the United States were believed to be under increasing threat from the Japanese, with the consequences that we now know well: black-out curtains, air raid sirens, intense propaganda leading to the internment of Japanese-Canadians, and the stationing of troops in the Northwest.

The differences between the 1940 and the 1947 *Volcano* are many and profound, and it is not my purpose now to examine them in detail.[8] However, a few observations will suggest the degree to which the subject of war informed the 1940 text, where and how Lowry initially introduced the subject, and the extent to which he carried the subject forward into the final novel. The initial thing to strike a reader of the 1940 novel will be its two epigraphs. The first is a quotation from a Henry James letter of 4 August 1914:

> The plunge of civilization into this abyss of blood and darkness … is a thing that so gives away the whole long age during which we have supposed the world to be, with whatever abatement, gradually bettering, that to have to take it all now for what the treacherous years were all the while really making for and *meaning* is too tragic for any words. (*1940 UV*, 3)

The second epigraph is the last two stanzas of Matthew Arnold's "Dover Beach" with its frightening conclusion: "And we are here as on a darkling plain / Swept with confused alarms of struggle and flight, / Where ignorant armies clash by night." (*1940 UV*, 3).

Lowry's point in choosing these passages is to remind us, not only of the Great War, and of the persistence of "treacherous years" and constant threats from "ignorant armies," but also to show from the start that the novel we are reading is about war, about civilization plunged into another abyss, about betrayals, incertitude, and pain. Such epigraphs are perhaps obvious (at least moreso than the ones for the final novel) and certainly bereft of hope. More importantly, Lowry created his Jacques Laruelle character for his new chapter one; he established Laruelle as the French filmmaker about to return home to fight for his country in World War Two; and he positioned Laruelle as the central remembering consciousness for the story of Geoffrey's life and death. Through Laruelle, his conversations with Dr. Vigil, his thoughts, memories, and visit to the bar of the Cinema Morelos, Lowry establishes a heavy, pervasive presence for the war, for the "inescapableness of conflict," "the darkening … horizon of the world," and "the thunder of war growing always nearer" (*1940 UV*, 32–33). As Laruelle notes when he enters the bar—"everyone was talking about the war" (26). However, like the James and Arnold epigraphs, all this "talking about war" seems too obvious, somewhat heavy-handed, and Lowry would overhaul the way he introduced the subject until, by 1947, war in general and the three wars central to the story were woven carefully, judiciously, and *effectively* into the very fabric of the text.

As Asals noted, the war in Spain is much less present in this version and losing the Battle of the Ebro is not yet a refrain. Talk about the politics and economics behind wars is already in place, but it is too preachy and finally sounds banal. The *Samaritan* memory is there in chapter six (complete with German officers in the ship's furnace), but it has none of the vaguely sinister, haunting quality that it will acquire by 1947. Nevertheless, many references to various wars and to the general subject of war are already mobilized by Lowry; they just aren't strategically placed and repeated.[9] Among these references are the Consul's string of accusations hurled at Hugh about do-gooders interfering in "poor defenceless Spain," "poor little defenceless Ethiopia," and

> Before that, it was little defenceless Belgium, although always bear in mind before that, it was poor little defenceless Flanders. And what about the poor little defenceless Belgian Congo? Leopold I the Great emancipator, eh? And tomorrow it will be poor little defenceless Luxembourg. Or Latvia. Or Piddledee—[…] And in Tolstoy's day it was poor little defenceless Montenegro. Poor little defenceless Serbia! (*1940 UV*, 309)

Another ringing phrase to appear here and echo back to "June 30th, 1934" and forward to the final *Under the Volcano* is the Consul's disgusted pronouncement that "there's a sort of determinism about the fate of nations" and that they "get what they deserve" (*1940 UV*, 304). By 1947 this phrase will once more be formulated as a question, as it was in the short story—"Can't you see there's a sort of determinism about the fate of nations?" (*UV*, 322)—with the result that it sinks back into the narrative fabric of the novel instead of sticking out like a sore thumb. Tolstoy's *War and Peace* plays a more obvious intertextual role in this version than it does in the final text, but that hardly means it is less important here than there. In 1940 the frequent references and chatter about Tolstoy's novel are obtrusive; by 1947, when they surface suddenly, the impact is more startling and more ominous. When it came to the concluding vision of death, war, and destruction, Lowry retained the 1940 version but once more he made small but judicious changes: gone are the "million crackling aeroplanes slanting across the stars," and one million burning bodies becomes ten million (see *1940 UV*, 376–77, and *UV*, 390–91). Smaller adjustments to punctuation, word order, and slightly increased repetition (notably "falling") serve to make the 1947 text more subtle, more terrifying, more final—and yet, paradoxically, more hopeful.

Thus far, I have focused on war—on what Lowry thought about and did with *his* historical moment—and on some of the ways in which war appears as a theme, or an issue to debate, or as a source of imagery in his work. In turning now to the final *Under the Volcano*, I want to shift my focus to the function of memory, remembering, and memories because *Volcano* is a memory-text, by which I mean that it is a narrative about memory and forgetting, about the process of remembering, and about the role of this process in constituting identity (individual, communal, national, or broadly human). Memory in the novel, be it the memory of direct, personal experience, or what we now call, after Marianne Hirsch, the post-memory of generationally distant influences (see Hirsch, 22), is fundamental to the structure, story, purpose, and meaning of the text. Memory (including remembering, forgetting, and post-memory) operates in the following ways:

a. to produce a foundational "landscape of memory" built up from several *lieux de mémoire* and existing within the metaphoric *milieux de mémoire* of the text;[10]
b. to thematise and narrativise the loss or maintenance of a fully functioning, responsible human identity;
c. to dramatise the crippling effect of melancholia and the urgent need to work through grief, guilt, and trauma into a state of mourning; and,
d. to warn its readers that the consequences of refusing to mourn include a form of ethical paralysis in the face of what Agamben calls a "state of exception" (see *State of Exception*, 50)

Let me take up each of these four descriptions of the novel in turn, with particular attention to memories of war.

Memory is critical to the tightly woven fabric of themes in *Under the Volcano*—themes such as marriage, family relations, love, friendship or brotherhood, alcoholism, sin and guilt, damnation and salvation—as well as the theme of war. Readers, like the characters, are constantly being asked to think about, by remembering, the past, the dead—it is after all the Mexican Day of the Dead in 1938 and 1939—their sins of omission as well as commission, and the significance of a bewildering number of recurring quotations, signs, symbols, references, and elusive, haunting voices, seen or heard once, twice, or more often, but fleetingly, almost *en passant*. We can be forgiven if, like Geoffrey (or is it Hugh?), we cannot remember *War and Peace* well enough to distinguish it from *Anna Karenina*, or cannot quite recall the punctuation on, or the exact translation of, that sign in the garden—"Le gusta este jardín?"—or when we last saw it. Just reading the novel is a test of one's memory. Chapters two through twelve can be seen as Jacques Laruelle's remembering of the last day in his old friend's life; they may also represent (as Lowry told Jonathan Cape, *SC* I, 510–11) Jacques's creation of a Faust film, but they are, I suggest, his biographical commemoration of Geoffrey Firmin and, to a degree, his own memoir insofar as Geoffrey's biography is closely intertwined with Jacques's autobiography. Outside Jacques, orchestrating *his* memories, subject position, and intradiegetic perspective, is of course Malcolm Lowry, the author.[11] But my chief concern is with the subject of war and the ways in which war is explored through remembrance, so I must leave the other themes and narratological matters to the side to focus on a few instances of the characters' remembering and, at times, willful forgetting, of war.

It is significant that each of the characters has one war or another in his or her life and that each character is haunted by that fact. Jacques, for example, can no more forget World War One (he served in the French artillery under Guillaume Apollinaire [33]) than he can ignore his imminent departure for France and World War Two, the evidence all around him in 1939 Quahnahuac (Cuernavaca) of the "pro-Almazán, pro-Axis" newspaper put out by the fascist Unión Militar (24), or that German "hieroglyphic of the times" *The Hands of Orlac* (26). He sees the people around him at the Cinema as "warriors waiting for the show to begin" (30) and believes that "if the Allies lost" the coming war, life would be worse than if they won (10). Visiting, one last time, the ruins of Maximilian's Palace, he remembers the ghosts of Maximilian and Carlotta, of Geoffrey and Yvonne, and of Archduke Ferdinand, who also met with a "violent death" (15). His walk through the surrounding fields and the streets of the town becomes a type of frightening walk down a grotesque memory lane in which, he realizes, "wherever you turned the abyss was waiting for you" (16). Through Jacques's walk and his re-visiting of key *lieux de mémoire* (like the Palace), Lowry establishes the general outlines of a "landscape of memory" that he will develop, fill in, and explore throughout the novel, and without which the various traumas of the novel cannot be understood.

One of the most important memories buried in this landscape that surfaces through Jacques (the other crucial one is Geoffrey's unsent letter to Yvonne in the book of Elizabethan plays, the letter Jacques will burn) is the story of the SS *Samaritan*. During World War One, this "unarmed merchantman ... with a cargo of antimony and quicksilver and wolfram" was loitering close to interesting islands in the Pacific near the East China Sea, when the periscope of a German U-boat appeared and the innocent *Samaritan* turned into a Q-ship "belching fire": "The U-boat did not even have time to dive," or so Jacques recalls the story. "Her entire crew was captured. The *Samaritan* ... sailed on leaving the submarine burning helplessly" (33–34). Moreover, Geoffrey, possibly a "lieutenant-commander" by this point in the war, was "largely responsible for this escapade" and received a medal (Jacques cannot remember which one) for this naval success (34). However, as anyone who knows *Volcano* will recall, the story does not end there; something dreadful and illegal happened to the German officers from the U-boat. Although these men had time-honoured rights to protection and respect (the second treaty of the Geneva Convention, adopted in 1906, addressed armed forces at sea), they were "kidnapped by the *Samaritan*'s stokers and burned alive in the furnaces" (34). Whether or not Geoffrey had ordered their murder, as commander he was blamed and "had not received his decoration without first being court-martialled" (34). Jacques remembers Geoffrey discussing "the incident" with him and dismissing the whole affair as a joke—"People simply did not go around ... putting Germans in furnaces" (35)—until, in the months before his death when he was in such a state of alcoholic despair (according to Jacques's memory) that "his life had become a quixotic oral fiction," Geoffrey not only proclaimed his guilt but confessed that he had "always suffered horribly on account of it" (35).

The truth about Commander Firmin's role in the *Samaritan* incident will never be clarified in the novel. Instead, the horror, guilt, illegality, and shame associated with it will hover over Geoffrey and provide some of the most haunting and disturbing reverberations in the text. The ironically named *Samaritan* symbolizes the hatred, violence, and brutality of war; the deaths of the German officers foreshadows all too horribly the fate of millions of Jews at the hands of the Nazis, and it is no accident that Hugh's memory is troubled by his past anti-Semitism or that Geoffrey will be accused of being "a Jew chingao" (386) by the fascist Unión Militar moments before they kill him. Both Ackerley and Bowker (relying on Russell Lowry's memory) have traced the probable source for the Q-ship story to an actual World War One scandal involving the HMS *Baralong*, a British warship masquerading as "a nondescript tramp ship" flying "the neutral American flag" (O'Neill, 8). In fact, the *Baralong*, captained by Commander Godfrey Herbert, was armed with three twelve-pounder guns and depth charges; it tricked the U-boat, sank it, and then its Royal Marines shot the German sailors as they swam towards another ship, the *Nicosian*, which the U-boat had originally stopped and boarded. The German *Kapitänleutnant* Bernard Wegener, according to some reports, was shot as he tried to swim to the *Baralong* and the Germans who had boarded the *Nicosian* were cornered in the engine room by the Marines and shot on the spot. No member of the German crew survived because Herbert had ordered that his men take no prisoners. According to Gerry O'Neill, the "scandal of the *Baralong* incident was hidden [behind a] veil of secrecy." Other reports claim that Herbert demanded silence from all who witnessed the executions, his report to the Admiralty was censored, the *Baralong*'s name was changed to protect it from German revenge, and the Q-ship's crew received a bounty prize for sinking the U-boat. However, word about the fate of the Germans leaked out to the newspapers, gossip spread along the Merseyside docks, and the incident became well-known, albeit never officially acknowledged, in England and the United States. The German government rightly called the execution of the U-boat crew a British war crime (a term still used to characterize what happened); they issued a medal commemorating the *U-27*, and it has been suggested that the incident led to increased German cruelty at sea during World War Two.[12]

The importance of the *Samaritan* memories in *Volcano* cannot, I think, be over-emphasized. Although we get the fullest recollection of what happened and of what Geoffrey's role may have been in chapter one, echoes and half-submerged memories surface several times in the novel. For example, in chapter three, Geoffrey, whose mind is besieged by "blown fragments of … memories" (71) and of many things he has "tried to forget" (82), is jolted into awareness of his present existence (and Yvonne's presence) by a partial, accusatory recollection: "Ah, what a world it was, that trampled down the truth and drunkards alike! [he thinks.] A world full of bloodthirsty people, no less! Bloodthirsty, did I hear you say bloodthirsty, Commander Firmin?" (89). Except that Geoffrey has not spoken out loud. Instead, he represses this ugly memory of his past bloodthirstiness and guilt—the "truth," if you will—to speak to Yvonne about his drinking. It is as if, to his mind at least, his getting drunk is the lesser, the more acceptable, of the two evils linked by this memory of his World War One Q-ship, and that his drinking is, in part, explained or excused by his guilty past. A bit later in the morning (chapter five), while he pretends to inspect his garden, this memory surfaces once more, but this time the name "Liverpool" triggers his memory:

> Liverpool, whence sailed so often during the war under sealed orders those mysterious submarine catchers Q-boats, fake freighters turning into turreted men-of-war at a moment's notice, obsolete peril of submarines, the snouted voyagers of the sea's unconscious … (138)

On the previous occasion, the memory seemed to gesture towards the truth and an excuse for drinking. This time, the persistent memory definitely stands as an image of Geoffrey and of what he has become as a consequence of the Q-boat atrocity: he is not what he seems, an innocent, betrayed husband, an Adam about to be evicted from Eden because of a sinful Eve. In fact, who or what he really is, is no longer clear, not even to himself. He has, as we are told in many ways, lost himself, just as he will apparently lose the documents that attest to his legal citizenship and official identity on the ferris wheel of chapter seven. When we next read about the *Samaritan*, in chapter six, we are looking through Hugh's eyes at a photograph on the wall of Geoffrey's bedroom "of a small camouflaged freighter" (193) and hearing Geoffrey explain to Hugh that "*everything* about the *Samaritan* was a ruse" (193, my italics). The Consul claims to have "cut that picture out of a German magazine" (193), and for some vague reason Hugh assumes that the existence of the framed photograph hanging in this room discounts "most of the old stories" (193) swirling around his brother's World War One command. But there are other plausible assumptions one could make, especially in light of Geoffrey's insistence that "everything" about the ship was a ruse. Despite his peripatetic life and propensity to lose things or leave them behind, he has kept this picture of his past because that was the time, in those ship's quarters, when he lost himself by betraying the man he should have been and suspending the laws of the sea and of war. That picture serves as a *mise en abyme* of his former *lost* identity and of his duplicitous, bloodthirsty one. It is also an *aide mémoire* to a past he is still unable to fully account for but keeps revisiting. It is yet another form of writing on the wall (among several such writings) reminding him of his guilt and warning him of the consequences.

Before I move on to consider matters of melancholia, mourning, and *Volcano*'s portrayal of ethical paralysis that produces what Agamben calls a "state of exception," I should pause to reflect on where remembering and forgetting have left readers of the *Volcano* and Laruelle's three main characters. By the time we have finished chapter one, Laruelle (Lowry) has mapped the terrain for his story (film) and situated his three characters within it. He has, in fact, established a "landscape of memory" for the entire work. I have borrowed this term from Laurence Kirmayer's study "The Landscapes of Memory: Trauma, Narrative, and Dissociation" because it captures the crucial nexus between physical/real and narrative/fictional settings (the more familiar term for novels and films) and the function of memory. Kirmayer uses this concept to identify "the metaphoric terrain that shapes the distance and effort required to remember affectively charged and socially defined events that initially may be vague, impressionistic, or simply absent from memory."[13] He argues that memories of certain kinds of extreme trauma (such as Holocaust survival or battle experiences) cannot be acknowledged, let alone managed, if a narrative template for that trauma is absent in society. Put simply, if an individual or a society lacks a familiar or appropriate narrative form for telling certain kinds of stories, extreme personal or group experiences of trauma remain untold and unacknowledged, with the consequence that public and private validation and healing cannot begin. Indeed, an individual's attempt to describe the memories of such experiences may be met with denial and shaming by the family, community, or nation. Kirmayer's theory is more complex and nuanced than my brief outline suggests and his psychoanalytic goals are different from mine. Nevertheless, I find this notion of "landscape of memory" (originally borrowed from literary and artistic practices) useful and productive when re-applied to novels (and other art forms) that deal with war.

In the case of *Under the Volcano*, we have stories about wars, traumatic experiences, grief, guilt, shame, and suffering that *must* be told through memories—Jacques's memories and post-memories of his own and the others' lives and Yvonne's, Hugh's, and Geoffrey's memories and post-memories—if they are to be told, shared, understood, and managed at all. Moreover, to tell this story, which is at once shocking, terrifying, deeply personal, and manifestly public, the artist/rememberer must create a "landscape of memory," a narrative ground, that produces and validates events, that brings forgotten or lost memories to the surface of language and consciousness and situates these memories securely within an increasingly familiar and meaningful (interpretable) landscape. A central and artistically effective way of creating this landscape is through the establishment of what I am calling (after Pierre Nora) *lieux de mémoires*—sites (real and fictional) like Maximilian's Palace, the Cinema Morelos, Señora Gregorio's bar, Jacques's *zacuali*, the *Samaritan* photograph and caption, and, most importantly, the Farolito in Parián. Throughout the novel, these sites, or places, will be revisited, remembered, and re-inscribed with accumulating significance, and all are permeated with a range of memories, be they historical and national, local and indigenous, or personal. Memory, then, the remembering and forgetting, the post-memories, and the haunting of tomorrow by today and yesterday, is the sustaining infrastructure for developing the themes, producing the stories, and establishing the characters that, together, are *Under the Volcano*.

Within the novel and its landscape, war is a constant presence, and wars haunt, and determine, the lives of all four characters. World War One surfaces constantly from the past; the Spanish war intrudes persistently in the present; and World War

Two hovers menacingly ahead in the immediate future. The story of the *Samaritan* incident, although tied emphatically to the Great War and the Consul, links Laruelle and Hugh with Geoffrey, and impinges upon Yvonne. As is so often true with Lowry's material, this story derives from historical facts, which I might add is also the case with most artistic representations of war.[14] But more importantly, the *Samaritan* incident establishes the crucial moral and legal position of Geoffrey Firmin; it symbolizes the long shadow of World War One as a cause of the war and horror to follow; it illuminates what Geoffrey represents and why he dies as he does, and it opens the basic questions posed by the text: how does Geoffrey deal with his past and how should we? The answer, I suggest, is that he doesn't, that to return to Timothy Findley's words from *The Wars* with which I began, he takes "refuge in tragedy," and he so obsessively returns to past trauma that he cannot distinguish past from present. Lowry, Laruelle, and possibly the readers are the ones who must deal with this past, this "landscape of memory," this story, and work through its sorrow. Moreover, Geoffrey exemplifies existence as "bare life," as "*homo sacer*," beyond the limits of law (see Agamben, *Homo Sacer*, 8). Having once authorized (or so I believe) a "state of exception" from the bridge of his Q-ship, he is now living in such a state himself and he will be killed with impunity. To demonstrate how I reach this conclusion, I must return to the novel and to Geoffrey's inability to mourn.

I have come to see Geoffrey, neither as the hero of the story nor as a victim or scapegoat for the sins of humanity, but as a symbol of a negative condition associated with a loss of identity and responsibility. He also represents a warning for anyone who pays attention. To be sure, he has suffered and failed, he has been hurt and abandoned (by mother, father, brother, wife), but his response to these events in his life is to withdraw into a melancholic state in which he obsessively repeats and revisits the behaviours and places associated with trauma and loss. He becomes possessed by the ghosts of his past, unable and unwilling to distinguish past from present, or personal failings from historical crimes, and incapable of genuine mourning. As Dr. Vigil tells Laruelle, "Poor your friend, he spend his money on earth in such continuous tragedies" (5), and as he shouts at Hugh and Yvonne, "I love hell. I can't wait to get back there" (327). He is damned, but his damnation, like his hell, is largely of his own making. By contrast, Yvonne, Hugh, and especially Laruelle, are able to mourn; each remembers the past and grieves (or regrets) past events, and none of them conflates past and present. Instead, and in distinct ways, each acts out and works through the past in an effort to move on into an active, responsible future. Yvonne has returned to her past in the hope of laying the ghosts to rest, healing the trauma of betrayal and divorce, overcoming loss (of father, child, and husband) and moving into a new future in that northern, Canadian home she and, for a fleeting moment, Geoffrey envision. Hugh chooses to fight, however belatedly by November 1938, for Spain, and by doing so atone for his past. Yvonne dies without reaching Geoffrey, and yet because of him; Hugh seems less than convincing as a man of action and honour. But both, as LaCapra might put it, seek to come "to terms with trauma including its details" (as Yvonne says: "I haven't forgotten, *anything*!" [334]) and "critically [engage with] the tendency to act out the past and to recognize why it may be necessary" to do so (LaCapra, 144).

Laruelle, however, represents the most significant contrast to Geoffrey and the most successful example of how one should manage trauma through memory. He demonstrates what LaCapra calls the "empathetic unsettlement" of the "attentive secondary witness" (78) because he mourns the past, the loss of his friend, of Yvonne, and of Hugh (who he came to see as a son), but he never *identifies* with Geoffrey or mistakes himself as entitled to the subject position of a "surrogate victim" (78). Instead, "through memory work, especially the socially engaged memory work involved in working through" (LaCapra, 66), he is able to create art (whether we read chapters two to twelve as his film or, as I prefer, as his commemorative elegy/biography of his friends) in which the past is "performatively regenerated or relived" in what LaCapra calls an "experimental, nonredemptive" (179) narrative and in what I have been calling a "landscape of memory." Jacques Laruelle, then, is the connecting thread, the narrational centre of *Under the Volcano*.[15] Not only does he succeed where the others, especially Geoffrey, fail, but by using memory to confront the "traumatic dimensions of history" (LaCapra, 95) he also makes an "ethically desireable" contribution to our understanding of human nature and humanity's responsibility to the times through which we live and to the future. Although I cannot quite agree with LaCapra when he claims that much modern literature and art is "a relatively safe haven in which to explore post-traumatic effects" (180) of such catastrophic events as war, the Holocaust, and terrorism because *Under the Volcano* does not feel like a safe haven to me, I do agree with him that by remembering and mourning the "traumatic dimensions of history" (95), we can write history and fiction that "helps to make possible a legitimate democratic polity in the present and the future" (91). *Under the Volcano* exemplifies that kind of writing of history and trauma, and Laruelle (at least as I see him) is Lowry's mediating representative within the text.

But why does Geoffrey deliberately reject the idea of a future in any form (be it Yvonne and his marriage, a new life in Canada, or just a trip to Guanajuato), and what does his murder signify? To address these questions, and move on to my conclusions, I want to recruit three concepts developed by Giorgio Agamben in two of his recent books, *Homo Sacer: Sovereign Power and Bare Life* (1995; 1998) and *State of Exception* (2003; 2005) in which he elaborates on the history, meaning, and uses of states of exception. These three concepts are called by Agamben the condition of "bare life," which produces "*homo sacer*," and the implementation of a "state of exception" that makes "bare life" and "*homo sacer*" possible. My turn to Agamben not only enables me to trace the connections between *Volcano*'s "landscape of memory" and Geoffrey's destructive melancholia, but also helps me retain my focus on war, the processes of memory, key events like the *Samaritan* incident, and a collection of allusions to wars, to totalitarianism, and annihilation, remembered moments (such as Hugh's anti-Semitic behaviour or Laruelle's World War One service), and brief phrases or seemingly casual epithets such as losing the Battle of the Ebro, mistaking Geoffrey for Trotsky, or calling Geoffrey a Jew and an "espider" (386).

III: Remembering Tomorrow

"What for you lie?" the Chief of Rostrums repeated in a glowering voice. "You say your name is Black. No es Black. You say you are a wrider .... You no are a wrider .... You are no a de wrider, you are de espider, and we shoota de espiders in Méjico .... You no wrider .... You Al Capón. You a Jew chingao."

(UV, 386)

In *Homo Sacer*, Agamben describes the condition of "bare life" as one in which an individual is reduced to mere physical existence, stripped of all aspects of identity and value as a socio-political being and a citizen of a state with rights and subject-hood, and placed outside the law or at the boundary, or limit, of law even while existing within the geographical boundaries of the nation state. The most familiar English literary image to capture Agamben's meaning seems to me to be Lear's description of Edgar: "unaccommodated man is no more but such a poor, bare, forked animal as thou art" (III, iv, lines 100–101). Such an individual, Agamben argues, is a *homo sacer*: he "who may be killed and yet not sacrificed" (*Homo Sacer*, 8), "an outcast, a banned man, tabooed, dangerous" (*Homo Sacer*, 79) because he is polluted and contaminating. No one can be held accountable for killing a *homo sacer*. Agamben claims that the *homo sacer* is "the figure proposed by our age" (114), and he warns that "we are all virtually *homines sacri*" (115). In order for this radical devaluation to occur, what Agamben calls (after Walter Benjamin) a "state of exception" must be established by the executive branch of government (or of some other power) abrogating legislative processes to create "a permanent state of emergency" (*State*, 2). While Agamben can trace such practices back to classical times, he insists that what we experience today as states of exception began with World War One, intensified in all western nations but most emphatically in Germany before and during World War Two, and have now "become essential practices of contemporary states, including so-called democratic ones" (*State*, 2). What's more, he defines "modern totalitarianism ... as the establishment of the state of exception ... that allows for the physical elimination ... of entire categories of citizens" (*State*, 2).

Not surprisingly, Agamben's sharpest example of a state of exception is the Third Reich, and he describes the concentration camp as "*the space that is opened when the state of exception begins to become the rule*" (*Homo Sacer*, 168). "The Jews," he describes as examples of "bare life" or *homines sacri* who were exterminated "'as lice'" (Hitler's term, *Homo Sacer*, 114), and for whose killing no one could be held responsible by the Reich: "the Jews are the representatives par excellence and almost the living symbol of ... bare life that modernity necessarily creates within itself but whose presence it can no longer tolerate" (*Homo Sacer*, 179). Agamben's discussion of "bare life" and the "state of exception" is chilling in part because it rises from his passionate response to World War Two but also, in part, because he predicts that unless democracies stop betraying basic principles of law, human rights, and freedom (in places like Guantanamo or detainee camps—not prisoner of war camps, as defined by the Geneva Convention—in Afghanistan) a state of exception will become the "dominant paradigm" for handling "global civil war" (*State*, 2).

When Geoffrey Firmin is shot by the military police and thrown into the barranca with other garbage (like the dead dog), he becomes a *homo sacer*. No one will be prosecuted or held accountable for his murder because he has first been reduced to "bare life"—an espider, a Jew, a creature without identity or a real name, a thing of no value who may even be a spy and, thus, a danger to the powers that be. And the powers who control the square in front of the Farolito at Parián are the same fascist Unión Militar who have appeared threateningly at other points in the landscape. Both the Farolito and the square function as "an anomic space in which what is at stake is a force of law without law" (*State*, 39) controlled by this police force. In short, the military police has established this space as a state of exception within the nation of Mexico. How did this Englishman—a Consul no less and a decorated veteran of World War One—end up in such a space? Well, on the level of plot, he chose to *return* there to his Hell, to his melancholic refuge; he is now seriously drunk; he has lost his papers; he is wearing the jacket he had lent Hugh earlier, in the pocket of which is that incriminating telegram; and he has repeatedly rejected offers of help and safety from everyone who cares for him (Dr. Vigil, Jacques, Hugh, Yvonne). But there are other reasons, ones more germane to his past, to his refusal to remember, mourn, and work through to a clear separation between past and present so he can begin to imagine a future. He has taken "refuge in tragedy," become paralysed by melancholia, and betrayed the values he should have upheld. Worse still, or perhaps more fittingly, as the officer in command of the *Samaritan* he created a state of exception in which prisoners were reduced to "bare life" and disposed of as so many *homines sacri*. I might say, therefore, that he got what he deserved, or I might agree with Lowry that "you can even see the German submarine officers taking revenge on the Consul in the form of the sinarquistas and semi-fascist brutos at the end." (*SC* I, 527). However, states of exception are far too dangerous to evoke as an image of righteous punishment.

Fortunately, Geoffrey's is not the only example of this behaviour in *Under the Volcano*, and his fate (determined, as he is fond of saying, like the fate of nations) is a warning, not an example of constructive action to be emulated. Hugh, after all, did leave in 1938 to fight for the Republican forces in Spain; Yvonne died as a result of her persistent desire to help her husband and save their marriage; and Laruelle /Lowry creates the commemorative work of art—novel, film, opera, biography—to tell us about the past and warn us about the future. To create this work of art, *he* has orchestrated a wealth of memories and engaged his readers in sharing with him the demanding memory work of mourning which can produce understanding, if not also closure or redemption. And if we have not understood by the time we read the last sentence—"Somebody threw a dead dog after him down the ravine" (391)—then we should go back to the beginning and start again with "Wonders are many, and none is more wonderful than man" or "Whosoever unceasingly strives upward ... him can we save" (np, epigraphs).

Lowry always insisted that there was hope and humour in *Under the Volcano*, and while I have said little about his sense of humour, I do want to stress his idea of hope because, in the face of war, atrocity, inhuman brutality, and destruction, this text holds out hard-won hope. If we can engage with Laruelle/Lowry's creative memory work, if we dare to read the writing on the wall, to remember and mourn the past without taking "refuge in tragedy" (as Findley so aptly puts it), then there is hope. If we can recognize and resist those forces within ourselves and our democratic cultures that mine the ethical ground on which we stand, then we *may* be able to create a better world, but first we must ask, as Goodyear did in "June 30th, 1934": "What is wrong with *us*? ... And what is wrong with me?" (43). Agamben, a philosopher, calls for us to develop a "new politics," if we hope for peace, without saying precisely how to do this (see *Homo Sacer*, 11, and *State*, 86–88), and Lowry, an artist, will not preach or pronounce. But like Agamben, Lowry was apocalyptic in his final vision of what the future held in store *unless* .... And we are now living in that future produced by the past of twentieth-century wars. At his best, as here with *Under the Volcano*, Lowry's tools for facing the future were his ability to remember the past and to create a work of art which asks us Yvonne's question— "Do you remember tomorrow?" The answer in *Volcano* is that tomorrow is an anniversary (their wedding anniversary, the Mexican Day of the Dead) a day on which to remember and mourn, so we can understand how to move forward. Outside the novel, in Lowry's life, moving forward became impossible; the Consul after all is, in part, Lowry and, sadly, the part that he succumbed to.

But unlike the Consul Lowry *was* a "wrider" who continued to write and to remember, and among his more poignant memories was his youthful admiration for Nordahl Grieg. So, I will close by returning to the ghost of Grieg, to Lowry's terse inclusion of Grieg's death in that December 1944 letter to Aiken (*SC* I, 469), and to a Lowry poem: "In Memoriam: Invald Bjorndal and his Comrades—For Nordahl

Grieg." In 2002 the remains of the wreckage of the plane in which Grieg was shot down on 2 December 1943 near Berlin were found, and a monument was created from the wreckage and placed in the Norwegian Embassy in Berlin (see Figure 2). Would Lowry have cherished this memorial to a man of action, or would he have preferred to remember Grieg with poetry? Lowry wrote:

> Mother, Father, I have come
> A long way to die in the blood and rain.
> Buy me some earth in the graveyard at home.
> Goodbye. Please remember me with these words
> To the green meadows and the blue fjords. (*CP*, 186)

(2009)

FIGURE 2: Nordahl Grieg Monument, Norwegian Embassy, Berlin.

NOTES

* All references to *Under the Volcano* are to the 2007 Harper Perennial edition.

[1] It is never made clear which war or wars Captain Constable served in, but that he was in the American army and, as Yvonne remembers him, felt traumatized by some failure in his service, is stressed. This father in many ways parallels Geoffrey and explains, in part, Yvonne's attraction to the Consul.

[2] Freud's essays on mourning and melancholia and on remembering and working through have been fundamental to several contemporary theorists of memory, post-memory, and trauma, even when they refute or modify Freud's statements. I find LaCapra's use of Freud convincing and clear, especially as regards memory and working through (see LaCapra, 90–96). Judith Butler's comments on mourning and violence are also interesting and relevant to issues of war and trauma; see *Precarious Life*, 19–49.

[3] Aiken's *The Soldier: A Poem* was first published in the United States in 1944, and Aiken described it as "a prosy affair, but I hope timely" in an August 1943 letter to Lowry; in the same letter, he also asks if Lowry has seen any "Japs" (Sugars, 175).

[4] Arthur Lowry was terminally ill with cancer and would die on 11 February 1945. Nordahl Grieg served as a war reporter but was classified as missing in action when the plane in which he was flying was shot down near Berlin on 2 December 1943. In 2002, pieces of the wreckage were indentified in a farmer's field outside Berlin, and a monument to Grieg, which now hangs in the Norwegian Embassy in Berlin, was built from these pieces. Russell Lowry has left a description of the impact of World War Two on the family and on Liverpool and Merseyside (UBC Special Collections, Lowry Family Fonds, 1:19). Liverpool was reduced to rubble during the 1941 blitz of the city, and Russell tried to enlist three times but was rejected due to poor eyesight; he did serve with the Civil Guard. He had no sympathy for Malcolm's whining about money from the safety of Vancouver while their father was seriously ill and England was being bombed.

[5] In a letter to Conrad Aiken (ca November 1939), Lowry explains that he has "made every attempt to enlist here" but has been turned down; his plan is to get to Boston and enlist in the east or return to England to enlist (*SC* I, 246–47). He wrote to his father in March 1940 making a lengthy appeal for money to travel east. In this letter, he describes his attitude towards Hitler, his willingness to enlist, and his awareness that the family in England is suffering while he is safe (*SC* I, 300–302). This may well be the whining letter that Russell Lowry resented; see note 4.

[6] In "Hollywood and the War," first published in Vancouver's *Daily Province* on 12 December 1939, Lowry quotes an article he had read in *Time* magazine, and the sentence is identical to the one about "dreams unfulfilled" that he used in this letter to Margerie.

[7] It is very clear from Tom Taylor's book *Glimpses* that the local newspapers carried constant reports of the war in Europe, the bombing of England, and the post-Pearl Harbor fears of Japanese invasions along the Canadian west coast; see in particular the reproduction of a major article for 25 June 1942, titled "The War Is Here" in which the Japanese are described as worse than the Germans (119). In *The Great War of Words*, Peter Buitenhuis examines the extensive propaganda in England and Canada during World War One, and one of the most familiar recruitment posters of the period shouts: "Remember Belgium.

Enlist Today." Geoffrey's sarcastic remarks about "poor little Belgium" hearken back to this kind of propaganda ploy; see Buitenhuis, 9–11.

[8] The changes Lowry made to the 1940 manuscript are radical and extensive. For a detailed analysis, see Asals's *The Making of Malcolm Lowry's Under the Volcano*.

[9] Whether or not Lowry knew the military history of the twentieth century well, he certainly managed to work relevant and meaningful references to these wars into much of his fiction, and especially *Ultramarine* and *Under the Volcano*. In addition to the two World Wars and the Spanish Civil War, he makes frequent references to the Sino-Japanese wars of the late nineteenth and early twentieth century, as well as the major Asian conflict of 1937 to 1945, during which period Japan invaded China and committed atrocities similar to the Nazi murder of Jews.

[10] Kirmayer's theory of a "landscape of memory" as a necessary *narrative* condition for the validation of traumatic experience and the healing of trauma is developed in the context of Holocaust and incest survival. However, the trauma experienced in war by both combatants and civilians can also be examined in these terms; see also note 13. Nora's terms *lieux* and *milieux de mémoire* are developed in the context of French post-World War Two history; for a specific analysis of the distinctions between these two terms, see Nora's "Between Memory and History."

[11] In Genette's narratological system, Laruelle is the intradiegetic narrator, who is a character inside the story as well as the frame narrator standing in for Lowry, and "Lowry" is the extradiegetic narrator; see Genette, *Narrative Discourse*, 228–31.

[12] In addition to O'Neill's article on the *Baralong* incident, a considerable amount of material is available on the web from the German perspective, and military enthusiasts still debate the rights and wrongs of the case; see the web sites listed in my Works Cited. The second treaty of the Geneva Convention, adopted in 1906, addressed protocols for armed forces at sea, but the third treaty addressing the treatment of prisoners of war was not adopted until 1929. In 1949 the Geneva Convention was updated and expanded.

[13] Kirmayer applies his landscape concept to his studies of memories by Holocaust survivors and incest survivors. What he refers to as "absent" from memory, however, I prefer (after LaCapra) to classify as "lost" to memory because the experiences remembered were real and can be found, or recalled and articulated; see LaCapra, 46–49.

[14] My studies of war art and literature to date confirm that, unlike other categories of artistic representation, the subject of war demands adherence to known facts and a ratified historical record. This need to respect the truth claims of history places certain constraints on a novelist, playwright, painter, or filmmaker and can lead to debates over whether the creative work is art, memorial, or simply record-keeping.

[15] Lowry scholars continue to debate the role of Laruelle in *Under the Volcano* and many argue that Laruelle is not a key figure, let alone the creator of chapters two to twelve. This debate erupted in a lively manner during the July 2009 centenary conference on Lowry at the University of British Columbia with no decisive conclusion emerging. This is not the place to launch a thorough discussion of the Laruelle question, but a few comments are in order. Far from being a trivial matter, an opinion on the role, position, and perspective of Laruelle affects how one reads and interprets the story of Geoffrey's life and death. If Laruelle is seen as a morally weak character who is tangential to the main story, then Geoffrey becomes a more positive and tragic figure; if Laruelle is seen as a crucial mediator for the reader and

a witness to the memories and post-memories of the other characters, then he carries considerable weight as a moral lens through which to judge events. Lowry's own comments in his letter to Cape are not always helpful, but it seems to me that if all four characters represent aspects of one larger image of humanity, then credence must be given to Laruelle's role as the *surviving mourner* and the one who bears witness and imagines—brings back to life for one day—the other characters and their stories. Lowry positions Laruelle strategically on the margins of the story from where he can see and understand the larger picture and help us to see what is at stake. Despite his failings as a man—his affair with Yvonne, his dallyings in Mexico, his less than great film-making career—he has fought for France and will fight against fascism once more, he tells Geoffrey how foolish and destructive he is being, and he lives to clean up the mess Geoffrey leaves in his wake. To be consistent with my reading of Laruelle's importance, I would add that his burning of Geoffrey's unsent letter to Yvonne, found a year after his and Yvonne's deaths, symbolizes his capacity to release the fruitless grip of the past on the present and, thereby, to clear the way forward. It is a ritual act of purgation and leave-taking.

Works Cited

Achad, Frater (Charles Stansfeld-Jones). *Q.B.L. or The Bride's Reception.* New York: Samuel Weiser, 1972.

———. *The Anatomy of the Body of God.* Chicago: Collegium ad Spiritum Sanctum, 1925.

Ackerley, Chris and Lawrence J. Clipper. *A Companion to Under the Volcano.* Vancouver: University of British Columbia Press, 1984.

Agamben, Giorgio. *Homo Sacer: Sovereign Power and Bare Life.* Trans. Daniel Heller-Roazen. Stanford: Stanford University Press, 1998.

———. *State of Exception.* Trans. Kevin Attell. Chicago: University of Chicago Press, 2005.

Aiken, Conrad. *Selected Letters of Conrad Aiken.* Ed. Joseph Killorin. New Haven: Yale University Press, 1978.

———. "Introduction." *Mr. Arcularis, A Play.* Cambridge, MA: Harvard University Press, 1957. v–ix

———. *The Soldier: A Poem.* The Poets of the Year Series 39. Norfolk: New Directions, 1944.

———. *Blue Voyage.* London: Gerald Howe, 1927.

———. *The House of Dust: A Symphony.* Boston: Four Seas, 1920.

Asals, Frederick. *The Making of Malcolm Lowry's Under the Volcano.* Athens. University of Georgia Press, 1997.

———. "Introduction." In *Malcolm Lowry: The 1940 Under the Volcano.* Eds. Paul Tiessen and Miguel Mota, ix–xxxv. Waterloo, ON: The Malcolm Lowry Review and Wilfrid Laurier University Press, 1994.

Asals, Frederick and Paul Tiessen, eds. *A Darkness That Murmured: Essays on Malcolm Lowry and the Twentieth Century.* Toronto: University of Toronto Press, 2000.

Atwood, Margaret. *The Handmaid's Tale.* Toronto: McClelland and Stewart, 1987.

Bakhtin, M.M. *The Dialogic Imagination: Four Essays by M.M. Bakhtin.* Ed. Michael Holquist. Trans. Caryl Emerson and Michael Holquist. Austin: University of Texas Press, 1981.

———. *Problems of Dostoevsky's Poetics.* Ed. and trans. Caryl Emerson. Minneapolis: University of Minnesota Press, 1984.

———. *Speech Genres and Other Late Essays.* Trans. Vern W. McGee. Eds. Caryl Emerson and Michael Holquist. Austin: University of Texas Press, 1986.

————. "The Problem of Speech Genres." In *Speech Genres and Other Late Essays*, ed. Caryl Emerson and Michael Holquist, trans. Vern W. McGee, 60–102. Austin: University of Texas Press, 1986.

Bareham, Terence. "After the Volcano: An Assessment of Malcolm Lowry's Posthumous Fiction." *Studies in the Novel* 6 (1974): 349–62.

Barthes, Roland. *Image, Music, Text*. Trans. Stephen Heath. New York: Hill and Wang, 1977.

————. *The Pleasure of the Text*. Trans. Richard Miller. New York: Farrar, Straus, and Giroux, 1975.

————. *S/Z: An Essay*. Trans. Richard Miller. New York: Hill and Wang / Farrar, Straus, and Giroux, 1974.

Baudelaire, Charles "Épigraphe pour un livre condamné." *Fleurs du mal*. In *Baudelaire: Selected Poems*, trans. Joanna Richardson, 186–87. Harmondsworth: Penguin, 1975.

Baudrillard, Jean. "The Ecstasy of Communication." Trans. John Johnson. In *The Anti-Aesthetic: Essays on Postmodern Culture*, ed. Hal Foster, 126–34. Seattle: Bay Press, 1983.

Bloom, Harold. *The Anxiety of Influence: A Theory of Poetry*. New York: Oxford University Press, 1973.

Bock, Dennis. *The Communist's Daughter*. Toronto: Harper Perennial, 2006.

Bock, Martin. "Syphilisation and Its Discontents: Somatic Indications of Psychological Ills in Joyce and Lowry." In *Joyce/Lowry: Critical Perspectives*, ed. Patrick McCarthy and Paul Tiessen, 126–44. Lexington: University Press of Kentucky, 1997.

Bowker, Gordon. "Lowry and Shelley." *Malcolm Lowry Review* 38–39 (Spring–Fall 1996): 44–45.

————. *Pursued by Furies: A Life of Malcolm Lowry*. Toronto: Random House, 1993.

————, ed. *Malcolm Lowry Remembered*. London: BBC/Ariel, 1985.

Bradbrook, Muriel. "Intention and Design in *October Ferry to Gabriola*." In *The Art of Malcolm Lowry*, Ed. Anne Smith, 56–65.

————. *Malcolm Lowry: His Art and Early Life*. Cambridge: Cambridge University Press, 1974.

Bradbury, Malcolm. "Malcolm Lowry as Modernist." *Possibilities: Essays on the State of the Novel*. London: Oxford University Press, 1973, 181–91.

Bronner, Stephen Eric, and Douglas Kellner. *Passion and Rebellion: The Expressionist Heritage*. London: Croom Helm, 1983.

Brooke, Rupert. "John Donne." *Poetry and Drama* 1.2 (1913): 185–88.

————. "John Donne, the Elizabethan." *The Nation* 12.28 (1913): 825–26.

————. *John Webster & the Elizabethan Drama*. 1916. New York: Russell, 1967.

Brown, Frederick. *An Impersonation of Angels: A Biography of Jean Cocteau*. New York: Viking, 1968.

Brunswick, Ruth Mack. "The Preoedipal Phase of the Libido Development." In *The Psycho-Analytic Reader: An Anthology of Essential Papers with Critical Introduction*, ed. Robert Fliess, 231–53. New York: International University Press, 1948.

Buitenhuis, Peter. *The Great War of Words: Literature as Propaganda, 1914–18 and After*. Vancouver: University of British Columbia Press, 1987.

Bulwer-Lytton. *Zanoni*. New York: Little Brown, 1898.

Butler, Judith. *Precarious Life: The Powers of Mourning and Violence*. London: Verso, 2004.

Cocteau, Jean. *The Hand of a Stranger (Journal d'un Inconnu)*. Trans. Alec Brown. New York: Horizon, 1959.

————. *The Infernal Machine and Other Plays by Jean Cocteau*. Trans. Albert Bermel. New York: New Directions, 1963.

————. *La Machine infernale*. Paris: Bernard Grasset, 1934.

Collier, Graham. *The Day of the Dead*. London: Mosaic Records, 1978.

————. "Lowry, Jazz and the 'Day of the Dead.'" In *Swinging the Maelstrom: New Perspectives on Malcolm Lowry*, ed. Sherrill Grace, 243–48. Montreal: McGill-Queen's University Press, 1992.

Connell, Richard. "The D Box." *The 20-Story Magazine* 8.44 (1926): 39–42.

————. "The Yes-and-No Man." *The 20-Story Magazine* 8.47 (1926): 47–53.

Costa, Richard Hauer. "The Grisly Graphics of Malcolm Lowry." In *Apparently Incongruous Parts: The Worlds of Malcolm Lowry*, ed. Paul Tiessen, 71–79. Metuchen, NJ, and London: Scarecrow, 1990.

————. "Lowry's Forest Path: Echoes of Walden." *Canadian Literature* 62 (Autumn 1974): 61–68.

————. *Malcolm Lowry*. New York: Twayne Publishers, 1972.

Cowan, David. "Malcolm Lowry's Aggregate Demon: A Study in the Psychology of Influence." Diss. University of Michigan, 1981.

Cross, Richard K. *Malcolm Lowry: A Preface to his Fiction*. Chicago: University of Chicago Press, 1980.

————. "*Ulysses* and *Under the Volcano*: The Difficulty of Loving." In *Joyce/Lowry: Critical Perspectives*, ed. Patrick A McCarthy and Paul Tiessen, 63–83. Lexington: University Press of Kentucky, 1997.

Dahlie, Hallvard. "Lowry's Debt to Nordahl Grieg." *Canadian Literature* 64 (1975): 41–51.

————. "'A Norwegian at Heart': Lowry and the Grieg Connection." In *Swinging the Maelstrom: New Perspectives on Malcolm Lowry*, ed. Sherrill Grace, 31–42. Montreal: McGill-Queen's University Press, 1992.

Day, Douglas. *Malcolm Lowry: A Biography*. New York: Oxford University Press, 1973.

Debussy, Claude. *Pelléas et Mélisande*. Opera. Text by Maurice Maeterlinck. Trans. by Paul Myers. Berlin Philharmonic. Dir. Herbert von Karajan. EMI Records, 1979.

Derrida, Jacques. *The Post Card*. Trans. Alan Bass. Chicago: University of Chicago Press, 1987.

————. *La carte postale: De Socrate à Freud et au delà*. Paris: Flammarion, 1980.

————. "Of an apocalyptic tone recently adopted in philosophy." Trans. John P. Leavey, Jr., *Semeia* 23 (1982): 63–97.

Dostoevsky, Feodor. *Poor Folk*. Trans. Robert Dessaix. Ann Arbor, MI: Ardis, 1982.

Doyen, Victor. "Fighting the Albatross of Self: A Genetic Study of the Literary Work of Malcolm Lowry." Diss. Katholicke Universiteit to Leuven, 1973.

Dunne, J.W. *An Experiment with Time*. London: A. & C. Black, 1927.

Duplay, Mathieu. "The Operatic Paradigm: Voice, Sound, and Meaning in Lowry's Fiction." In *A Darkness That Murmured*, ed. Frederick Asals and Paul Tiessen, 162–69. Toronto: University of Toronto Press, 2000.

Durrant, Geoffrey. "Aiken and Lowry." *Canadian Literature* (Spring 1975): 24–40.

————. "Death in Life: Neo-Platonic Elements in 'Through the Panama.'" In *Malcolm Lowry: The Man and his Work*, ed. George Woodcock, 42–55. Vancouver: University of British Columbia Press, 1971.

Eliot, T.S. *Selected Essays*. London: Faber, 1951.

————. "Whispers of Immortality." In *Collected Poems, 1909–1962*, 55–56. London: Faber, 1963.

Ellmann, Richard. *James Joyce*. New York: Oxford University Press, 1983.

Epstein, Perle. "Swinging the Maelstrom: Malcolm Lowry and Jazz." In *Malcolm Lowry: The Man and his Work*, ed. George Woodcock, 150–51. Vancouver: University of British Columbia Press, 1971.

Findley, Timothy. *The Wars.* Toronto: Clarke, Irwin, 1977.

Fort, Charles. *The Books of Charles Fort.* New York: Holt, 1941.

Foster, Hal. *Recodings: Art, Spectacle, Cultural Politics.* Seattle: Bay Press, 1985.

———. *The Anti-Aesthetic: Essays on Postmodern Culture.* Seattle: Bay Press, 1983.

Foucault, Michel. *The Archeology of Knowledge.* Trans. A.M. Sheridan Smith. London: Routledge, 1972.

———. *The Order of Things: An Archaeology of the Human Sciences.* New York: Pantheon-Random, 1970.

Freedman, Ralph. *The Lyrical Novel: Studies in Hesse, Gide, and Woolf.* Princeton, NJ: Princeton University Press, 1963.

Freud, Sigmund. "Leonardo Da Vinci and a Memory of His Childhood (1910)." *The Standard Edition of the Complete Psychological Works by Sigmund Freud.* Ed. and trans. James Strachey et al, Vol. XI, 63–81. London: Hogarth, 1957.

———. "Mourning and Melancholia." *The Standard Edition.* Vol. XII, 243–58. London: Hogarth, 1958.

———. "Remembering, Repeating and Working-Through." *The Standard Edition.* Vol. XIV, 147–56. London: Hogarth, 1958.

———. *The Interpretation of Dreams.* Ed. and trans. James Strachey et al. Vol. 4 Penguin Freud Library. London: Penguin, 1991.

———. "Fetishism." *Collected Papers: Miscellaneous Papers, 1888–1938.* Vol. V. Ed. and trans. James Strachey, 198–204. The International Psychoanalytical Library Series Number 37. London: Hogarth Press and The Institute of Psychoanalysis, 1952.

———. *Beyond the Pleasure Principle.* Ed. and trans. James Strachey. New York: Liveright, 1961.

Gabrial, Jan. *Inside the Volcano: My Life with Malcolm Lowry.* New York: St. Martin's Press, 2000.

Genette, Gérard. *Palimpsestes: La littérature au second degré.* Paris: Éditions du Seuil, 1982.

———. *Narrative Discourse: An Essay in Method.* Trans. Jonathan Culler. Ithaca, New York: Cornell University Press, 1980.

Gilmore, Leigh. *Autobiographics: A Feminist Theory of Women's Self-Representation.* Ithaca: Cornell University Press, 1994.

Gironella, Alberto. *Alberto Gironella: El Via Crucis del Cónsul.* Barcelona: Círculo de Lectores, 1992.

———, Illustrator. *Bajo el Volcán.* Trans. Raul Ortiz y Ortiz. Barcelona: Círculo de Lectores, 1992.

Goethe, Johann Wolfgang von. *Faust: parts one and two.* Trans. John Clifford. London: N. Hern Books, 2006.

Grace, Sherrill. "The Legacy of *Under the Volcano:* An Afterword." Malcolm Lowry. *Under the Volcano.* New York: Perennial Classics, 2000, 391–97.

———. "Three Letters Home." *A Darkness That Murmured: Essays on Malcolm Lowry and the Twentieth Century.* Eds. Frederick Asals and Paul Tiessen. Toronto: University of Toronto Press, 2000, 14–28.

———. "'The Daily Crucifixion of the Post': Editing and Theorizing the Lowry Letters." In *Editing Canadian Texts,* ed. John Lennox, 26–53. New York: AMS Press, 1993.

———. "Putting Lowry in Perspective: An Introduction." In *Swinging the Maelstrom: New Perspectives on Malcolm Lowry,* 3–18. Montreal: McGill-Queen's University Press, 1992.

———. "Respecting Plagiarism: Tradition, Guilt, and Malcolm Lowry's 'Pelagiarist Pen.'" *English Studies in Canada* xviii 4 (1992): 461–82.

————, ed. *Swinging the Maelstrom: New Perspectives on Malcolm Lowry.* Montreal: McGill-Queen's University Press, 1992.

————. "Thoughts towards the Archeology of Editing: 'Caravan of Silence.'" *Malcolm Lowry Review* 29–30 (Fall 1991–Spring 1992): 64–77.

————. "'A Strange Assemble of Apparently Incongruous Parts': Intertextuality in Malcolm Lowry's 'Through the Panama.'" In *Apparently Incongruous Parts: The Worlds of Malcolm Lowry*, ed. Paul Tiessen, 187–228. Metuchen, NJ and London: Scarecrow, 1990.

————. *Regression and Apocalypse: Studies in North American Literary Expressionism.* Toronto: University of Toronto Press, 1989.

————. "Confabulation (1)." *Malcolm Lowry Review* 17–18 (Fall 1985–Spring 1986): 59–66.

————. *Malcolm Lowry and the Voyage That Never Ends.* Vancouver: University of British Columbia Press, 1982.

————. "The Creative Process: Time and Space in Malcolm Lowry's Fiction." *Studies in Canadian Literature* 2, 1 (1977): 61–68.

————. "*Under the Volcano*: Narrative Mode and Technique." *Journal of Canadian Fiction* 2 (Spring 1973): 57–61.

Graves, Robert. *Greek Myths.* London: Cassell, 1955.

Grieg, Nordahl. *The Ship Sails On.* Trans. A.G. Chater. New York: Knopf, 1927.

————. *De unge døde (They Died Young).* Oslo: Gyldendal, 1932.

————. *War Poems of Nordahl Grieg.* Trans. G.M. Gathorne-Hardy. London: Hodder & Stoughton, 1944.

Guerard, Albert. "Notes on the Rhetoric of Anti-realist Fiction." *Triquarterly* 30 (Spring 1974): 3–50.

Hassan, Ihab. *The Dismemberment of Orpheus: Toward a Postmodern Literature.* Madison: University of Wisconsin Press, 1982.

Henke, Suzette. *Joyce's Moraculous Sindbook: A Study of "Ulysses."* Columbus: Ohio State University Press, 1978.

Hesse, Hermann. *Demian.* Trans. W.J. Strachan. London: Vision Press, 1960.

Hirsch, Marianne. *Family Frames: Photography, Narrative, and Postmemory.* Cambridge, MA: Harvard University Press, 1997.

Houghton, Geoff and Pat Houghton. *Well-regulated Minds and Improper Moments: A History of The Leys School.* Cambridge: The Governors of The Leys School, 2000.

Hutcheon, Linda. *A Poetics of Postmodernism: History, Theory, Fiction.* New York: Routledge, 1988.

————. *A Theory of Parody: The Teachings of Twentieth-Century Art Forms.* New York and London: Methuen, 1985.

Huyssens, Andreas. *After the Great Divide: Modernism, Mass Culture, Postmodernism.* Blooming-ton: Indiana University Press, 1986.

Irigaray, Luce. "This Sex Which Is Not One." Trans. Claudia Reeder. *New French Feminisms.* Ed. Elaine Marks and Isabelle de Courtivron. Brighton: Harvester Press, 1980, 99–106.

Isaak, Jo Anna. *The Ruin of Representation in Modernist Art and Texts.* Ann Arbor: UMI Research Press, 1986.

"Jean Marais, Jean Cocteau et *La Machine infernal.*" *Paris-Théâtre* 81 (February 1954): 3–66.

Joyce, James. *Finnegans Wake.* New York: Viking, 1959.

————. *Ulysses: The Corrected Text.* Ed. Hans Walter Gabler. New York: Random House, 1986.

Kaiser, Georg. *From Morning to Midnight. German Expressionism: Plays Volume One—Georg Kaiser.* Trans. B.J. Kenworthy, Rex Last, and J.M. Ritchie. London: John Calder, 1985. 17–73.

Kandinsky, Wassily. *Concerning the Spiritual in Art.* Trans. M.T.H. Sadler. New York: Dover, 1977.

Kendrick, W. "God Must Be Crazy." *Voice Literary Supplement* (May 1990): 33.

Kenner, Hugh. *Joyce's Voices.* Berkeley and Los Angeles: University of California Press, 1978.

Keyserling, Hermann. *The Recovery of Truth.* Trans. Paul Fohr. New York and London: Harper & Bros., 1929.

Kilgallin, Tony. *Lowry.* Erin, ON: Press Porcépic, 1973.

Kim, Suzanne, "Les Oeuvres de jeunesse de Malcolm Lowry." *Etudes Anglaises* XVIII (1965): 383–94.

Kirmayer, Laurence J. "Landscapes of Memory: Trauma, Narrative, and Dissociation." In *Tense Past: Cultural Essays in Trauma and Memory*, ed. Paul Antze and Michael Lambek, 173–98. New York: Routledge, 1996.

Kristeva, Julia. *Desire in Language: A Semiotic Approach to Literature and Art.* Ed. Leon S. Roudiez. Trans. Thomas Gora, Alice Jardine, and Leon S. Roudiez. New York: Columbia University Press, 1980.

———. *Σημειωτική /Recherches pour une sémanalyse.* Paris: Éditions du Seuil, 1969.

LaCapra, Dominick. *Writing History, Writing Trauma.* Baltimore: Johns Hopkins University Press, 2001.

Landers, W.M. "Introduction." *La Machine infernale.* London: George C. Harrap, 1957.

Laplanche, J. and J.B. Pontalis. *The Language of Psychoanalysis.* Trans. Donald Nicholson-Smith. New York: Norton, 1973.

Lawrence, Karen. *The Odyssey of Style in "Ulysses."* Princeton: Princeton University Press, 1981.

Leavis, F.R. *The Great Tradition: George Eliot, Henry James, Joseph Conrad.* London: Chatto & Windus, 1948.

Lodge, David. *The Modes of Modern Writing: Metaphor, Metonymy, and the Typology of Modern Literature.* Ithaca: Cornell University Press, 1977.

Lorenz, Clarissa. *Lorelei Two: My Life with Conrad Aiken.* Athens: University of Georgia Press, 1983.

———. "Call It Misadventure." In *Malcolm Lowry Remembered*, ed. Gordon Bowker, 82–88. London: BBC/Ariel, 1985.

Lowry, Malcolm. "The Bravest Boat." In *Hear us O Lord from heaven Thy dwelling place*, 13–27. Vancouver: Douglas & McIntyre, 1987.

———. *The Collected Poetry of Malcolm Lowry.* Ed. Kathleen Scherf. Vancouver: University of British Columbia Press, 1992.

———. *Dark as the Grave Wherein My Friend Is Laid.* New York: Meridian Books, World Publishing, 1969.

———. "Elephant and Colosseum." In *Hear us O Lord from heaven Thy dwelling place*, 115–73. Vancouver: Douglas & McIntyre, 1987.

———. "The Forest Path to the Spring." In *Hear us O Lord from heaven Thy dwelling place*, 215–83. Vancouver: Douglas & McIntyre, 1987.

———. "Ghostkeeper." In *Malcolm Lowry: Psalms and Songs*, ed. Margerie Lowry, 202–27. New York: Meridian Books, 1975.

———. "Haitian Notebook." Malcolm Lowry Collection. The University of British Columbia Special Collections. Ms 7:9.

———. *Hear us O Lord from heaven Thy dwelling place.* London: Jonathan Cape, 1962.

———. *Hear us O Lord from heaven Thy dwelling place.* Harmondsworth, Middlesex: Penguin, 1969.

————. *Hear us O Lord from heaven Thy dwelling place*. Vancouver: Douglas & McIntyre, 1987.

————. "Hollywood and the War." In *Malcolm Lowry: Vancouver Days*, ed. Sheryl Salloum, 142–44. Madeira Park, BC: Harbour, 1987.

————. "In Ballast to the White Sea." Malcolm Lowry Collection. The University of British Columbia Special Collections. Ms. 12:15.

————. "June 30th, 1934." In *Malcolm Lowry: Psalms and Songs*, ed. Margerie Lowry, 36–48. New York: Meridian Books, 1975.

————. *Lunar Caustic*. London: Jonathan Cape. 1968. Rpt in *Malcolm Lowry: Psalms and Songs*. Ed. Margerie Lowry. New York: Meridian Books, 1975.

————. *Malcolm Lowry: Psalms and Songs*. Ed. Margerie Lowry. New York: Meridian Books, 1975.

————. *Malcolm Lowry: The 1940 Under the Volcano*. Eds. Paul Tiessen and Miguel Mota. Waterloo, ON: The Malcolm Lowry Review and Wilfrid Laurier University Press, 1994.

————. *October Ferry to Gabriola*. New York: World Publishing, 1970.

————. "The Ordeal of Sigbjørn Wilderness." Malcolm Lowry Collection. The University of British Columbia Special Collections. 13:7.

————. "Satan in a Barrel." In *Satan in a Barrel and other early stories by Malcolm Lowry*, ed. Sherrill Grace, 28–38. Edmonton: Juvenilia Press, 1999.

————. *Satan in a Barrel and other early stories by Malcolm Lowry*. Ed. Sherrill Grace. Edmonton: Juvenilia Press, 1999.

————. *Selected Letters of Malcolm Lowry*. Ed. Harvey Breit and Margerie Bonner Lowry. Philadelphia and New York: J.B. Lippincott, 1965.

————. *Selected Poems of Malcolm Lowry*. Ed. Earle Birney. San Francisco: City Lights Books, 1962.

————. "Strange Comfort Afforded by the Profession." In *Hear us O Lord from heaven Thy dwelling place*, 99–113. Vancouver: Douglas & McIntyre, 1987.

————. *Sursum Corda! The Collected Letters of Malcolm Lowry*. 2 vols. Ed. Sherrill Grace. London and Toronto: Jonathan Cape and University of Toronto Press, 1995 and 1996.

————. "Through the Panama." In *Hear us O Lord from heaven Thy dwelling place*, 29–98. Vancouver: Douglas & McIntyre, 1987.

————. "Travelling Light." *Satan in a Barrel and other early stories*. Ed. Sherrill Grace. Edmonton: Juvenilia Press, 1999.

————. *Ultramarine*. 1933. Revised edition. London: Jonathan Cape, 1963.

————. *Under the Volcano*. London: Jonathan Cape, 1947.

————. *Under the Volcano*. Harmondsworth, Middlesex: Penguin, 1963.

————. *Under the Volcano*. New York: Perennial Classics, 2000.

————. *Under the Volcano*. New York: HarperPerennial, 2007.

Lowry, Margerie. "Introductory Note." *Ultramarine*. London: Jonathan Cape, 1963. 5–8.

Lowry, Russell. "Brother Malcolm." In *Malcolm Lowry Remembered*, ed. Gordon Bowker, 17–22. London: BBC/Ariel, 1985.

Lyotard, Jean-Francois. *The Postmodern Condition: A Report on Knowledge*. Trans. Geoff Bennington and Brian Massumi. Minneapolis: University of Minneapolis Press, 1984. 79–81.

McCarthy, Patrick A. *A Forest of Symbols: World, Text and Self in Malcolm Lowry's Fiction*. Athens: University of Georgia Press, 1994.

McCarthy, Patrick A. and Paul Tiessen, eds. *Joyce/Lowry: Critical Perspectives*. Lexington: University Press of Kentucky, 1997.

McClintock, Anne. *Imperial Leather: Race, Gender and Sexuality in the Colonial Context.* New York and London: Routledge, 1995.

McKenzie, D.F. *Bibliography and the Sociology of Texts.* The Panizzi Lectures. London: The British Library, 1986.

McMichael, Charles T. and Ted R. Spivey. "'Chaos-hurray!-is come again': Heroism in James Joyce and Conrad Aiken." *Studies in the Literary Imagination* 3 (Oct. 1970): 65–68.

Mallon, Thomas. *Stolen Words: Forays into the Origins and Ravages of Plagiarism.* New York: Ticknor, 1989.

Markson, David. *Malcolm Lowry's "Volcano": Myth, Symbol, Meaning.* New York: Times Books, 1978.

———. *Wittgenstein's Mistress.* Elmwood Park, IL: The Dalkey Archive Press, 1988.

Martin, Jay. *Conrad Aiken: A Life in his Art.* Princeton, NJ: Princeton University Press, 1962.

Melville, Herman. "Bartleby the Scrivener." *Great Short Works of Herman Melville.* New York: Harper & Row, 1969. 39–74.

Miller, David. *Malcolm Lowry and The Voyage that Never Ends.* London: Enitharmon Press, 1976.

Mitchell, Breon. "Expressionism in English Drama and Prose Literature." In *Expressionism as an International Literary Phenomenon*, ed Ulrich Weisstein, 181–92. Paris: Didier, 1973.

Nadel, Ira. "Joyce and Expressionism." *Journal of Modern Literature* 16 (1989): 141–60.

New, William. "Gabriola: Malcolm Lowry's Floating Island." *Articulating West.* Toronto: New Press, 1972. 189–95.

Nichols, Roger and Richard Langham Smith. *Pelléas et Mélisande.* Cambridge: Cambridge University Press, 1989.

Nora, Pierre. "Between Memory and History: Les Lieux de Mémoire." Trans. Marc Roudebush. *Representations* 26 (Spring 1989): 7–25.

O'Kill, Brian. "Aspects of Language in *Under the Volcano.*" In *The Art of Malcolm Lowry*, ed. Anne Smith, 72–92. London: Vision Press, 1978.

O'Neill, Gerry. "Scandal of the Baralong Incident was Hidden in Veil of Secrecy." *Journal of the Sea* 1.4 (2006): 8–10.

Ortega y Gasset, José. *Toward a Philosophy of History.* New York: W.H. Norton, 1941.

Osborne, Richard. "Karajan conducts *Pelléas et Mélisande.*" Notes and Libretto. Claude Debussy. 10–13.

Ouspensky, P.D. *A New Model of the Universe.* New York: Vintage, 1971.

———. *Tertium Organum: A Key to the Enigmas of the World.* New York: Vintage, 1970.

Patterson, Michael. *The Revolution in German Theatre, 1900–1933.* New York: Routledge & Kegan Paul, 1981.

Paz, Octavio. "Testimonial." In *Alberto Gironella: El Via Crucis del Cónsul*, 43. Barcelona: Círculo de Lectores, 1992.

Peckham, Morse. "Reflections on the Foundations of Modem Textual Study," *Proof* 1 (1971): 122–55.

Poe, Edgar Allan. "The Purloined Letter," *Selected Writings of Edgar Allan Poe.* Boston: Houghton Mifflin, 1956. 208–25.

Ponce, Juan Garcia. "Testimonial." In *Alberto Gironella: El Via Crucis del Cónsul*, 44. Barcelona: Círculo de Lectores, 1992.

Porter, Andrew. "Gleams amid the Shadows." San Francisco Opera, 1997–1998 Season Program, 10–12, 41.

Railo, Eino. *The Haunted Castle.* London: Routledge, 1927.

Rios, Julián. "Esto es gallo (This is a rooster)." In *Alberto Gironella: El Via Crucis del Cônsul,* 22. Barcelona: Círculo de Lectores, 1992.

Santayana, George. *Three Philosophical Poets.* Cambridge, MA: Harvard University Press, 1927.

Salloum, Sheryl. *Malcolm Lowry: Vancouver Days.* Madeira Park, B.C.: Harbour, 1987.

Schneider, Michel. *Voleurs de mots: Essai sur le plagiat, la psychanalyse et la pensée.* Paris: Gallimard, 1985.

Scholes, Robert and Robert Kellogg. "The Narrative Tradition." In *The Novel: Modern Essays in Criticism,* ed R.M. Davis, 16–29. Englewood Cliffs, NJ: Prentice-Hall, 1969.

Schreber, Daniel Paul. *Memoirs of My Nervous Illness (Denkwürdigkeiten eines Nervenkranken).* Trans. Ida Macalpine and Richard A. Hunter. London: William Dawson & Sons, 1955.

Sedgwick, Eve Kosofsky. *Between Men: English Literature and Male Homosocial Desire.* New York: Columbia University Press, 1985.

Shakespeare, William. *The Tragedy of King Lear.* Ed. George Lyman Kittredge. Waltham, MA: Ginn-Blaisdell, 1967.

Smith, Anne, ed. *The Art of Malcolm Lowry.* London: Vision Press, 1978.

Sokel, Walter H. *The Writer in Extremist Expressionism in 20th Century German Literature.* Stanford: Stanford University Press, 1959.

Spender, Stephen. "Introduction." *Under the Volcano.* Philadelphia: J.B. Lippincott, 1965. vii–xxvi.

Stanwood, Paul. "Fantasy & Fairy Tale in Twentieth-Century Opera." *Mosaic* 10.2 (1977): 183–95.

Steegmuller, Francis. *Cocteau: A Biography.* Boston: Little, Brown, 1970.

Steiner, Wendy. *The Colors of Rhetoric: Problems in the Relation between Modern Literature and Painting.* Chicago: University of Chicago Press, 1982.

Sugars, Cynthia, ed. *The Letters of Conrad Aiken and Malcolm Lowry, 1929–1954.* Toronto: ECW Press, 1992.

Swan, Jim. "Mater and Nannie: Freud's Two Mothers and the Discovery of the Oedipus Complex." *American Imago* 31.1 (1974): 1–64.

Swinburne, Algernon Charles. *The Complete Works of Algernon Charles Swinburne.* Vol. 11. Ed. Sir Edmond Gosse and Thomas James Wise. London: Heinemann, 1926. 20 vols.

Taylor, Tom. *Glimpses: World War II West Vancouver.* Vancouver: Private Publisher, 2004.

Thurston, E. Temple. *The Wandering Jew.* London: Putnam, 1920.

Tiessen, Paul, ed. *The Letters of Malcolm Lowry and Gerald Noxon, 1940–1952.* Vancouver: University of British Columbia Press, 1988.

———, ed. *Apparently Incongruous Parts: The Worlds of Malcolm Lowry.* Metuchen, NY: Scarecrow Press, 1990.

Vane, Sutton. *Outward Bound.* New York: Boni & Liveright, 1924.

Vice, Sue. "The Construction of Femininity in *Ulysses* and *Under the Volcano*: A Bakhtinian Analysis of the Late Draft Versions." In *Joyce/Lowry: Critical Perspectives,* ed. Patrick A. McCarthy and Paul Tiessen, 96–108. Lexington: University Press of Kentucky, 1997.

———. "The Volcano of a Postmodern Lowry." In *Swinging the Maelstrom: New Perspectives on Malcolm Lowry,* ed. Sherrill Grace, 123–35. Montreal: McGill-Queen's University Press, 1992.

Virgili, Carmen. "El Día de los Muertos." In *Alberto Gironella: El Via Crucis del Cónsul,* 9–31. Barcelona: Círculo de Lectores, 1992.

Voloshinov, V.N. *Marxism and the Philosophy of Language.* Trans. Ladislav Matejka and I.R. Titunik. Cambridge, MA: Harvard University Press, 1986.

Voltaire, Francois. *Dictionnaire Philosophique.* Vol IV. Paris: Firmin Didot, 1829, 224.

Weisstein, Ulrich, ed. *Expressionism as an International Literary Phenomenon.* Paris: Didier, 1973.

White, Harold Ogden. *Plagiarism and Imitation during the English Renaissance.* Cambridge, MA: Harvard University Press, 1935.

White, John. *Mythology in the Modern Novel.* Princeton, NJ: Princeton University Press, 1971.

Wildman, Carl. "Introduction." *Jean Cocteau: Orpheus, Oedipus Rex, The Infernal Machine.* London: Oxford University Press, 1962.

Willett, John. *Expressionism.* New York: McGraw-Hill, 1970.

Wood, Barry. "Malcolm Lowry's Metafiction: The Biography of a Genre." *Contemporary Literature* 19 (1978): 1–25.

Woodcock, George, ed. *Malcolm Lowry: The Man and his Work.* Vancouver: University of British Columbia Press, 1971.

Yeats, W.B., trans. *Sophocles' King Oedipus: A Version for the Modern Stage.* London: Macmillan, 1928.

Films:

From Morn till Midnight. Dir. Karl-Heinz Martin. Ilag-Film. 1920.

Isn't Life Wonderful. Dir. D.W. Griffith. United Artists. 1924.

Looping the Loop. Dir. Arthur Robison. Universum-Film. 1928.

Outward Bound. Dir. Robert Milton. Jack L. Warner. 1930.

The Student of Prague. Dir. Henryk Galeen. Sokel-Film. 1926.

The Wandering Jew. Dir. Maurice Elvey. Julius Hagen. 1933.

Websites:

http://forum.axishistory.com. "Axis History Forum: Unpunished Royal Navy war crimes of WW1 and WW2."

http://www.nmm.ac.uk/collections/displayRepro.cfm. "National Maritime Museum: Coins and Medals."

http://www.vlib.us/wwi/resources/archives/texts/t050925/Baralong. "Memorandum of the German Government" January 1916.